365 Daily

Whispers of Wisdom for SINGLE MOMS

ISBN 978-1-60260-136-9

Published by Barbour Publishing, Inc., P.O. Box 719, Uhrichsville, Ohio 44683, www.barbourbooks.com

Our mission is to publish and distribute inspirational products offering exceptional value and biblical encouragement to the masses.

Printed in the United States of America.

Introduction

Nobody has to tell a single mother that her job is a tough one. You're already well aware of that.

What you might need to hear, though, are some regular reminders of God's love for you. . .of the vital importance of the job you're doing. . .of the incredible blessings of motherhood in spite of the daily struggles. That's what *Whispers of Wisdom for Single Moms* is all about—providing encouragement to help you face your challenges with confidence, hope—even joy.

These 365 devotional readings will turn your thoughts to the unchanging wisdom of the Bible and its heavenly Author—who longs to write a success story for you. You'll find insights into the emotions you face and practical ideas for leading your family. You'll be refreshed by the real-life triumphs of single moms and gently challenged at times to make beneficial changes to your own attitudes and actions.

"Single motherhood" is a huge responsibility—and also a bit of a misnomer. With your heavenly Father by your side, you have access to all the wisdom, resources, and strength you need to accomplish everything He's called you to do—to be the best mom you can be. We hope *Whispers of Wisdom* is an encouragement along the way!

The Publishers

My Thirsty Soul

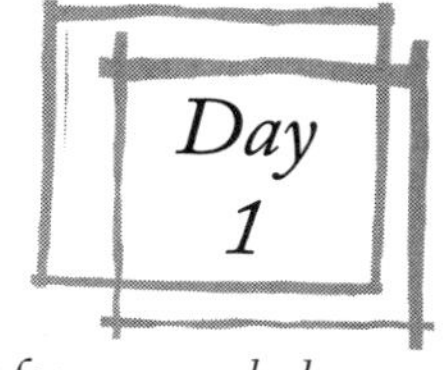

O God, you are my God, earnestly I seek you; my soul thirsts for you, my body longs for you, in a dry and weary land where there is no water.
Psalm 63:1 NIV

Let's face it—single motherhood provides us little leisure time. Days slip away from us until we find ourselves falling exhausted into bed—often, without having spent any time with the Lord. But our connection with God through prayer and Bible study is an absolute necessity.

God doesn't expect us to spend three hours a day in intense prayer or devote an entire evening to an in-depth study of the Bible's original Hebrew and Greek words. But He does ask for a little of the time we have. If the only "alone moments" we can offer Him are during our drive time to work, He'll take them!

Finding quiet time with God is crucial for our spiritual, mental, even physical health. Let's think of our alone time with Him as a period of refreshing for whatever strength, wisdom, or encouragement we'll need to succeed in the day before us.

The psalmist describes a "dry and weary land," ready to absorb an evening rain or morning dew. What a picture of our lives, eagerly awaiting our Lord's life-giving sustenance.

Lord, though I truly need You, I'm not always quick to recognize that truth. Cause me to see that You alone meet my deepest needs. Then shower me with Your living water and refresh my spirit until my cup overflows.

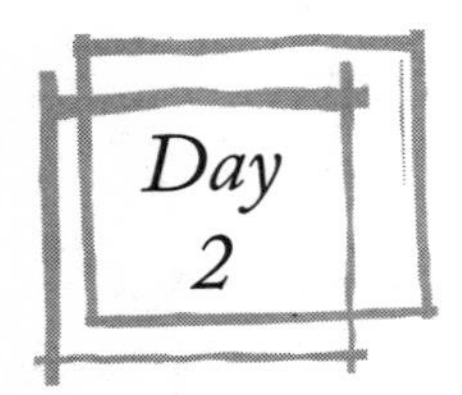

The Sports Page

I try to find common ground with everyone,
doing everything I can to save some.
1 Corinthians 9:22 NLT

In *Beyond Ourselves*, author Catherine Marshall described a great regret in how she parented her son after her husband, Peter, died. She had trouble finding ways to relate well to Peter Jr. During his teen years, the gulf between them widened. Too late, Catherine wished that she would have forced herself to become knowledgeable about the things that interested her son. Things like the sports page. She realized that if she had tried to learn about sports from the angle that *did* interest her—the personalities, the stories behind the athletes—she probably could have enjoyed it. In turn, she probably would have had a better relationship with her son. She should have met Peter Jr. at his level, rather than expect him to meet hers.

The great apostle Paul understood the need to find common ground with others. On a missionary trip to Athens, he was stumped about how to hook his audience. The Athenians believed in so many gods, how could he possibly interest them in learning about the one true God? Paul finally came across the Tomb of the Unknown God. Voila! He found his hook. Paul could tell them who this unknown God was! Paul preached one of the greatest sermons he had ever preached using that tomb as common ground.

Dear Lord, open my eyes to things that interest my children,
to open up pathways of communication between us,
letting them know that what is important to them is important to me.

Food, Glorious Food

As one who is in the Lord Jesus, I am fully convinced that no food is unclean in itself. But if anyone regards something as unclean, then for him it is unclean.
Romans 14:14 NIV

A wise person once said that you couldn't spell *diet* without d–i–e. That's pretty much how many of us feel about cutting back on those wonderfully bad-for-us entrees and desserts we all love so much.

The apostle Paul writes in Romans that no food is unclean in itself—but if a person regards something as unclean, she shouldn't eat it. At the time, Paul was talking about food sacrificed to idols, but today he could just as easily be referring to fast foods and sweets. We know those foods aren't good for us, but we sure enjoy eating them.

Good foods, though, don't have to be unpleasant. And they're definitely better for God's temple—our bodies.

Start small. Stock the fridge or cupboards with fruit, low-fat yogurt, and other healthy snacks. Avoid the temptation to stop at a fast-food chain for lunch. Or, if you must eat quickly, choose a salad instead of a burger—and skip the fries entirely.

Your body—and maybe even your kids—will thank you later.

Dear Lord, help me to choose healthy foods for my children and myself. I know that no food is "unclean" on its own, but eating the wrong things could harm the body You have given me.

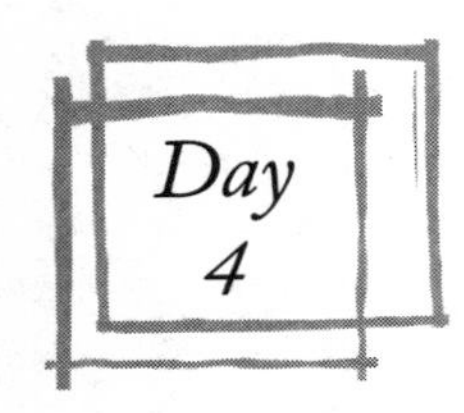

Time Clocks

Is not the Lord your God with you?
and hath he not given you rest on every side?
1 Chronicles 22:18 KJV

The time clock is a wonderful invention. You clock in and (here is the best part) you clock out! While we're "on the clock," we're aware that our time is not our own. Whether cooking for a hungry throng of customers, typing on a keyboard, or emptying trash, for a set time we must do another's bidding. Then we go home, off the clock at last.

At home, there is no time clock. No way to "punch out" for the day. Our duties seem endless: picking up dry cleaning, rushing to a soccer game, folding the millionth load of laundry, trying to find an interesting way to use hamburger *again,* reading to the kids, helping with homework. . . Where's the time clock to put an end to this work?

God promises to give His people rest. The laundry will be there tomorrow. We can occasionally live with cereal for dinner. The vacuuming can wait for the weekend. Algebra will always be hard.

Slow down. Rest. Catch your breath. Allow God to renew you. You have His permission to clock out for the day.

Father God, teach me how to slow down. There are so many pressing needs, yet I know I must find a way to clock out for my day. Enable me to rest in You.

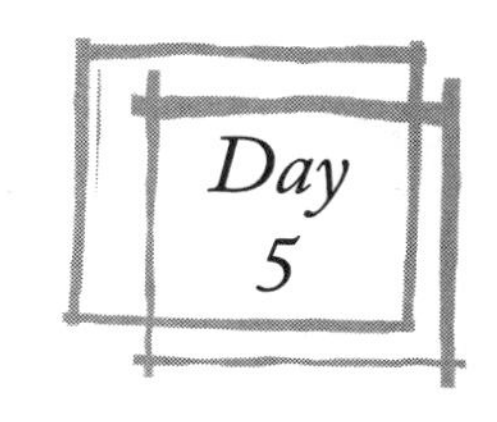

Christ, My Identity

"The Lord your God is with you, he is mighty to save. He will take great delight in you, he will quiet you with his love, he will rejoice over you with singing."
Zephaniah 3:17 NIV

As women, we love to love. We tend to trust easily. If we were married, we expected our husbands to look after our children and us, to admire and desire us as wives, always to be our protectors. Even if we've never been married, most of us have dreamed of such relationships.

But when our expectations fall short and we find ourselves parenting alone—whatever the reason—our spirits shatter into a million little pieces. Often, we lose our identity. Any self-esteem we may once have had evaporates along with our dreams.

But God Himself, the maker of all creation, the very One who hung the stars in space and calls them by name, looks at each one of us with love. In His eyes are delight and joy. Because the Father has created us in His own image, He knows every hurt we feel—and He will quiet us with His love. He rejoices that we are His daughters and He delights in us—not because of anything we do but simply because we are His.

Lord Jesus, though I sometimes feel alone and without an identity, I trust that You are with me. I ask that You will quiet my spirit with Your mighty peace and allow me to know the depth of Your love for me.

A Disciplined Mom

The wise woman builds her house, but the foolish tears it down with her own hands.
Proverbs 14:1 NASB

Being a lazy parent creates more work! Shortcuts often seem easier, but taking the time to make the tough choices now and to consistently discipline our children will prevent bigger problems down the road.

Compare lackadaisical parenting shortcuts to the effects of a poor diet. One bag of potato chips won't kill you. But a bag of chips, every day, over a period of years, will certainly cause trouble. The same is true in our jobs as mothers.

Lazy choices return negative effects over time—effects that can devastate our homes. The trouble may go unnoticed for some time. But when we realize the problems, it can be too late.

Determine now to make wise decisions, every day. Exercise simple, daily disciplines in your parenting. Make a commitment to consistency. Maintain your commitment to those daily disciplines, lest one poor choice lead to another—and you begin to tear down your home with your own hands.

The wise woman builds her house.

Lord, let me honor You by my discipline in my daily responsibilities.
Help me to consistently build up my household rather than tear it down.
Please show me what You would have me do and then give me the strength to do it.

The Rubber Meets the Road

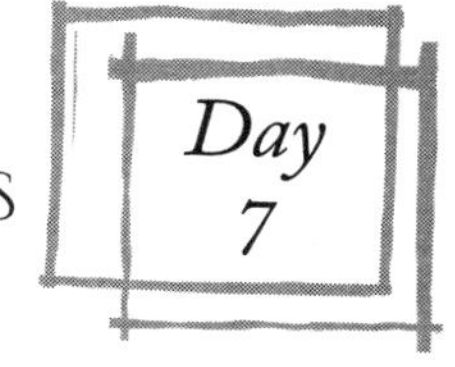

Then the woman said to Elijah, "Now I know that you are a man of God and that the word of the Lord in your mouth is truth."
1 Kings 17:24 NASB

Lynn stared up at the ceiling from her hospital bed, too filled with anxiety to sleep. Tomorrow's surgery would bring answers, but it might also bring more questions. If cancer was found, what would that diagnosis mean to her three young children? Alone and scared, Lynn came to an important conclusion that night. "Who else do I have but You, God, as You have promised?" she asked aloud. A flicker of faith flamed into a fire. Lynn believed God's word.

Trusting God in the midst of a hard reality is where the rubber meets the road. Are we going to truly believe the promises of God?

The widow of Zarepheth was facing a hard, impoverished reality when the prophet Elijah invited himself to be her long-term houseguest. This widow experienced God's daily provision of food because of her hospitality to Elijah. Her flicker of faith grew until, suddenly, her son died. Elijah held out his hands to her, asking for her dead child. What other choice did she have but to release him to God's servant? Elijah prayed and God breathed life into the boy, restoring him to his mother. God did not fail her.

You, Great God, are our life. I choose to believe that my children and I are held in Your strong embrace for all eternity.

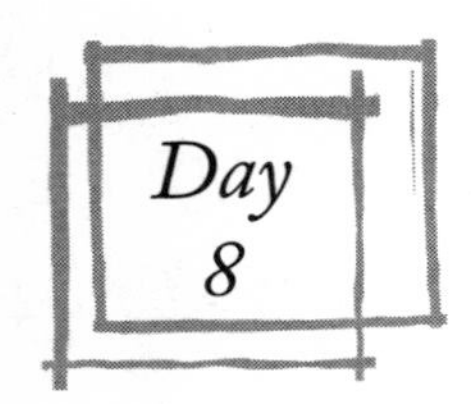

Hurt by Others' Choices

God heard the boy crying. The angel of God called from Heaven to Hagar, "What's wrong, Hagar? Don't be afraid. God has heard the boy and knows the fix he's in."
Genesis 21:17 MSG

A slave during early biblical times, Hagar had little say in her life decisions—others made them for her. Because of the infertility of her mistress, Sarah, Hagar became the concubine of Sarah's husband, Abraham, and gave birth to Ishmael.

At first, Hagar's hopes soared. Her son would become Abraham's heir, rich and powerful beyond her wildest dreams! However, the surprise appearance of Isaac, the late-life son of Sarah and Abraham, destroyed Hagar's fantasies of a wonderful future. Sarah wanted Hagar and Ishmael out of their lives. Abraham, though upset, loaded Hagar with water and food and told her to take Ishmael into the unforgiving desert.

When their water supply failed, Hagar laid her dehydrated son under a bush and walked away crying because she could not bear to watch Ishmael die. But God showed Hagar a well of water. Quickly she gave her child a drink. Both survived, and "God was on the boy's side as he grew up" (Genesis 21:20 MSG).

God is also on our side when we and our children suffer because of others' choices. Even when we have lost hope, God's plan provides a way for us and those we love.

Heavenly Father, when my world seems out of control, please help me love and trust You—even in the deserts of life.

Belly Laughs

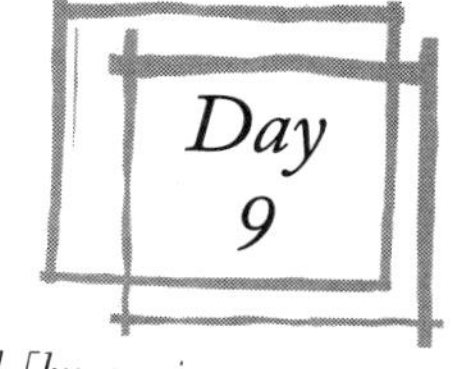

All the days of the desponding and afflicted are made evil [by anxious thoughts and forebodings], but he who has a glad heart has a continual feast [regardless of circumstances].
Proverbs 15:15 AMP

Do you know how to relax? Have you built a time for laughter into your schedule?

Maybe that sounds silly and unimportant with the demands of motherhood caving in on you. But it's not! In fact, relaxation and fun are vital to your health—and, by extension, the health of your family. We may face challenges, but as Proverbs reminds us, we can have a continual feast regardless of circumstances. Don't wait for laughter to find you—seek it out!

Find a clean comedy show to loosen up. Maybe get into a tickling match with the kids. Perhaps it's as simple as scheduling a popcorn and movie night with the kids to melt away the day's pressure.

A good laugh is health to our bones and gives our kids permission to lighten up, too. Do it now—not when life is in perfect order. Our families need to see us loosen up and enjoy ourselves now and then.

*Heavenly Father, You are a God of laughter and enjoyment.
Why does it seem frivolous to giggle with my children?
Enable me to have a continual feast regardless of my circumstances.*

Commitment Challenges at Church

Remember me for this, my God, and do not blot out what I have so faithfully done for the house of my God and its services.
Nehemiah 13:14 TNIV

Have you ever sacrificed precious "leisure" hours to serve on a church committee, count offerings, or weed church flower beds? Despite your work schedule and double duty at home as a single mom, you agree to co-teach Bible school—only to receive a phone call the night before from your partner. She has decided to go on vacation instead! Now, surrounded by hyper kindergarteners, you wonder what you did to deserve this.

Nehemiah felt the same way. A governor during Old Testament times, he spearheaded the rebuilding of Jerusalem's broken walls, then spent years encouraging his countrymen to worship Yahweh. He organized priests and Levites and served as a spiritual lay leader. He managed the practical affairs of the temple, including schedules, payments, and distributions. Nehemiah fought enemies, settled internal squabbles and—and—*and!* His days never seemed long enough. He grew discouraged when trusted fellow workers in God's house placed their priorities elsewhere. Between crises, Nehemiah took a deep breath and prayed the above prayer.

More than twenty-five hundred years later, God tells the story of Nehemiah's perseverance in the Bible. Like you, Nehemiah may not have seen his reward as soon as he wanted. But now he is enjoying it forever.

So will you.

Lord Jesus, when I feel tired and unappreciated as I serve others, let Your applause be enough for me.

Bible 101

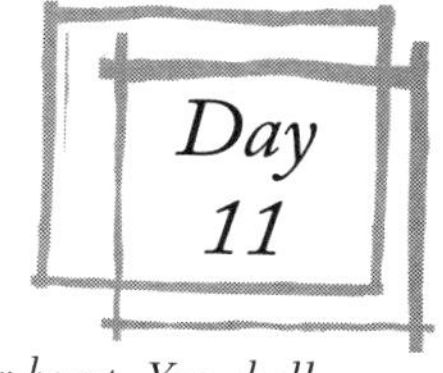

"And these words which I command you today shall be in your heart. You shall teach them diligently to your children, and shall talk of them when you sit in your house, when you walk by the way, when you lie down, and when you rise up."
Deuteronomy 6:6–7 NKJV

Every week, a young girl ran next door to share her Sunday school lesson with her elderly neighbor. He was lonely, so he enjoyed the girl's stories of Jesus' calming the seas and feeding the masses. The man treasured that time for the spiritual intimacy they shared. The little girl had built a bridge that spanned generations.

God commanded the parents of ancient Israel to spend their time sharing His words with their children. In today's busy world, that may seem impractical. But think of the moments each day that could be used for eternal purposes: How about turning off the car radio and talking about Jesus? Maybe singing songs and practicing memory verses while stirring spaghetti sauce? What about playing a Bible story game instead of checkers?

There are practical ways to accomplish what seems impractical—and make it enjoyable. Follow the Lord's commands and spend your days impressing the words of God on your children's hearts. They'll certainly benefit—and you might just learn something yourself.

Lord, please give me the patience and the energy to teach Your Word. Give me the creativity to do it well. Please help me to learn as I teach my child.

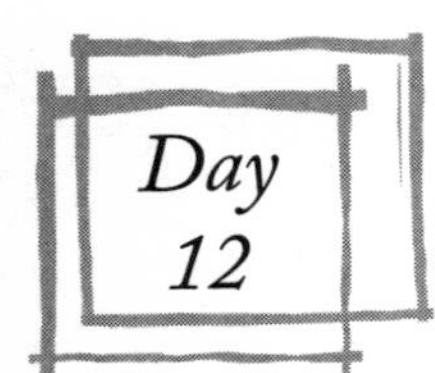

Called to Be a Mom

"Before I formed you in the womb I knew you;
before you were born I sanctified you."
JEREMIAH 1:5 NKJV

Raising children alone, working a job, managing a household—mothers often feel lost in the shuffle. The kids need gym clothes, help with math, and clean underwear. They seem to require signed permission slips to go to the restroom. And, if a mom *really* cares, she attends every single solitary school play in which her daughter plays the role of a bush.

No wonder she finds it difficult to make room in her tired brain for lofty thoughts of God or His purpose for her life. And deep inside, Mom might assume that God has forgotten her, as well.

Jeremiah probably felt forgotten, too, because God had to remind him that He designed Jeremiah in his mother's womb—and set him apart for a special purpose. Reading his story, we learn that God Himself touched Jeremiah's mouth and called him to speak His Word to kings and nations.

"No wonder God's eye was on Jeremiah!" we object. "Jeremiah was a great prophet! All I do is pick up kids at basketball practice!"

But if we reexamine the scripture, we realize God also called Jeremiah's unnamed mom to give birth to this great prophet and nurture him. Without her, Jeremiah's profound ministry would never have existed.

And he wouldn't have gotten a ride home from basketball practice.

Lord, You not only called me as a mother, but You, the infinite Son of God, died for me. Thank You, Jesus, for reminding me how special I am, and for sacrificing Your life so that I might live!

Do the Next Thing

You, O Lord, *keep my lamp burning;*
my God turns my darkness into light.
Psalm 18:28 niv

Single mothers work hard. They go to a job for forty hours (or more) a week, maintain their homes, raise their children, and often mediate with the other parent. They wish they could go to bed the same day as they get up and not get up the same day that they go to bed.

One shining example of their work ethic is Elisabeth Elliott, perhaps least recognized in her role as a single mother. A young widow, she returned to Ecuador to bring the gospel to the same Indians who had murdered her husband and four other missionaries. Her struggles are recounted in her book, *The Savage, My Kinsman*. Often lost in the dramatic story is the fact that Ms. Elliott brought her preschool daughter with her. She faced the same challenges as any other single mother, only in a hostile and primitive environment.

Her secret to surviving the daily grind? "Do the next thing." She didn't look past breakfast or getting her daughter to bed. She trusted God to keep her lamp burning long enough to finish the task at hand.

Dear God, like the psalmist I beg You to keep my lamp burning long enough to do the next thing. Only You can give me the strength and wisdom I need, and I know You will.

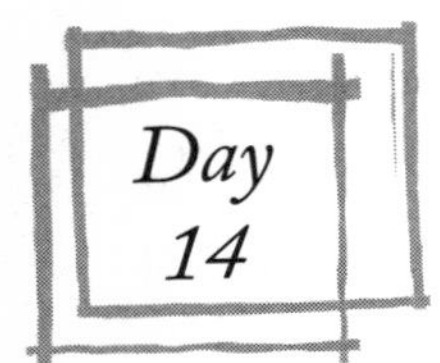

Day 14

POWER IN WEAKNESS

God is my strength and power: and he maketh my way perfect.
2 SAMUEL 22:33 KJV

Being the primary disciplinarian and authority figure can be such a daunting task. We desperately desire our children to "like" us, yet realize some choices we make will not exactly endear us to them. Sometimes we're left feeling overwhelmed and inadequate for the task.

There are times when, no matter how much strength, willpower, and wisdom we muster, our power is insufficient. Our ability falls short of the need at hand. But that's okay. None of us are supermoms—able to leap mounds of dishes and piles of homework in a single bound, effortlessly handling board meetings, homework hassles, the supermarket dash, and upset tummies without breaking a sweat.

Our precious heavenly Father holds us up and walks with us through the minefield of our circumstances. His strength is sufficient and equal to whatever task we face. He understands the pressures we face. He knows that we do not always feel competent for our life's challenges. So He beckons us to come to Him for strength, for direction, for patience and wisdom.

Our obvious lack draws us to the Father—who meets our needs abundantly in and through Him.

Father God, I am often left feeling overwhelmed and drained by the sheer responsibility before me. I cry out to You for my needs. Strengthen me and fill me with Your wisdom.

Have a Heart!

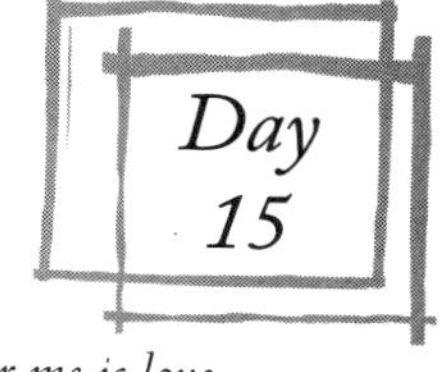

He has taken me to the banquet hall, and his banner over me is love.
Song of Solomon 2:4 NIV

After New Year's Day, the dreaded invasion began.

Hearts. Hundreds of them.

Whenever Megan entered the post office, grocery store, or Wal-Mart, those hearts reminded her she would spend another Valentine's Day alone. Well, not really alone. Her ten-year-old twins Abby and Andi, now asleep, would argue over valentines and candy. Megan couldn't wait for February 15! Chocolate would be cheap. And the hearts would all disappear for another year.

But deep inside, Megan yearned for more. "Lord, I don't mean to complain. But I wish I had a special someone on Valentine's Day!" Her mind painted the picture: a restaurant with china and cloth napkins. Soft lights. Sweet music. Her imaginary beloved held her hand and told Megan she meant more to him than anything.

All Christians experience seasons of deep loneliness. Like Megan, we can forget that our Bridegroom gave His very life for us! Although we sometimes doubt Jesus, His promise remains as real as if He had placed a ring on our finger: *I will come for you soon. Wait for Me.* Jesus is planning a magnificent heavenly wedding reception in a banquet hall only the angels can envision.

The earthly "heart invasion" will come and go—but His heart for you is forever!

Lord Jesus, I can't wait for Your arrival! Help me become the beautiful Bride You long to hold in Your arms.

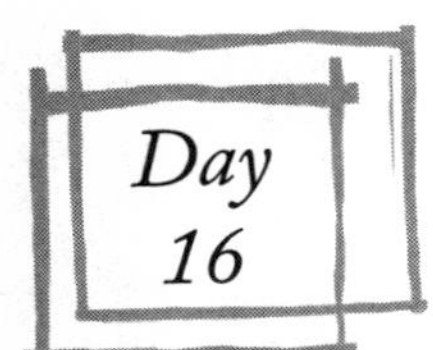

Sufficient Grace

But he said to me, "My grace is sufficient for you, for my power is made perfect in weakness." . . . For when I am weak, then I am strong.
2 Corinthians 12:9–10 NIV

It was after midnight when Dawn finally slumped into her unmade bed, exhausted and discouraged. Not accomplishing half of the day's to-do list, she knew that the next day would be even more hectic. With three small boys and no husband to help with the daily chores, Dawn was both mommy and daddy to the three little angels who trusted her. *How can I possibly make it through another day?* Dawn wondered as she finally drifted off to sleep.

Our lives as single parents can be discouraging and overwhelming. We find ourselves wondering how we will make it through another day. The answer is God's grace.

In His Word, God assures us that His grace is sufficient. It is when we are at our weakest that He has the greatest opportunity to show His strength. We can step back and let Him be all the strength we need. No, He's not going to do our laundry or mow our lawn, but He will give us the power to get through each day with peace and confidence.

His grace is always sufficient—just as He promised.

Abba Father, I am weary and I don't know how to keep going. My kids need more than I can give; I need You to help me. Please show me Your grace and make it sufficient for me. Give me Your strength because I cannot make it without You.

Clap Your Hands!

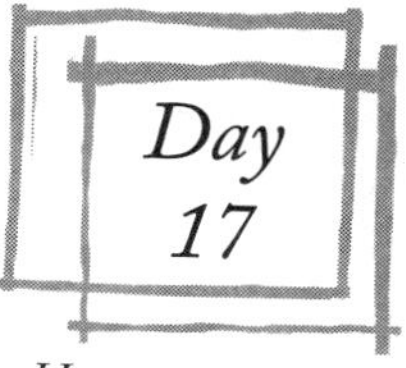

Clap your hands, all you nations; shout to God with cries of joy. How awesome is the Lord Most High, the great King over all the earth! . . . God has ascended amid shouts of joy, the LORD amid the sounding of trumpets. Sing praises to God, sing praises; sing praises to our King, sing praises.
PSALM 47:1–2, 5–6 NIV

In 1931, German theologian Dietrich Bonhoeffer spent a year at a seminary in New York City. While there, he was introduced to a church in Harlem. Astounded, then delighted, at the emotion expressed in worship, he returned to Germany with recordings of gospel music tucked in his suitcase. Bonhoeffer knew that the worship he observed was authentic and pleasing to God.

King David would have loved gospel music! Many of the psalms were meant to be sung loudly and joyfully. David appointed four thousand professional musicians—playing cymbals, trumpets, rams' horns, tambourines, harps, and lyres—for temple worship. We can imagine they would have rocked the roofs off of our modern-day church services!

Dancing was a part of worship in David's day, too. David angered his wife, Michal, with his spontaneous dance in the street, as the Ark of the Covenant was returned to Jerusalem (1 Chronicles 15:29). The world, in David's viewpoint, couldn't contain the delight that God inspires. Neither could he!

How often do we worship God with our whole heart? Do our children ever see us burst forth in a song of praise? Have they witnessed us clapping our hands and lifting them up high? Probably not often enough. Let's try that today!

O Lord, great is Your name and worthy of praise!

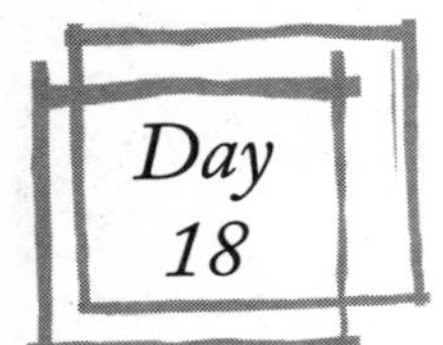

God's Mirror

Charm is deceptive, and beauty does not last;
but a woman who fears the Lord will be greatly praised.
Proverbs 31:30 NLT

A woman admitted that she spent much of her attention on how she looked and who was looking at her. She even watched her reflection in store windows to see how passersby reacted as she walked down the street.

Her overwhelming focus on appearance was driven by a fear of being alone. The woman was afraid that if she wasn't outwardly attractive, she might never find a husband. But she misunderstood what really determined her value.

Proverbs 31:30 shares a very important truth about charm and beauty: They fade. If a woman marries primarily on the basis of physical beauty, the couple will eventually be left wanting. Much more fulfilling to a marriage is the woman's spiritual focus.

May our minds be focused on the qualities that last: honesty, faithfulness, loyalty, and spiritual growth. Mr. Right will define beauty as God does—and will value good personal qualities above physical perfection.

Today, gaze into the mirror of scripture. Allow your true beauty to be that inner beauty of soul—a reflection of Christ—that never fades.

Father, thank You for the beauty that You reflect from my soul. Help me to place less importance on my outward appearance and more value on the inner qualities that You are developing in me.

IDEAL PLACE

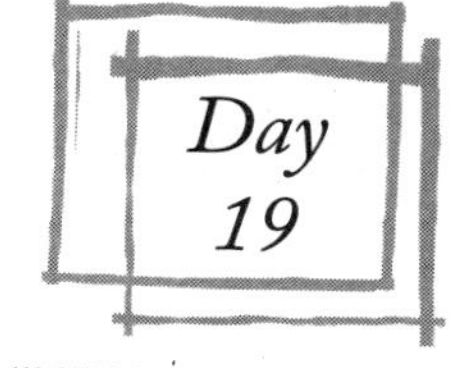

For consider your calling, brethren, that there were not many wise according to the flesh, not many mighty, not many noble; but God has chosen the foolish things of the world.
1 CORINTHIANS 1:26–27 NASB

Once my life is running smoothly. . .

If I didn't have toddlers underfoot. . .

As soon as I get this anger problem under control. . .

When I get enough money. . .

As soon as I (fill in the blank). . .then I can be used by God.

We are *where* we are, *when* we are, because our Father chose us for such a time as this. Our steps are ordered by Him. Whether He has called us to teach a Sunday school class, pray with other moms, lead a Bible study, or sing in the choir—we need not wait for the ideal time and place to serve Him. The only "ideal" is where you are right now.

God delights in using His people—right in the middle of all that appears crazy and wrong and hopeless. *Now* is the time to serve God, not next week or next year or when things get better. He wants our cheerful, obedient service right in the midst of—even in spite of—our difficult circumstances.

Father, help me see that there is no "ideal" place or circumstance to serve You. You can, and will, use me right where I am. Thank You that I do not have to have it all together to be used by You.

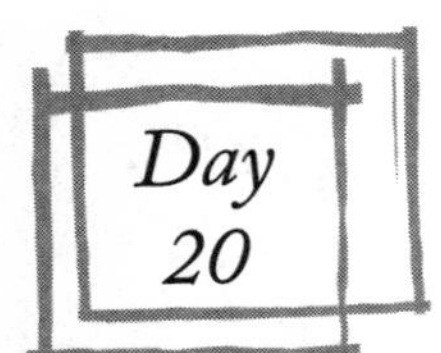

Hard Time Loving

When the Lord *saw that Leah was unloved, He opened her womb.*
Genesis 29:31 NKJV

Leah knew that Jacob didn't love her. He hadn't wanted to marry her in the first place.

As soon as Leah's father gave her sister Rachel to Jacob as his second wife, Jacob abandoned Leah emotionally. Not physically, though—she was now pregnant for the fourth time, the physical discomfort of carrying a baby adding to the pain of not being loved.

Like every man of the time, Jacob wanted a bevy of sons. When Leah gave birth to her first child, Reuben, she thought, *He'll love me now. I've given him what he wants.* Similar thoughts filled her mind with the next two boys, but with this fourth pregnancy, she accepted reality. Jacob didn't love her and never would. One child more or less wouldn't make a difference.

How do we react to our circumstances as single mothers? It's not what we wanted or planned—any more than Leah wanted or planned a loveless marriage. Are we tempted to become bitter or blame God for what happened?

Leah did neither. Instead, she turned to Jacob's God: "Now I will praise the Lord." And God honored her faith. From that son, Judah, God gave the world the Savior.

Praising God puts our troubles in perspective.

Heavenly Father, You are good even when I don't understand.
Fill my lips with praise for You, even in the midst of trials.

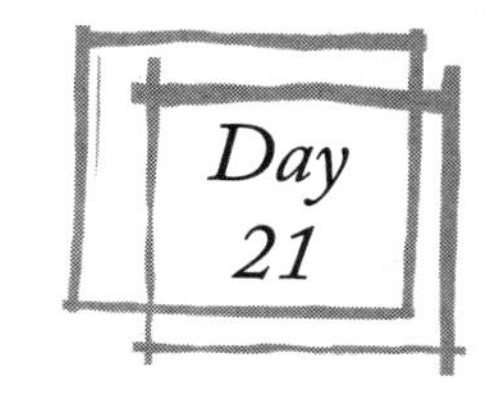

God in the Details

"When we heard of it, our hearts melted and everyone's courage failed because of you, for the LORD your God is God in heaven above and on the earth below."
JOSHUA 2:11 NIV

The people of Jericho had reason to be worried. They had seen evidence of God's strength and support of His children—and knew that Joshua planned to conquer Canaan. As residents of the key military fortress in the land, they understood that Joshua would soon be at their gates.

Yet only Rahab seemed to recognize the right course of action: to embrace the Lord and open her home to Joshua's agents. In return, they made sure she and her family survived the attack. Because of her courage and faith, Rahab became an ancestress of Jesus.

Sometimes, when our own lives seem to be under siege from the demands of work, bills, and children, finding the work of God amid the strife can be difficult. Even though we acknowledge His power, we may overlook the gentle touches, the small ways in which He makes every day a little easier. Just as the Lord cares for the tiniest bird (Matthew 10:29–31), so He seeks to be a part of every detail in your life. Look for Him there.

Father God, I know You are by my side every day, good or bad, and that You love and care for me. Help me to see Your work in my life and in the lives of my family.

The Undercover Mission Trip

If I rise on the wings of the dawn, if I settle on the far side of the sea, even there your hand will guide me, your right hand will hold me fast.
Psalm 139:9–10 NIV

Lindsey had to beg her mom to go on a summer mission trip. "Please, Mom," Lindsey pleaded. "I really believe God wants me to go."

It wasn't that Lindsey's mom wanted to hold her back or interfere with God's plans, but Lindsey was considering a Third World country where Christianity was illegal! For eight long weeks, there could be no phone calls, e-mails, or letters because they might jeopardize the safety of those on the trip. The undercover mission trip.

After praying, Lindsey's mom agreed to let her go. But it still wasn't easy. She missed her daughter. She worried about Lindsey, prayed to hand those worries over to God, and often snatched them back again.

At midsummer, a friend called unexpectedly. "Would you believe that my nephew is on that same mission trip as Lindsey? And his sister had gone on that trip, a few years ago."

"And she returned home," Lindsey's mom asked, "safe and sound?"

"Safe and sound," her friend reassured her.

As Lindsey's mom hung up the phone, she almost laughed. God had delivered just the right encouragement at just the right moment.

Lord God, You are faithful even when I am not. And You are faithful to my children, even when I have doubts. I praise You for Your providential care today.

Power Over the Plastic

Better is a little with the fear of the LORD, than great treasure with trouble. Better is a dinner of herbs where love is, than a fatted calf with hatred.
PROVERBS 15:16–17 NKJV

Many of us receive more mail from credit card companies than from our relatives! We toss the letters out, but dozens more materialize in our mailboxes with tempting offers.

The pressure on Mom mounts as children beg to go to Disney World. Teens sigh for jeans like those worn by popular kids, *the* jeans with perfect designer rips. Meanwhile, the car threatens to give up the ghost. The Salvation Army sofa sags like the last bank account balance. A glance into the refrigerator reveals scanty rations until payday. *Sigh.* Mom feels so weary, so discouraged. Dinner at a restaurant without cardboard crowns or curly slides sounds wonderful! All she has to do is hand over the plastic and sign on the dotted line. . . .

God's Word comes to our rescue when we face little temptations that can add up to big trouble. Lovingly He reminds us that unrealistic expectations and overspending can destroy a family. Even macaroni and cheese—again!—with those we love tastes better than costly meals out that strain the budget and rob us of our peace.

Lord Jesus, thank You for Your concern in every area of our lives. Help us as a family to live within our means and enjoy the riches of a happy home.

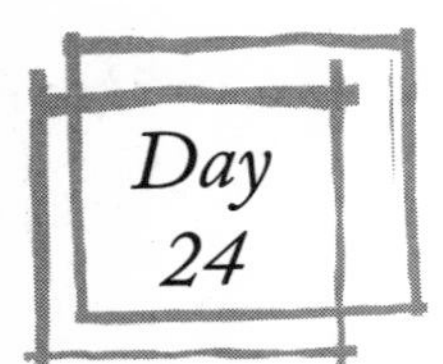

Budget Breaker

Then the Lord said to Moses, "Behold, I will rain bread from heaven for you; and the people shall go out and gather a day's portion every day, that I may test them, whether or not they will walk in My instruction."
Exodus 16:4 NASB

The month lasted longer than the paycheck. The grocery bill exceeded the budget. Childcare expenses surpassed the rent. It's not an easy road to travel, yet one that many of us walk.

Isn't it interesting that we can trust God for eternal life, yet find it harder to trust Him for help with the mortgage?

In the Old Testament, God told the wandering Israelites He would feed them "manna from heaven," but with one caveat: He would only allow them to gather enough food for one day. No storing food away for the dreaded "what if's" of tomorrow. They would simply have to trust their God to faithfully supply their needs.

They didn't always pass the "trust test"—and neither do we. But thankfully, God is faithful in spite of us! He will meet our needs when we come to Him in simple trust. Then we can bask in His faithfulness.

Father, Your Word promises to supply all my needs. I trust You in spite of the challenges I see. You are ever faithful. Thank You!

Laugh Out Loud

He will yet fill your mouth with laughter
and your lips with shouts of joy.
Job 8:21 NIV

Laughter is the best medicine, so the old saying goes. How true that is, especially for us. Being a single mother is absolutely indescribable. Sleepless nights, sinks full of dirty dishes, unfinished to-do lists, meals scraped together from last week's leftovers, lawns that always need mowing, flat bicycle tires. . . You name it, we deal with it. We do it all—from yard work and pet grooming to floor scrubbing and car repair. Nobody else can begin to understand our world.

When we become run-down and frustrated, impatience and short-temperedness toward the precious children we care for are the unfortunate side effects. Thankfully, God gives us His Word saying He will fill our mouths with laughter and our lips with joy—regardless of our circumstances.

Imagine what a heartfelt belly laugh would do for us after the third glass of spilled milk or the snapping of the mousetrap—again. Being upset won't cause the milk to miraculously return to the glass, but a lighthearted giggle will cause your spirit—and that of your children—to glitter. Laughter is always good medicine for a worn-out single mom. Try it and watch your attitude rise—along with the corners of your children's mouths.

Father, sometimes I get so tired and weary. I want to find joy, rather than discouragement, in everyday things. Please help me see the bright side of every circumstance and keep laughter in my home.

A Pattern Worth Repeating

So know that the Lord *your God is God, the faithful God.*
He will keep his agreement of love for a thousand lifetimes for people who love him and obey his commands.
Deuteronomy 7:9 NCV

We all know that patterns repeat in families, even to the "third and fourth generation" (Exodus 20:5 NIV.) We worry over negative patterns, like abuse and divorce, that have hurt our children the same way they hurt us. We long to replace those negative patterns with godly, joyful living.

God wants that for our families, as well. He encourages parents with a God-sized promise, the kind every mother wants for her family but thinks is impossible.

Think beyond a legacy for our grandchildren and great-grandchildren. God's vision extends far past that. He will show "love for a *thousand lifetimes*" (emphasis added). The idea of a "thousand lifetimes" boggles the mind. Taken literally, at twenty-five years times one thousand, it endures for twenty-five thousand years—longer than people have lived on the earth.

God takes our hands and says, "Love Me. Obey Me. I will show love to your family as long as you have descendants on the earth." And when we demonstrate our love for God by doing what He says, we guarantee His faithfulness and love to generations yet unborn, until the Lord returns to take us home.

That's a legacy worth passing on.

Heavenly Father, I praise You that You will be faithful to my children and their children after them. I pray that they also will love You and obey You.

Little Miss Perfect

To all perfection I see a limit.
Psalm 119:96 niv

Dana's mom was not exactly a model mom. Dana felt she was raised by the parenting philosophy of "benign neglect." She was on her own from an early age. She promised herself that she would be the kind of mother to her own kids that she had always wanted. She had very high expectations for herself. And her children. It mattered to Dana how her children dressed, how they behaved in public, even the schools that they attended. It all had to be perfect. . .though nothing ever was.

Her children struggled against such tight control. They felt smothered and resentful—which only fueled Dana's frustrations. She was trying so hard! Why couldn't her children appreciate her? She was giving them so much more than she had ever received.

One day, after a bitter fight with her son, Dana happened to watch an old family video. She felt as if she was seeing herself objectively for the first time. Her son's shoelace came untied and she bent to tie it. Ice cream tipped out of her daughter's cone and she hurried to fix it. She saw the pressure she put on herself and, by extension, on her kids. She realized she was trying to fill a gap in herself that only God could provide: the knowledge that she was loved and valued, just for being her.

Continue Your beautiful work in my life, O Lord.
May I be an agent of love.

What about My Dad?

"If you obey my commands, you will remain in my love, just as I have obeyed my Father's commands and remain in his love."
John 15:10 NIV

Her daughter had been watching television—a show about a family with a mom, dad, and children all living together in a pleasant house outside town. When the final credits began to roll, the daughter looked up to her mother and asked an innocent question: "Why doesn't Daddy live with us?"

It's an honest question from a curious child, one that is inevitable for a single mom. Explaining the situation can be challenging, especially for younger kids. But the truth of the matter is that your child's Father—notice the capital *F*—does live in your home, and in your hearts.

When kids ask "What about my dad?" explain that even though a biological father may not be present, our heavenly Father is always with us. In those times when an earthly father leaves a noticeable void, every child of God can turn to his or her heavenly Father. His love is perfect, unchanging, and always available.

Dear God, thank You for being our heavenly Father. Even when we are without an earthly dad, You are there to comfort and protect us. Thank You for living in our hearts—and help us to remember Your presence each day.

PERFECT PRAYERS

Pray, therefore, like this: Our Father. . .
Out of the depths have I cried to You, O LORD.
MATTHEW 6:9 AMP; PSALM 130:1 AMP

How many messages have you heard on prayer? Have you ever come away thinking, *Did you hear how eloquently they prayed? How spiritual they sounded? No wonder God answers their prayers!*

Sometimes we take the straightforward and uncomplicated idea of prayer—the simple give and take of talking with God—and turn it into something hard. How many times have we made it a mere religious exercise, performed best by the "holy elite," rather than what it really is—conversation with God our Father.

Just pour out your heart to God. Share how your day went. Tell Him your dreams. Ask Him to search you and reveal areas of compromise. Thank Him for your lunch. Plead for your kids' well-being. Complain about your car. . . . Just talk with Him. Don't worry how impressive (or unimpressive!) you sound.

Talk with God while doing dishes, driving the car, folding laundry, eating lunch, or kneeling by your bed. Whenever, wherever, whatever—tell Him. He cares!

Don't allow this day to slip away without talking to your Father. No perfection required.

Father God, what a privilege it is to unburden my heart to You.
Teach me the beauty and simplicity of simply sharing my day with You.

Smiles Bring Joy

A cheerful look brings joy to the heart,
and good news gives health to the bones.
Proverbs 15:30 NIV

The teenage girl nervously walked backstage. It was her turn next. She had practiced for hours. This song was perfect, her teacher had said. But the butterflies in her stomach were telling a different story. Fear began to grip her throat. She couldn't breathe. It was then that she saw her mother sitting in the front row. There she was, eyes sparkling, smiling that goofy smile, and proudly saying, "My daughter is next! She is so talented!" The young girl took a deep breath and closed her eyes. The fear melted and confidence took over. *I can do this,* she thought as she boldly walked onstage.

Smiles can say so many things in a quiet, gentle form. They can give comfort and support and bring joy and strength to someone who is weary. Courage and confidence are given by the love that smiles portray. They can simply remind a person that someone really does care. And more often than not, a smile is immediately returned to the giver.

Joy is contagious; spread it around. Smile at someone today. Go ahead and chuckle at that joke. Laugh with someone. Not only will you be blessing another, but also you will be blessed yourself.

Dear Lord, fill me with Your joy today that I may bless others with my smile and laughter and portray Your love to those around me. Amen

Best Dressed Secret

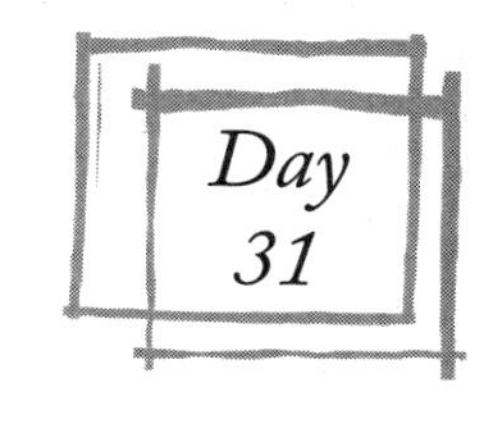

Those who go to him for help are happy, and they are never disgraced.
Psalm 34:5 NCV

Little Orphan Annie, dressed in threadbare hand-me-down clothes, gets the other girls in the orphanage to sing along with her. "You're never fully dressed without a smile."

We could all learn a lesson from Annie. Maybe we need to add it to our morning checklist: Make breakfast, pack lunches, get children ready for school, apply makeup, and, oh yes—put on a smile.

Smiling does the heart good. Age will not dim our smiles, and they announce our happiness to the world.

But we're not happy, we might argue. We worry when there's too much month left at the end of the paycheck. Our children's misbehavior weighs us down. We long for adult companionship and suffer loneliness. We battle anger, regret, and bitterness over our life situation.

Maybe we could choose another word and say we're joyful. Unlike happiness, joy depends on God rather than our circumstances. As the psalmist points out, God never disappoints anyone who comes to Him for help. He may not help us in quite the way we expect, but He will always give us exactly what we need.

When we wear a happy face despite our circumstances, we may find that our inward spirit changes to match the outward smile.

Dear Lord, let our smiles come from the inside out.
Our circumstances change, but You never do. Thank You, Lord!

The Gift of Friends

Two are better than one, because they have a good return for their work: If one falls down, his friend can help him up. But pity the man who falls and has no one to help him up!
Ecclesiastes 4:9–10 NIV

As our children grow, we want good things—including good friends—for them. Many of us have been praying for a spouse for our child while our kid's still in diapers. We meet our kids' friends, and often the parents of those friends, to be sure our kids are surrounding themselves with positive influences.

Sometimes, though, we forget that adults have a similar need for good friends. Single moms especially would benefit from that one special friend who will be there, no matter what. Maybe it's someone to shop with or borrow a sweater from, or maybe it's that trusted friend who will answer the phone in the middle of the night when little Jillian has a high fever or we simply need to vent our frustrations.

Jesus is our helper and our hope, undoubtedly. But often He works through sincere and trusted friends—especially that one special friend for whom the blessings are mutual.

Lord, sometimes I feel lonely and in desperate need of a friend who will be honest with me and yet not judge me. . .someone who will send me a note on Valentine's Day or find time to join me for coffee or a movie. Please bless me with one true friend, a gift from You, to fill some of the void I feel in my life.

A Mom, a Minivan, and a Mercedes Benz

Has God forgotten to be gracious,
or has He in anger withdrawn His compassion?
Psalm 77:9 NASB

A sporty Mercedes Benz recklessly cut off Connie's minivan as she was driving her son to basketball practice. At the school, she noticed that Mr. Mercedes himself had parked and was walking toward the buildings. Dressed in a button-down shirt and tie, he looked like somebody's dad.

Connie unrolled her car window and politely asked, "Sir? Did you even realize that you cut me off?" The man stopped, narrowed his eyes, and swore at her.

Connie was stunned. How *dare* he treat a woman like that?

Sitting in the parking lot, trying to decide what to do about Mr. Mercedes, Connie prayed. And then, calming down, she listened. The situation became clearer. It was as if the Lord was saying, "Stop personalizing this. Look beyond the behavior. Look at what it tells you about him."

Connie felt a wave of pity for the man. Anyone who would act that way, especially toward a mom in a minivan on a bright, sunny morning, must be a pretty miserable guy.

On his windshield, Connie left a note, inviting him to church. *Who knows?* she thought. *Maybe he'll try it.*

Lord, help me to turn to You even faster when I am upset or angry.
Thank You for intervening in my life and giving me the perspective that I need.

Blessings or Burdens?

The people brought children to Jesus, hoping he might touch them. The disciples shooed them off. But Jesus was irate and let them know it: "Don't push these children away."
Mark 10:13–14 MSG

"Did you get your homework done?" "Clean your room!" "Stop teasing your sister!" "No, you cannot have potato chips for dinner." "You did *what* to the neighbor's dog?" "If I have to change one more diaper, I'm gonna scream."

Sound familiar?

Not exactly the picture-perfect family scenario you were hoping for—but this is reality. Not just for you, but for all of us at one time or another. Picture-perfect families occur only in pictures!

Like all of us, Jesus had a busy schedule. Yet He took time for children. Think about it—the Lord of glory bounced kids on His lap! The disciples tried to shoo the children away. After all, there were more important matters to attend to, and they couldn't be bothered by giggling kids with runny noses.

Are we sometimes so caught up in "being mom" that we forget to stop and enjoy the moments we have with our children? Would a potato chip dinner over a board game knock us out of the running for "Mom of the Year"?

Let's make sure our children know they're not a burden, but a blessing.

Father God, what a blessing You have given me in my children. Teach me how to enjoy my time with them.

All in Good Time

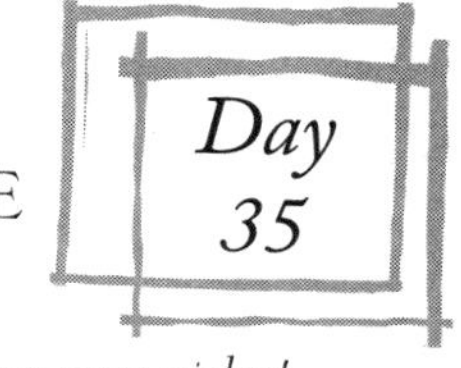

What a Day that will be! No more cold nights—in fact, no more nights! The Day is coming—the timing is God's—when it will be continuous day. Every evening will be a fresh morning.
Zechariah 14:6 MSG

Susan put her son to bed then tiptoed to her own room. There, she couldn't contain her emotions any longer. "God, when will you send me a husband?" she pleaded. "When will this time of being alone end? I need help now, Lord."

Through the tears, it can be hard to see that God has a plan for our lives. If that means a better job, a physical healing, or a new husband and father for our kids, that will happen—but only in God's perfect time.

In today's Bible passage, Zechariah is talking about the Lord's return—but the lesson is applicable in a much broader context. God's timing is perfect. While our situations may seem hopeless, to God, they're just part of the bigger picture. Our job is to trust God's timing for every circumstance of life—including the building of a new family unit. God knows our situation, and He will not forsake us.

Dear God, help me to remember that Your timing is perfect. In every situation, whether looking for a partner or taking care of my family unit, I pray that You would help me to seek Your will and Your perfect timing.

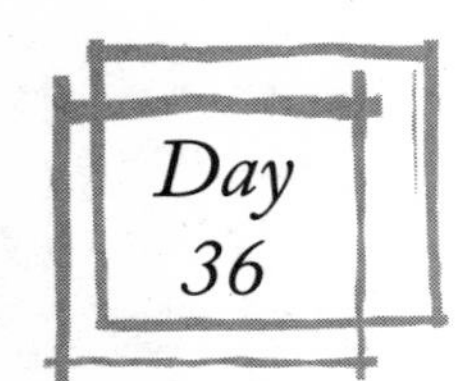

Meeting My Needs

And my God will meet all your needs according to his glorious riches in Christ Jesus.
PHILIPPIANS 4:19 NIV

Jillian strapped her two small girls into their car seats, then settled into the driver's seat. She glanced at the gas gauge, its needle pointing frighteningly close to empty. Jillian had to visit the store for milk, bread, and diapers. How she could pay for those and still find enough to cover the phone bill was anyone's guess. *God,* Jillian cried silently, *I need your help.*

Rest assured, moms—God hears our silent cries. While He never promised to meet our wants or desires, He does promise to meet our *needs.* That great new pair of black slingbacks in the shoe store window may not qualify as a need in God's sight. But if we sincerely ask His help, with a thankful heart, God miraculously covers us with His riches. We find, somehow, that our needs are met. After all, He owns the cattle on a thousand hills. And that's a lot of shoe leather.

Though we may not immediately appreciate *how* He does it, God always comes through for us.

Dear Lord, at times I find myself in need with bills that need to be paid and cupboards that are bare. Please do a miraculous work and cover me today and every day. Your Word says You will meet my needs, so I put my faith in You and stand firmly on Your Word. Thank You.

Sweet Sleep

When thou liest down, thou shalt not be afraid: yea, thou shalt lie down, and thy sleep shall be sweet.
Proverbs 3:24 KJV

Betty never gets enough rest. She's busy from the moment she awakens until she lies down late at night. After she puts the children to bed, she tackles one more chore before she can call it a day.

Betty may allow herself a half hour of television before bedtime, but when she lies down, her mind still races with unfinished business. She tallies her fears. *What if the car breaks down? What will I do when the heating bill comes? Will the boss let me leave work early for the parent-teacher conference?* Betty tosses and turns and falls into a fitful sleep, only to be awakened by the alarm's clamor all too soon.

Sound familiar? Many of us have not learned how to release fear and find sweet sleep. The secret? Believing that God is greater than our greatest fear.

Does our way seem dark? God is light.

Do our bills exceed our income? Our God shall supply all our needs.

Do we fear for our children? The Lord is faithful to a thousand generations.

The more we focus on God's character—not our own weakness—the sweeter our sleep will be.

Oh, Lord, may I always keep Your wisdom, not my concerns, before me. May I always rest in peace and joy.

Start Over

Jesus said, "Neither do I condemn you;
go, and from now on sin no more."
John 8:11 ESV

Patty heard a thunderous cry from downstairs. Her two sons were fighting again and someone had gotten hurt. She hurried downstairs to referee. Instead of listening to their litany of complaints, she told them to "start over." Whoever began the discussion that led to the argument needed to begin again. The boys looked at her with a blank stare. Finally, the older one complied, asking the younger one to move his things. This time, the attitude that ignited the flare-up was missing.

"Start overs" became Patty's parenting tool to teach her boys to think about *how* they said things. Little by little, she noticed a reduction in the number of petty arguments.

God gives us opportunities for daily start overs.

One morning while teaching at the temple, Jesus was interrupted by some self-righteous Pharisees. They had dragged along a woman caught in adultery, insisting that she be stoned. "What do you say?" they asked Jesus.

Jesus quietly suggested that the man without sin had the right to throw the first stone. One by one, the accusers silently left. Jesus asked the woman, "Where are they? Has no one condemned you?" (John 8:10 ESV).

She answered, "No one."

What was Jesus' response? "Neither do I condemn you; go, and from now on sin no more" (John 8:11 ESV).

In other words, dear lady, start over.

Lord of second chances, thank You for not condemning me,
but for giving me daily opportunities to start over and do it right.

A Mother's Love

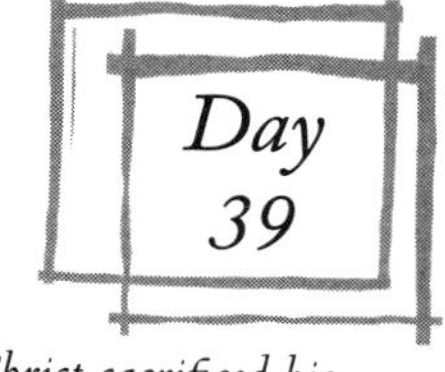

This is how we've come to understand and experience love: Christ sacrificed his life for us. This is why we ought to live sacrificially for our fellow believers.
1 John 3:16 msg

Recovering from surgery, a young boy reclined on the family sofa. As he described his anxiety leading up to the operation—and the pain following—his mother told him, "Son, I hate to see you suffer. If I could have taken your place, I would have."

The boy responded, "You must love me a lot to be willing to do that."

How that story echoes the Father's heart toward His children. He not only wanted to spare us agonizing, eternal pain, He actually bore the pain on our behalf. Suffering for us, taking our punishment. . . but not because we're so good or deserving. No—simply and purely because He loves us.

If we as moms are capable of such overwhelming compassion for our children, how much more does our heavenly Father care for us? God offers us the ultimate example of selfless love and infinite wisdom. And He'll help us with both in our own families.

Father God, thank You for leaving us such an example of love and selflessness. When I am weak and tired, grant me a heart of patience and compassion for my own children.

Jesus' Wristwatch

Look carefully then how you walk, not as unwise but as wise, making the best use of the time, because the days are evil. Therefore do not be foolish, but understand what the will of the Lord is.
Ephesians 5:15–17 ESV

Time is money, they say. Society preaches the value of making good use of our time—and the expense of wasting it.

In the Bible, Ephesians 5 speaks of using every opportunity wisely. But even though scripture teaches the value of time, Jesus never wore a watch. He didn't view His opportunities within the bounds of earthly time.

Have you ever ended a day with guilt and regret over the growing black hole of work yet to be completed? Or do you feel peace at the end of your day, having walked in the presence of the Lord?

Satan wants to consume you with endless lists of meaningless tasks. Fight back! Concern yourself less with the items you can cross off your to-do list, and more with those things the Lord would have you spend your time and energy on. You can strive to be a great multitasker or workhorse—but it's more important and fulfilling to be an efficient laborer for the Lord.

Father, help me to see where You are working and join You there. Let me place my list of tasks aside as I seek Your will for me today. Then give me the ability to show myself grace over the things I do not get done.

Remember This

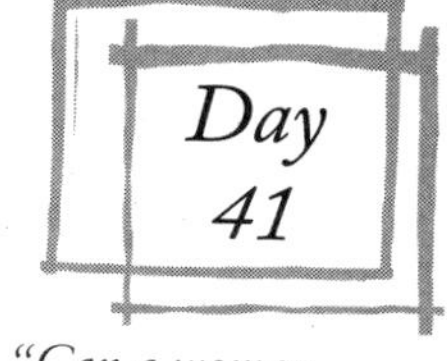

"The Lord *has left me alone. The* Lord *has forgotten me." "Can a woman forget her nursing child? Can she have no pity on the son to whom she gave birth? Even these may forget, but I will not forget you."*
Isaiah 49:14–15 NLV

One of the first lessons we try to teach our children is not to forget their homework. . .their lunch money. . .their shoes! Adults, too, struggle with remembering everyday responsibilities. We forget our keys. We forget to turn off the coffeepot. We may even forget to pay the electric bill until a terse final notice reminds us next week will be spent in utter darkness unless we send a check. *Now!*

A mom may forget a bill, but she never forgets the first time she held her baby in her arms. The fuzzy little head against her breast. The soft, perfect baby fingers and toes, all twenty of them!

Unthinkable as it seems, newspapers every day report mothers who abandon their children because of addiction to alcohol and drugs. Some desert their little ones out of frustration or fear for the future. Others crave a loose, carefree lifestyle.

But God tells us He will never leave or forsake us.

And that we should never forget it.

Father, You are the one who feeds and cares for us. Thank You for Your faithful, everlasting love. Help me to follow Your example and be there for my children when they need me.

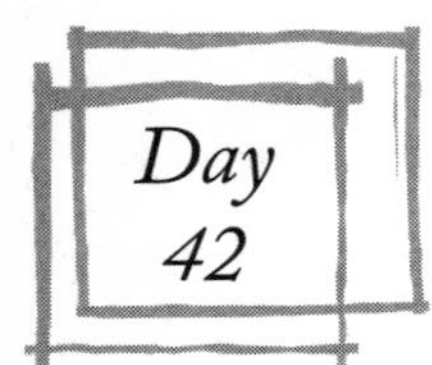

God's Wish List

For wisdom is better than jewels,
and all that you may desire cannot compare with her.
Proverbs 8:11 ESV

Whatever circumstance brought us to single motherhood, we all live in a single income household. And, like anyone else, the mania of materialism can hit us hard. Our desires often exceed our needs and our pocketbooks. Our wish list of all that we desire includes more than we could ever afford.

God has already identified what should be at the top of our wish list. It's not food or clothing; He's already promised to take care of those necessities. And it's not more money to give to missions, as spiritual as that may sound.

What we need most is something that money can't buy: God tells us to seek *wisdom*. Good sense, the ability to apply knowledge and experience to what is happening today—what could be more valuable?

Wisdom is rarer than the rarest jewel, and worth far more. Wisdom can guide us through a multitude of daily quandaries. It can help us differentiate between what we want and what we need. Tell us when to speak and when to be silent. Teach us how to live with our neighbors. Discipline us to avoid temptation and sin. Show us how to live on what we have.

God promises to give wisdom to everyone who asks (James 1:5). Pursuing wisdom means pursuing God.

Lord, I don't need more things.
Please grant me wisdom about the things I already possess.

Two Hopeless Sisters

Lot and his two daughters left Zoar and settled in the mountains, for he was afraid to stay in Zoar. He and his two daughters lived in a cave. One day the older daughter said to the younger, "Our father is old, and there is no man around here to lie with us, as is the custom all over the earth."
Genesis 19: 30–31 NIV

Those poor sisters. These girls had been raised in Sodom, a Canaanite city so corrupt that God sent angels to destroy it. Lot fled with his daughters and lived in a cave.

In that primitive culture, hope for a secure future rested entirely on a son's shoulders. Lot's daughters were out of luck. There were no bachelors hanging around the caves. Desperate, hopeless, and faithless, the daughters came up with an idea: get their father drunk, then sleep with him to conceive a child.

It's hard to feel anything but disgust for those two sisters. But how many times have we scrambled to find a man- (or woman-) made answer to our problems? How many times have we turned to God as an afterthought?

The Lord is faithful even when we are not. Scripture tells us that the older daughter had a son named Moab, father of the Moabites. Five hundred years later, a Moabite baby grew up to become Ruth, grandmother of Israel's great King David.

Heavenly Father, when will I learn to turn to You to solve my problems? When I go my own way, it ends in disaster. Thank You that even my poor choices are not beyond Your ability to redeem.

One Thing Is Needed

"Martha, Martha," the Lord answered, "you are worried and upset about many things, but only one thing is needed."
Luke 10:41–42 NIV

We are each given twenty-four hours in a day. Einstein and Edison were given no more than Joseph and Jeremiah of the Old Testament. The president and the paratrooper are all given an equal share. Even Mother Teresa and plain ol' moms are peers when it comes to time.

Time—we can't buy it, save it, or get a greater share no matter what we do. Its value is beyond measure. So we should learn to use it carefully. Do we tackle the laundry now or help the kids read *If You Give a Mouse a Cookie* one more time? Do we stay up late, cleaning the living room, or slip into bed early, knowing we need the rest? Do we fuss over our hair and makeup or find a moment to kneel before our Father?

Since God has blessed each of us with twenty-four hours, let's seek His direction on how to spend this invaluable commodity, wisely—giving more to people than things, spending more time on relationships than the rat race. In Luke, our Lord reminded dear, dogged, drained Martha that only one thing is needed—Him.

Father God, oftentimes, I get caught up in the minutia of life. The piled laundry can appear more important than the precious little ones You've given me. Help me to use my time wisely. Open my eyes to see what is truly important.

LADIES IN WAITING

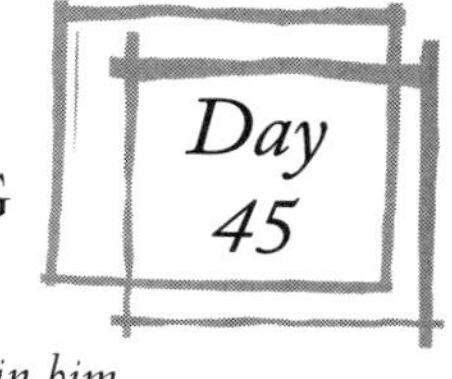

I will wait for the LORD. . . . I will put my trust in him.
ISAIAH 8:17 NIV

Modern humans aren't good at waiting. In our fast-paced society, if you can't keep up, you'd better get out of the way. We have fast food, speed dialing, and jam-packed schedules that are impossible to keep. Instant gratification is the name of the game—and that attitude often affects our own families.

The Lord Jesus Christ doesn't care about instant gratification. Our right-now attitudes don't move Him. Maybe He finds the saying, "Give me patience, Lord, *right now*," humorous—but He rarely answers that particular prayer.

Do we want joy without accepting heartache? Peace without living through the stress? Patience without facing demands? God sees things differently. He's giving us the opportunity to learn through these delays, irritations, and struggles. What a wise God He is!

We as single moms especially need to learn the art of waiting on God. He will come through every time—but in *His* time, not ours. The wait may be hours or days, or it could be years. But God is always faithful to provide for us. It is when we learn to wait on Him that we will find joy, peace, and patience through the struggle.

Father, You know what I need, so I will wait. Help me be patient, knowing that You control my situation and that all good things come in Your time.

Blessing, Not Blasting

Bless the Lord, *O my soul:*
and all that is within me, bless his holy name.
Psalm 103:1 kjv

Many people in our country claim they do not believe in God; others shrug and say they don't know if He exists. But whenever a copier jams at work, or a dish is dropped in a restaurant, or a flight is delayed, atheists and agnostics include God in the midst of their misery. They yell His name as if *He* messed up on the job—even though they believe He doesn't officially exist.

We, as Christians, are called to invest all our emotional energy in blessing God, rather than blasting Him. When others demean their day as "god-awful," we can choose to experience a "God-wonderful" day. When others swear at traffic, we can sing praises along with a CD or radio. With His help—because no one can praise God without tapping into the power of His Spirit—we can develop spiritual radar that detects daily God-moments worthy of applause: rainbows and roses, clean water to drink, and belly laughs with our kids.

Every day God stacks His gifts around us as if it were Christmas. Like children, we can't give Him much. But we can offer all we are to bless His holy name. And that's the present He loves most.

Lord, each day I encounter thousands of opportunities to bless You, the Lord of the universe. Help me seize the day and praise You whenever I can!

THE NEW ME

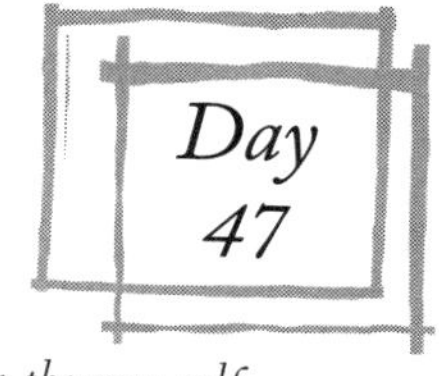

Be made new in the attitude of your minds; and. . .put on the new self, created to be like God in true righteousness and holiness.
EPHESIANS 4:23–24 NIV

It has been said that "attitude determines altitude." What does that mean? Simply this: Your attitude will either cause you to rise above life's circumstances or be buried by them.

We single moms face a mountain of circumstances that seem to range from barely bearable to completely unbearable. When our preschooler is kicking and screaming at the classroom door, it is barely bearable. And any mom who's had to tell her children that daddy won't be coming home anymore knows the completely unbearable.

But our choice of attitude can make even these seemingly unbearable circumstances bearable. We may not have control or power over our life situations—which can appear completely hopeless. But when we let the Holy Spirit renew our minds—when we choose an attitude of hope and peace—we can get through the worst circumstances with grace and beauty.

Jesus, my circumstances sometimes seem hopeless. Help me put on a new self and renew my mind's attitude so that I can find Your hope. Give me the ability to be like You in righteousness, and help me walk in the holiness and hopefulness that can only come from You.

Three Days without a Miracle

So the people grumbled against Moses,
saying "What are we to drink?"
Exodus 15:24 NIV

The Israelites were thirsty. Really, really thirsty. The kind of thirsty where they couldn't think of anything *but* water. Their tongues felt thick and their eyes burned under the relentless glare of the hot sun.

They had been wandering in the desert for three days without water, and they were about to snap. Could anyone blame them? Three million people, wandering in the desert without a road map, lacking such basic supplies as food and water. They did what people do when under stress. They blamed their leader. "Moses!" they complained. "It's all your fault!"

In reality, the Israelites had gone three days without a miracle. A few days prior, the Lord had parted the Red Sea, allowing the Israelites to escape, then closed it up again to drown the pursuing Egyptian army. Just three days ago! How had they forgotten God's just-in-time provision?

Moses didn't forget. His first response was to turn to God. "Then Moses cried out to the Lord, and the Lord showed him a piece of wood. He threw it into the water, and the water became sweet" (Exodus 15:25 NIV).

God held the answer to the Israelites' basic needs. He responded to Moses' prayer immediately, as if He had just been waiting.

What if we turned to God immediately with our basic needs, instead of waiting until the thirst set in? What if we remembered His faithfulness before, or better still, instead of, panicking? Most likely, we would have our sweet water sooner.

Lord, You are the supplier to my every need. Thank You for Your faithfulness.

ANXIETIES

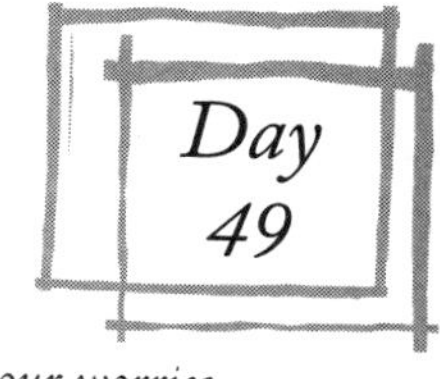

Casting the whole of your care [all your anxieties, all your worries, all your concerns, once and for all] on Him, for He cares for you affectionately and cares about you watchfully.
I PETER 5:7 AMP

Because He cares for you. Not because you have to. Not because it's the "right" thing to do. Not because it's what you're supposed to do. No. Read it again. . . Because He cares for you. That's right, He cares for you!

Our Father isn't standing there with His hand on His hip, saying, "All right, spit it out, I don't have all day," or worse. . .holding His hands to His ears, saying, "Enough! You have way too many problems."

The Amplified Bible puts it this way: "Casting the whole of your care [all your anxieties, all your worries, all your concerns, once and for all] on Him, for He cares for you affectionately and cares about you watchfully" (I Peter 5:7).

Because He cares for you. How humbling and emotionally overwhelming it is to realize that our Lord and God, Jesus Christ, actually wants us to unburden our hearts to Him. Not just because He knows that's what's best for us but simply because He cares. To know He isn't just informing us of one more requirement we have to meet. No. He asks each one of us to cast all our cares and anxieties on Him because He cares for us.

Father, I am overjoyed at Your concern for me. Thank You! Please teach me to cast my cares into Your arms. . .and leave them there.

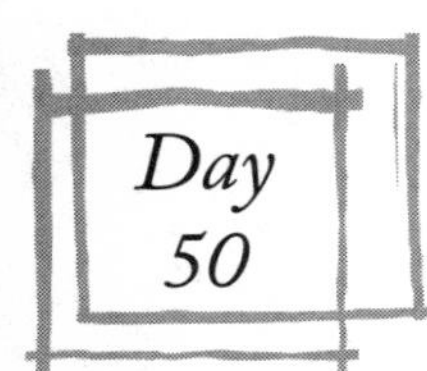

Patience Is a Virtue

And not only so, but we glory in tribulations also: knowing that tribulation worketh patience; and patience, experience; and experience, hope.
Romans 5:3–4 KJV

"Teach me patience, Lord." There are very few more dangerous words a Christian can utter. Patience can only be taught through tribulation.

In your life, what is God using to teach you patience? A crying baby? Endless diapers? Sleepless nights? Calls from the school principal? Spilled milk? Nonstop questions? You fill in the blank.

Trials produce experiences from which we can learn. The growth that comes through trials teaches us that every unsavory moment in life will eventually pass—and that, through Christ, there is victory in the endurance. That wisdom is true hope.

Can you find hope in the midst of your tribulations today? Let the Holy Spirit help you navigate your day with the wisdom to see that "this too will pass." And when it does, patience, maturity, and most of all, hope, will be the reward.

Lord Jesus, help me to be like the apostle Paul, welcoming the tribulations in my life as a means of becoming the person You've called me to be. Let me learn from my experiences and grow to be more like You.

THE THREE R'S

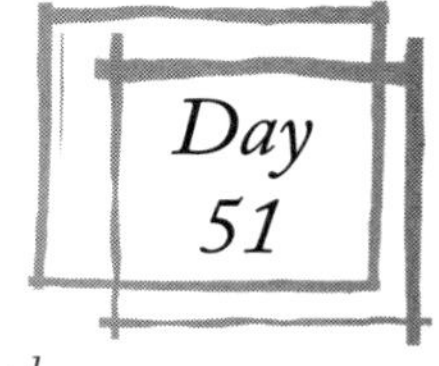

He who gives attention to the word will find good,
and blessed is he who trusts in the LORD.
PROVERBS 16:20 NASB

Not long ago, educators emphasized the three R's: reading, 'riting, and 'rithmetic. We believed that if we could succeed at higher learning, we would obtain good work and thus prosperity. Education was perceived as the solution to all social ills.

The Bible suggests a different path to prosperity: Heed God's Word. The dictionary defines the verb *heed* as "to give consideration or attention to." In other words, we mind what God says.

There are three ways we can heed God's Word.

Read it. The options for systematic Bible reading vary more than ever before. We can choose among a plethora of versions and even among audio renditions. Most Bibles contain a plan for daily reading. Whatever we choose, we must read the Word in order to heed it.

Remember it. Review the verses we learned as children. Tape favorite verses to our mirrors, on our computers, in our cars. We heed the Word by meditating on it and memorizing it.

Respect it. We heed the Word when we obey it. God did not give us a list of suggestions but rather commands for daily living.

These three R's are the path to prosperity.

Lord, in Your Word I find all that I need for peace and prosperity. Teach me the discipline of time spent in the Bible and then transform me through it.

Bone Tired

He said unto me, Son of man, can these bones live?
And I answered, O Lord God, thou knowest.
Ezekiel 37:3 KJV

Single mothers face each day as if they were running marathons: ready, set, go. . .and go. . . and go! Pack lunches. Drop children off at the sitter's or school. Finish the work project for an important meeting. After school, call the kids. Settle a fight over who takes out the trash. Pick up fast food on the way home. Dash to church for Bible study and children's night. By the time a mom wearily drops into a pew, her energy level has dropped below empty. Her body and spirit feel as if she can never, ever rise again.

Ezekiel experienced a similar feeling as he tried to bring God's messages to a group of Jewish exiles who did not want to hear it. The nation Israel languished, unresponsive as the dry bones Ezekiel saw in a vision. To his amazement, God's Spirit entered into the bones and turned them into a mighty army to accomplish His purpose.

Even on our worst days, God can revive our lifeless bones and transform us into courageous soldiers who can follow His commands. Like Ezekiel, we learn that He, the Lord of Life, is all we need.

Lord Jesus, thank You for being my Light and Life. I face this day knowing You will resurrect me at the end of it. Thank You for Your Spirit who gives me strength far beyond what I can imagine.

THE TREASURES OF WISDOM

The little child grew and became strong.
He was filled with wisdom, and God's goodness was upon him.
LUKE 2:40 NCV

What was Jesus like as a child? Did Mary and Joseph ever have cause to scold Him? As a toddler, did Jesus ever stick His hand in the fire? Or did He ever poke His baby brother to make him scream?

The Gospel of Luke is our only glimpse into Jesus' childhood. Our first peek into those years, from Luke 2, indicates that after Mary and Joseph returned to Galilee, Jesus grew, became strong, and was filled with wisdom.

Now fast-forward a few years. Jesus is twelve, a significant year in a Jewish boy's life—because He is now a man. With His parents, Jesus has traveled to Jerusalem for the Passover. After the weeklong festival, Mary and Joseph head home—only to discover, somewhere down the road, that Jesus is not among their group. Back they hurry to Jerusalem, fearing the worst. After three frantic days, they find Jesus calmly discussing theology in the temple. It almost seems as if the temple was the last place Joseph and Mary thought to search!

Luke closes this vignette with another description of Jesus' development: He "grew in wisdom and stature, and in favor with God and men" (2:52 NIV).

Does wisdom top the list of our goals for our children? Or is it stuffed underneath other hopes—for self-reliance, physical protection, or good grades? God Himself treasures wisdom—that one quality appears twice in the limited record of Jesus' childhood.

Lord, may my children commit themselves
to a lifelong search for Your wisdom.

Speak Kind Words of Love

A gentle answer turns away wrath, but a harsh word stirs up anger.
Proverbs 15:1 NIV

The young boy walked slowly into the kitchen. Head low, hands behind his back, he whispered, "Momma, I'm sorry."

She glared at the boy and said sharply, "What did you do?"

"I broke it," he said, showing her what he was hiding in his hand. It was a toy from a fast-food kids' meal that she had lovingly given to him just a few hours before. "I didn't mean to make you mad."

She saw the grief in her son's eyes and pulled him into her arms. "It's okay, baby," she said gently. "I'm not mad. But I am sorry—I shouldn't have yelled at you." Taking the broken toy, she said, "I think I can fix this if you'll help me. Would you go get the glue?"

The boy jumped up with a smile.

Ever been there? How often do we snap at our children when a kind word or a hug is what they really need? Today, let's plan ahead for such moments. When it seems like the kids are doing something wrong, first take a deep breath. Let go of the frustrations and remember that your children are still learning—not only from their mistakes, but from your reactions as well. Then speak kind words of love.

Heavenly Father, help me show my children Your loving-kindness in all things. When correction is necessary, help me discipline from a heart of compassion.

Bottles of Tears

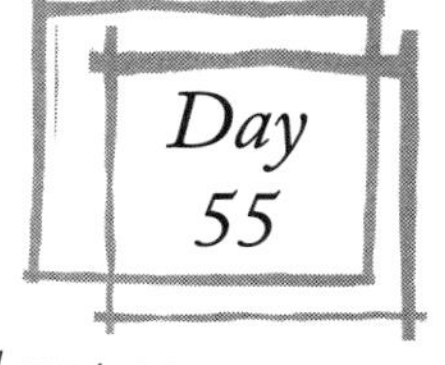

You keep track of all my sorrows. You have collected all my tears in your bottle. You have recorded each one in your book.
Psalm 56:8 NLT

Your workday is done, dinner is long over, and the dishes are washed. The last child has finally fallen asleep, and you quietly slip into your own bed. You've made it through another day. Silence.

And then it happens. . .again. The tears. In the night's solitude, you cry. You don't want to. Yet, as a single mom, alone, the tears flow freely.

The salty tears will dry before any other person knows of your pain. Can there be a more heart-wrenching scene?

But wait a minute. God promises that He is near the brokenhearted. He keeps track of your sorrows, making a record of them. He even bottles your tears. Did you catch that? He *bottles your tears.* You'll never be abandoned to face your pain alone. Your heavenly Father knows, and takes note, of all that troubles you. Jesus Himself is described as a "man of sorrows, acquainted with deepest grief" (Isaiah 53:3 NLT). Having endured such sorrow Himself, He can certainly offer you the comfort you need.

Go ahead, cry if you need to—but with the assurance that there is One who sees and is more than ready to comfort you.

Father, Your Word promises that You keep track of all that causes me sorrow—even to the point of bottling my tears. Thank You for never leaving me alone!

More Than Enough

Let us not become weary in doing good, for at the proper time we will reap a harvest if we do not give up.
Galatians 6:9 NIV

How often do we become impatient and give up? We stand in line at the coffee shop and find ourselves behind an indecisive person. Frustrated, we give up—but before we get to our car, that person—coffee cup in hand—walks past. If we'd only waited another minute, we, too, could be sipping a steaming caramel latte.

Or maybe we have a dream that we can't seem to make a reality—and rather than trying "just one more time," we give up. A piece of who we are drifts away like a leaf on the sea.

The Word of God encourages us to keep going, to press on, to fight off weariness and never give up. Jesus Christ has a harvest for each of us, and He eagerly anticipates blessing us with it—but we have to trust Him and refuse to give in to weariness.

We can only imagine what that harvest might be, because we know that God is the God of "immeasurably more than all we ask or imagine" (Ephesians 3:20 niv). We can be recipients of His "immeasurably more" if we press on in the strength He provides.

When you're tired, keep going—and remember that, in His perfect timing, you will reap an unimaginable harvest.

Father, You know that I'm tired and weary in this uphill struggle. Fill me with Your strength so I can carry on. I long to reap the harvest You have for me.

Do as I Do!

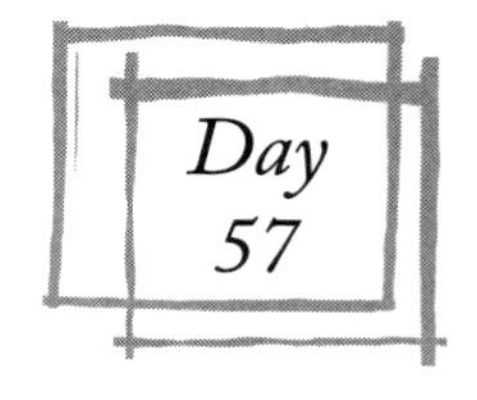

"'These people honor me with their lips,
but their hearts are far from me.'"
Matthew 15:8 NLT

"Because I'm the mom, that's why!"

We've all known mothers—perhaps we've been them ourselves—who expect their children simply to obey orders, even when the moms don't live up to their own standards. For example, we teach our children not to lie. But what will they think when they overhear us fibbing to get out of a commitment? The surest way for us to lose respect and erode the very values we're trying to instill is to expect one thing from our child while doing some other thing ourselves.

Children innately follow Mom. And they often allow mom's behavior, more than her words, to shape who they become. What might your child's behavior say about your home? Is it filled with joy and respect, or grumpiness and cursing? Are loyalty and honesty exemplified in daily choices, or are "harmless" lies and excuses the norm?

As moms, we need to live our own lives above reproach before we can expect godly behavior and good choices from each of our children. May our words and actions always be ones that we would be proud to see repeated by our child. . .because they will be!

Lord, please show me the ways in which I am not living up to my own expectations. Help me be a good example and a mom who deserves respect and obedience.

This House Is Too Crowded

"Agreed," she replied. "Let it be as you say."
Joshua 2:21 NIV

Rahab and her family were crowded inside her tiny house situated on the walls of Jericho. They were waiting for those two Israeli spies to return with their army.

The spies had promised Rahab they would keep her safe from the coming siege. That's all she had to rely on—the word of spies. But Rahab had come to believe that the Israelites' God was the true God. She was willing to stake her life, as well as the life of her crowded household, on that belief.

Still, she faced an indeterminate wait—probably with irritable family members who doubted her story. On the day the spies had departed, Rahab had tied that scarlet cord outside her window, to tip them off to her house. Had the cord grown faded, like the patience of her family?

Where were the Israelites? What was taking them so long? Rahab could have no idea what was happening in the camp of the Israelites where, in obedience to God, Joshua had ordered all the men to be circumcised, in a day without anesthetics. Huge numbers of men, each one requiring time to heal!

Rahab didn't know any of that, but she still remained steadfast. Ultimately, she did see God act—saving herself and her family.

There are times when all we have to rely on is the Word of God. When that happens, remember Rahab's steadfastness! We can have confidence that His promises will come true: Let it be as He says.

Lord, may my faith in Your Word benefit my family as Rahab's faith in the spies' word helped hers. Help me to remain steadfast regarding Your promises.

Casseroles and Kids

"Physical training is good, but training for godliness is much better, promising benefits in this life and in the life to come."
1 Timothy 4:8 NLT

The recipe is generations old, and it works perfectly: Grandma's creamy chicken casserole tastes exactly the same each time it's made. Whether Aunt Becky or Cousin Steve does the cooking, as long as they follow the recipe, the casserole turns out the same—delicious.

Raising children, however, is different. It's not simply a matter of following a "recipe." How many of us have seen a friend or family member carefully choose which television programs to watch, review school assignments for inappropriate material, scrutinize their children's friends, maybe even pursue private education or homeschooling, all in an effort to turn out perfect children. But there are times when at least one of those kids will go astray.

Why would such a child walk away? What makes the difference? Perhaps the "missing ingredient" is a freedom to choose.

We can meticulously follow a child-rearing "recipe" and still have a young person walk away from what he or she has been taught. What's most important for us as single moms is perseverance. We must never give up—forging ahead without unnecessary guilt over real or perceived mistakes.

Raising children is never as simple as following a recipe.

Father God, I surrender my children and my parenting skills to You. Please enable me to do the best I can and leave the rest in Your hands.

Cabbage Patch Love

The Lord said, "I have loved you."
But you ask, "How have you loved us?"
Malachi 1:2 NCV

Mouth gaping open, Jamie stared at the array of Cabbage Patch dolls at the toy store. She examined each doll until she came to an infant boy, complete with birth certificate. "I want this one. His birthday is the same day as mine." Her mother bought the doll, and Jamie doted on it, "feeding" it with the tiny bottle and wiping its face clean. She carried the doll at all times and bragged about it to everyone she met.

Imagine if such a doll could speak. Would it say to Jamie, "You say you love me, but I don't feel loved. How do you love me?"

Sometimes we ask God the same question. "Of course we know You love us, but with everything that's happened, we don't always feel loved."

God has a ready answer: "Before I created Adam, I chose you, as I once chose Jacob instead of Esau. Not only did I choose you, I also adopted you into My family. I gave My Son to make you Mine. I am always with you."

When we examine the facts, it's obvious that God loves us. He longs for us to love Him back. Let's open our eyes—and hearts—to that perfect love.

Father, You chose us to be Your own. You love us with all the tender compassion of a doting Father. Let us rest in Your love.

Seasons of Life

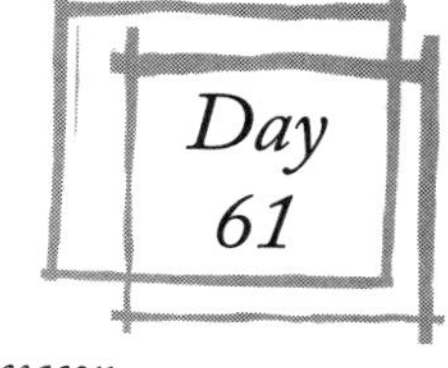

Everything on earth has its own time and its own season.
There is a time for birth and death, planting and reaping. . .
for crying and laughing, weeping and dancing.
ECCLESIASTES 3:1–2, 4 CEV

There is a time for work and play, spending and saving, even for relationships and, perhaps marriage. Interestingly, the Bible is relatively silent about dating guidelines. Maybe that's because singles in biblical times didn't find themselves in consuming, intricate, even potentially dangerous situations like singles today.

Frivolous intimacy and temporary emotional attachments waste energy that God might want us to use elsewhere. God does want His children to have every good and perfect thing that He has planned for them—but in His time. Waiting patiently, until God's will becomes clear, ensures that the energy spent growing close to another person will be a building block for the future rather than a failure to add to the pile of regret.

Strive for such a close walk with the Father—in prayer and Bible study—that the seasons He has designated for you will reveal themselves clearly. Eventually, with faith in His perfect plan for you, the waiting will become an acceptable part of life, of reaching with confidence toward the future.

Father, I trust in Your will, and I will wait until You lead me forward in a relationship. Please make Your will clear to me in all things. And please fill me with Your Spirit so that I never feel alone.

God My Refuge

But the Lord has become my fortress,
and my God the rock in whom I take refuge.
Psalm 94:22 niv

As single moms, we often feel that our fragile shoulders carry too much. We have more responsibility, more burdens, than anyone could imagine. We are both mom and dad; the soft shoulder and the hard hand of discipline; the house cleaner, cook, maintenance person, and gardener. When we fall short—when we don't accomplish in our one-parent homes what other families with two parents can—we feel like failures. And, often, other people make sure we're aware of our shortcomings.

In these times, go to the Lord to hide out for a while. Like a snow fort that protects kids from the flying snowballs of their playmates, God Himself becomes our fortress—and we can hide in Him anytime we need to. His lap is big and always available. We can find refuge under His wings.

When the world says, "You've fallen short," God says, "You are my daughter and I am so proud of you." He picks us up and shields us. We can take refuge in Him.

Lord, sometimes I feel so overburdened, doing so much yet still, falling short of all I need to do and be for my children. In this weary state, negative thoughts and words assail me. I come to You for refuge and safety. I need Your lap to comfort me and protect me from those who throw stones and judge. Be my fortress today, Lord.

NILE CROCODILES

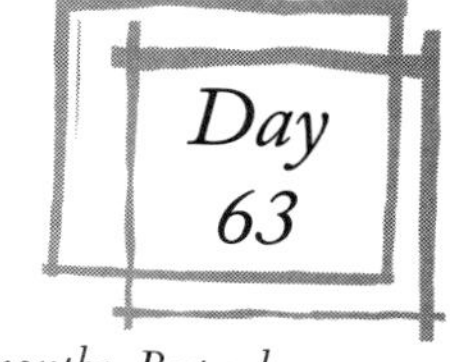

When she saw that he was a fine child, she hid him for three months. But when she could hide him no longer, she got a papyrus basket for him and coated it with tar and pitch. Then she placed the child in it and put it among the reeds along the bank of the Nile. His sister stood at a distance to see what would happen to him.
EXODUS 2:2–4 NIV

How did Moses' mother do it? How did she feel as she gently placed Moses into a (hopefully) waterproof basket and then lowered him into the murky waters of the Nile River?

Then how could she walk away? It was a dangerous river. All around swarmed birds, insects, and the frightening Nile crocodiles. How could his mother have resisted clutching that basket to her breast? Clearly, there was no other alternative for her.

Our children face risks, too, in their own rivers of life. The dangers are different than those Baby Moses may have encountered, but they're just as real: terrorists, car accidents, drugs and alcohol, even guns at school.

God had a plan for Moses' life. He wasn't like Miriam, watching her younger brother from far off; God had His hands on that little boy's basket the entire time. He has our children in His hands, too.

Thank You, Lord, that I can surrender my children to the dangers of life, knowing that You have a plan for them just as You did for Moses.

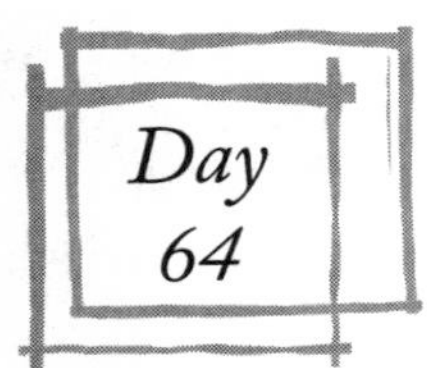

Examples Before Us

We are surrounded by a great cloud of people whose lives tell us what faith means. So let us run the race that is before us and never give up. We should remove from our lives anything that would get in the way and the sin that so easily holds us back.
Hebrews 12:1 NCV

They're all around us. Older women who have walked in our shoes and made it through life successfully. They have much wisdom to offer—if we are willing to ask. Experience alone fills them to overflowing with sage advice just ready to burst out.

So make a list of questions for them! Perhaps you could ask, "How did you enforce bedtimes? Did you deal with being 'alone' at school plays/soccer games/the grocery store/at night? How did you handle being the spiritual leader of the home? How do I 'pick the battles' with my kids? If you could have a 'do-over' in any area, what would it be?"

Let's look to the godly women that God graciously provides as examples for us, as we strive to raise our families according to His principles. The race set before us need not be a solo effort, when God has so richly given us "a great cloud of people whose lives tell us what faith means."

Father God, open my eyes to the people around me, those sent by You as examples to follow. Thank You for so richly providing for me.

Wise Guys

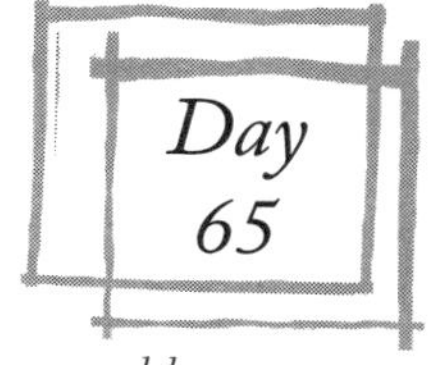

Who is wise, and he shall understand these things? prudent, and he shall know them? for the ways of the LORD are right, and the just shall walk in them: but the transgressors shall fall therein.
HOSEA 14:9 KJV

Have we read many headlines that include the words *wisdom* and *prudence*? Few "Ten Ways to Succeed" lists feature them—especially if we're talking about God's wisdom and prudence as defined in the Bible.

"Don't be so narrow-minded!" Coworkers laugh when we refuse to compromise Christian standards of honesty and diligence.

"The Bible? You've got to be kidding!" Friends roll their eyes. "It's about a zillion years old! What's the Bible got to do with today?" They pat us on the shoulder. "You need some fun in your life. Do what works for you."

God loves us, and He cares about our individual needs—and our fun! But His plan often stretches far beyond "what works" for each of us. If we choose to believe God and walk in His ways, He helps us deal with our weakness as we accept the scary challenges looming before us. God makes safe paths for our feet. But those who rebel against God stumble over His truth. The Word that heals us hurts unbelievers—and no one can offer them true relief until they "get wise" by turning back to God.

Father, even when I don't understand Your wisdom, help me believe Your loving heart. I pray for my friends who don't know You that they, too, may walk in safety.

Sleep on It

It is of the LORD's mercies that we are not consumed, because his compassions fail not. They are new every morning: great is thy faithfulness.
LAMENTATIONS 3:22–23 KJV

"Sleep on it." Researchers have found that to be sound advice. They believe that sleep helps people sort through facts, thoughts, and memories, providing a clearer look at the big picture upon waking. Sleep also separates reality from emotions like fear and worry, which can cloud our thinking and interfere with rational decision-making. Scientifically speaking, sleep is good medicine.

For Christians, the biological effects of sleep are outweighed by the spiritual benefits of the new day God gives us. At the end of an exhausting day, after the worries and the pressures of life have piled high, we may lie down, feeling as though we can't take another moment of stress. But God's Word tells us that His great mercy will keep our worries and problems from consuming us.

Through the never-ending compassion of God, His faithfulness is revealed afresh each morning. We can rise with renewed vigor. We can eagerly anticipate the new day, leaving behind the concerns of yesterday.

Heavenly Father, thank You for giving me a new measure of Your mercy and compassion each day so that my concerns don't consume me. I rest in You and I lay my burdens at Your feet.

Quiet Zone

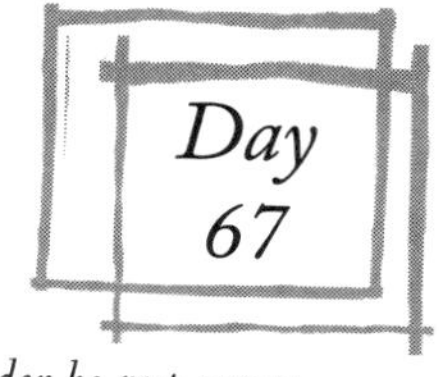

Let all bitterness and wrath and anger and clamor and slander be put away from you. . . . Be kind to one another, tenderhearted, forgiving one another.
Ephesians 4:31–32 ESV

Stacy stepped down from the bus. Her day at the office was over but her real workday—the evening at home with her children—had hardly begun. She slowed her steps, breathing in the fresh air, enjoying the few moments of quiet before the noise of two active preteens accosted her.

Carlie's music assaulted Stacy's ears before she even opened the door to her apartment. Then Stacy almost stumbled over her son, Matt, lying spread-eagled on the floor, face buried in a schoolbook. She reminded herself that the limited space in their two-bedroom apartment magnified every noise and movement.

An hour later, as the three of them sat down to dinner, Carlie read Ephesians 4:31–32 from a card Stacy provided. "Clamor?" she asked. "What does that mean?"

"It means when *you're* noisy!" Matt teased his sister.

Carlie reacted thoughtfully. "Maybe I could turn down the music," she said.

"And maybe I could work on my homework at the table," Matt added, looking at Stacy.

"And I can practice being more tenderhearted," Stacy admitted.

When we turn down the clamor, we can tune into kindness and forgiveness in our families.

Lord, may we remain tenderhearted in the clamor of our lives.

The Gift of Mirth

Parents, don't come down too hard on your children or you'll crush their spirits.
Colossians 3:21 MSG

Jill could be described as a serious gal. She had a strong work ethic, she diligently raised her children, she lived modestly, and she saved money like a miser. That meant she spent very little disposable income on vacations or dinners out or movie nights. She achieved many goals—but she forgot to have fun.

One day, Jill glimpsed her reflection in the mirror. She saw a face that was too harsh and careworn for a woman her age. She often caught herself snapping at the kids with a tone of annoyance. And, one day, with a jolt, she realized that tone had become a habit.

Jill loved her kids—but where was her joy? She was grateful to God for His blessings. But where was the outward evidence of her faith?

Soon, Jill made some changes. She turned Friday evenings into game nights with homemade pizza. And she made a conscious effort to not take herself so seriously. The first time she laughed at herself, her kids looked at her as if they were watching a rusty well starting to pump fresh water.

Little by little, joy and laughter grew in Jill's home, strengthening like a long-unused muscle finally getting some exercise. And as she saw the positive changes in her home, Jill praised God for prompting her to pursue joy.

Please help me, Father, not to crush spirits, but rather to fill my life and the lives of my children with joy!

Follow the Leader

I will instruct you and teach you in the way you should go;
I will guide you with My eye.
Psalm 32:8 NKJV

As children, most of us played the schoolyard game of "Follow the Leader." We ran around laughing, as others followed us wherever we went—down a sliding board, under a culvert, or maybe through poison ivy. It was fun to have control for a while.

As grown women, the game isn't quite as enjoyable. It goes along well for a while, but there's something exhausting about constantly being in charge. Of always being the go-to person, whether in our jobs or our homes. On occasion, it feels good to assign the role of leader to someone else.

In Psalm 32, God reminds us that He desires to be the real leader in our lives. He promises to instruct, teach, and guide us—always keeping His eye on us.

He doesn't casually toss out orders with His head buried in heavenly paperwork. God's eye is always on us as He guides us through both the mundane and major decisions of life.

Let's play "Follow the Leader" with God as our guide.

Father God, how I long to lay down the role of leader. I am under daily pressure to make difficult decisions. Thank You for the assurance that You are keeping an eye on me and are guiding me through this maze of life.

WIMPS FOR JESUS?

Wherefore lift up the hands which hang down, and the feeble knees; and make straight paths for your feet, lest that which is lame be turned out of the way; but let it rather be healed.
HEBREWS 12:12–13 KJV

God's discipline sometimes leaves us feeling limp—and not too bright.

"How could I do such a thing? Why didn't I stop to think, read the Bible, and pray about the situation?"

All Christians live through these humbling experiences, because we all make mistakes—sometimes big ones. Washed up and wiped out, we wonder why Jesus bothers with us. We want to give up.

Satan would like nothing better. "What's the use?" he whispers. "You've embarrassed yourself and God, and there's no way you will ever hold up your head again." We let our Bibles gather dust and stop going to church. When we see other Christians around town, we hide! We also find ourselves spending time and energy in paths that aggravate our pain rather than heal it.

As always, God presents better solutions for our problems. He disciplines us for the same reasons we correct our children: out of love. Ultimately, we want our kids to lead healthy, productive lives. How can we think God wants any less for us?

Lord Jesus, You gave Your life that I might be healed of my sin and weakness. Please help me to obey You, trusting that You know what You're doing in my life.

Press On

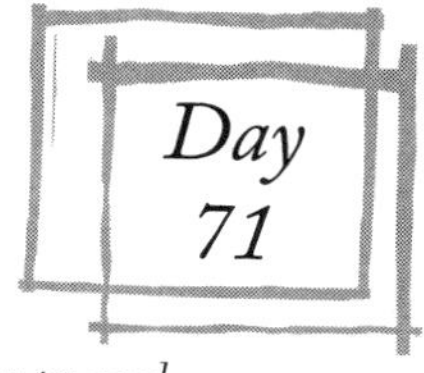

One thing I do: Forgetting what is behind and straining toward what is ahead, I press on toward the goal to win the prize for which God has called me heavenward in Christ.
PHILIPPIANS 3:13–14 NIV

Marcy sat alone on the park bench. Her husband had recently left her and their three young boys. Though Marcy and her husband had been members of a large church for many years, she now felt judged and rejected by her church friends. She had never felt so alone.

When tragedy strikes a marriage, the "Marcys" of the world are left feeling responsible and rejected. But other single moms often feel a similar disapproval from people around them. All of us as single mothers can spend too much time analyzing our pasts, wondering what we did wrong to deserve rejection and loneliness.

God knows we're not perfect—but He also knows that we aren't responsible for other people's behavior and decisions. God encourages us to forget what is behind, a past that can't be changed. Instead, He says, press on to what is ahead: His grace, His mercy, His forgiveness, and His peace. The light of His Word will lead us along the path to heavenly treasures.

Press on. Keep going. We will get to the end of our journey and hear the Lord God say, "Well done, my daughter, well done."

Abba Father, even though I feel a heavy load from the past, Your Word tells me to press on. Help me to forget what is behind and give me the strength and ability to press on in Your truth, power, and wisdom.

Walking in the Truth

I rejoiced greatly to find some of your children walking in the truth, just as we were commanded by the Father.
2 John 4 ESV

Sherry, infant son in her arms, joined other parents at the altar. The pastor challenged them to raise their children to love the Lord. The church promised to uphold them in prayer. She prayed silently, *Lord, help me to teach my child to love You.*

Melissa took her place beside her daughter. Mandy had asked Jesus to be her Savior during Vacation Bible School. Déjà vu swept over her. She remembered making the same decision at exactly the same age. Melissa rejoiced—she had been praying for this day since Mandy was born.

Carrie's daughter Lori joined the other high school seniors at the front of the church. Lori shared her testimony and the plans she felt God had for her future. Church members gathered around them and committed them to the Lord: "May they continue to walk in Your truth."

Dianne's son John called. "Mom, I have a question. . . ." They settled into a half-hour discussion over a point of theology. Dianne praised God that her grown son loved to talk about God.

The joy of seeing our children walking in the truth will surpass any hardship we face along the way. Always fight that good fight!

Father, we commit our children to You, and pray that they will walk in Your truth today and every day of their lives.

DOUBLE WALLS

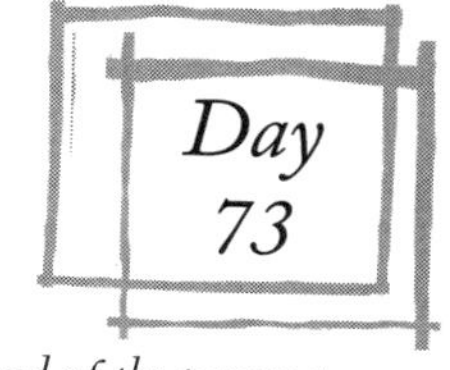

When the trumpets sounded, the people shouted, and at the sound of the trumpet, when the people gave a loud shout, the wall collapsed; so every man charged straight in, and they took the city.
JOSHUA 6:20 NIV

Among ancient fortified cities, Jericho stood out as the most fortified. Archaeologists suggest there were actually two walls surrounding the city, each one twenty feet high and twenty feet wide, with a large no-man's-land between. Anyone who might have succeeded in scaling the outer wall would have been an easy target for a skilled archer before reaching the inner wall.

Imagine the thoughts of the people of Jericho as they peeked over the walls and saw the Israelites marching around their city, day after day, with no weapons in sight. Did the city's residents have any worries about those rams' horn trumpets? Probably not. Maybe they even made jokes around the dinner table about those strange foreigners. After all, Jericho had the best security system in the known world. It was invincible.

Our kids often think they're invincible, too. They drive too fast, take unreasonable risks, and love the thrill of extreme. . .anything. They think they're living behind the thick, double walls of youthful protection.

But when anyone—at any age—dismisses God, no security system in the world can keep him or her safe. Let's remind our kids daily of God's protection—that only if they honor and obey Him will they be covered.

And then they're eternally safe.

Dear Lord, protect my children from their own foolishness.
Give them caution about the reliability of their own security system.
Guide my children to trust only You with their whole hearts.

From Bitterness to Freedom

Why do you say, "The Lord does not see what happens to me; he does not care if I am treated fairly"?
Isaiah 40:27 NCV

Bitterness. . .even the sound of that word, when spoken aloud, conveys unpleasantness. And we as single mothers are particularly prone to this toxic form of resentment.

Though it's not always the case, the circumstances that brought us to our single parent status often create a deep root of bitterness in us. Perhaps we faced betrayal, deception, or broken promises. Financial struggles, the emotional sorrow of loneliness, losing hope over what might have been—so many things can lead to bitterness in our lives.

We know bitterness is wrong, and our friends tell us to let go. But it's not always that easy. Especially because, well. . .it can feel good to be the injured party. For many people, there's a strange satisfaction in being the "victim."

Bitterness, whether conscious or unconscious, is clearly not a biblical feeling. It eats at us emotionally, spiritually, and even physically. So what should we do?

Tell God how badly you hurt—then ask Him for the capacity to forgive. Allow God to be your vindicator. Place all of your mistreatment into His hands, because He cares. And He'll work things out in the end.

Father, I admit I've been bitter at times as a single parent. Enable me to forgive when I need to. I know that will set me free.

THE GIFT OF RECEIVING

"In everything I did, I showed you that by this kind of hard work we must help the weak, remembering the words the Lord Jesus himself said: 'It is more blessed to give than to receive.' "
ACTS 20:35 NIV

You probably already know that, like Jesus said, it is better to give to others than to receive for yourself. But what if everyone gave and no one received? That would be impossible, actually. In order for some to give, others have to receive. God designed it perfectly so that the body of Christ would work together and help each other.

Have you ever turned down help of any kind—tangible goods like money or groceries, or intangible things like babysitting or wise counsel—out of pride? Are you trying to keep a stiff upper lip to show the world how strong you are? Maybe you are fully capable of succeeding with no outside help. But in doing so, you might rob others of the joy of giving.

Next time someone offers help, consider graciously accepting the extended hand. By your willingness to receive, others might enjoy the blessings of giving.

Lord, thank You for the times that You have sent help my way. Please give me the wisdom and the grace to know when to accept help from others—and even the courage to ask for it when I need it.

Forgiven and Free

Blessed is he whose transgressions are forgiven, whose sins are covered.
Psalm 32:1 NIV

Have you ever really pondered *freedom*? Every individual has a slightly different view of the concept. As women, we are free to vote and drive and earn a living. In western countries, we are free to walk down the street without hiding our faces; we are even free to abort babies and demand divorces. With many of our freedoms, however, come painful consequences.

God's Word shows that the freedom He offers is more far-reaching and eternally beneficial than our personal earthly freedoms we so often demand. When we find ourselves alone with children to feed, clothe, and love—and our children need so much more than we can give—God says we are free. When all we seem to receive from outsiders are glares and judgment, God says we are free. Whatever circumstances led us to this point in life—whether choices of our own or the choices of others—transgressions can be forgiven and we can find freedom. Freedom from judgment, guilt, past mistakes, and burdens.

Under God's umbrella, we are free to be who He created us to be. Nothing more, nothing less.

Father God, thank You for the freedom that comes from knowing You. You have forgiven my past and, even though I may live with consequences of that past, You say I am blessed. Thank You for the blessing of freedom that You give.

Waiting

Blessed are all who wait for him!
Isaiah 30:18 NIV

Some studies indicate we spend a total of *three years* of our lives just waiting!

That may seem hard to believe. But consider a typical day, with a few minutes stopped at traffic signals, a half hour in the doctor's waiting room, more time yet in a bottlenecked checkout line at the grocery store.

Some of us can handle that waiting through a natural patience. Others? Forget it.

Yet waiting is an inevitable part of everyone's life. And it's a necessary part, too. We wait nine months for a baby's birth. We wait for wounds to heal. We wait for our children to mature. And we wait for God to fulfill His promises.

Waiting for God to act is a familiar theme in scripture. Abraham and Sarah waited for a baby until a birth became humanly impossible. But it wasn't impossible to God. Joseph languished, unjustly accused, in Pharaoh's prison, while God ordained a far-reaching drought that would force Joseph's family to Egypt for survival. David spent years hiding from King Saul, but he matured into a wise and capable warrior during that time.

As frustrating as waiting can be, God is always at work on our behalf. Waiting time isn't wasted time. Whatever we might be waiting for—the salvation of our kids, provision for a physical need, a godly partner to help us with our parenting—we can wait with expectancy, trusting in God's timing.

By Your grace, Lord, help me to do the work You've called me to do and wait patiently for the good results You promise.

Boldly Enter the Throne Room

Sisters, we can boldly enter heaven's Most Holy Place because of the blood of Jesus. By his death, Jesus opened a new and life-giving way through the curtain into the Most Holy Place. And since we have a great High Priest who rules over God's house, let us go right into the presence of God with sincere hearts fully trusting him.
HEBREWS 10:19–22 NLT

Pressures come at us from every direction—a child needs braces, the car breaks down, the boss needs us to work more hours. The pressure seems unending—and can be overwhelming.

When the heavy weight of life falls on us, we have two options: to crumble in fear or stand up under it, in faith.

In His perfect wisdom, God has given us the role model we need: Jesus faced many pressures and temptations, yet remained unperturbed, sinless, and victorious. How? By continually seeking an intimate relationship with His Father.

Though we're certainly not sinless, we can approach our heavenly Father with boldness and confidence. Because we have a High Priest who is perfect, God doesn't see our faults and failures and weaknesses. He sees the perfection of the blood of Christ—and that gives us the right to enter His presence.

We approach God's throne by faith. His mercy flows as we come near, cleansing, refreshing, and strengthening us. All we must do is boldly open the door. Our help is inside.

Father, I stand at the foot of Your throne, boldly proclaiming Your goodness. Thank You for Your mercy and grace. Thank You for giving me the help I need.

I've Fallen and I Can't Get Up

The godly may trip seven times, but they will get up again.
Proverbs 24:16 NLT

Years ago, a famous television commercial depicted an elderly woman who had fallen, but, try as she might, she just couldn't get back up. Thankfully, she wore a device that connected her to an outside source of help. All she had to do was push the button! The dear grandma was just one click away from rescue.

In our lives, too, there are times when we fall down—not physically, but emotionally, spiritually, and relationally. We fall in our attempts to parent; we fall in our struggle with particular temptations. We may fall as we try to climb the ladder of success or in our effort to lead a consistently godly life.

But in whatever area we wrestle, however many times we fall, our heavenly Father never gives up on us. He never leaves us to ourselves, to stagger to our feet alone. God is always present with us, encouraging us to keep trying—regardless of past failures—picking us up, dusting us off, and setting us on our way again.

He is better than any button we could ever push!

Heavenly Father, it's such a comfort to know You will never leave me or forsake me. You are closer than the clothes I wear. I love You, Lord.

New Every Day

"See, I am doing a new thing!
Now it springs up; do you not perceive it?"
Isaiah 43:19 NIV

One of the blessings of motherhood is watching our children grow. Changes come quickly in infancy—the first tooth, the first word, the first step. Later, we see the first friendship, the first day at school, the first line in a class play. Eventually our precious babies will become teenagers, head off to high school, and then leave home. Then we'll get to enjoy the process all over again, as grandmothers.

God wants us to approach all of life with the same fresh wonder. If every baby affirms that God wants the world to go on, and every rainbow is a reminder of God's promise, every dawn represents a new start.

In fact, God gives us countless opportunities to start over. The word *new* appears over 150 times in the Bible. He puts a new song in our mouths (Psalm 33:3). He gives us a new heart and makes us new creatures in Christ (2 Corinthians 5:17). At the end of time, He will create a new heaven and a new earth (Revelation 21:1).

Instead of worrying about the past, God wants us to long for what will be. He is the God of all things new.

Eternal God, every day is a new opportunity from You.
Teach me to rejoice in what You promise us.

How Do I Love Thee?

This is what real love is: It is not our love for God; it is God's love for us. He sent his Son to die in our place to take away our sins.
1 John 4:10 ncv

If the word *love* were banned from popular music, radio stations and songwriters would go out of business. Even the Internet would shrink without this word, so key to human existence. All around the world, people search for someone to care. They chat with strangers, post videos, pay for profiles—anything to find the real love they crave.

Few prove successful—because we human beings are hard to love! Even our charity often wears a disguise. We give so we will receive attention, prestige, or assurance that other people will respect us. Some of us even think our little five-and-dime "love" will obtain a place for us in heaven, as if God were a headwaiter to be bribed.

The Bible tells us He does not *need* our love. He *is* love. God the Father, God the Son, and God the Spirit love each other in perfect eternal unity and joy. If God had done the logical thing, He would have wiped out us troublesome humans and created a new race, one that would worship Him without question.

But He would rather die than do that.

Oh, Lord, when I presume on Your love, please forgive me. Open my eyes to Your magnificent generosity so I can worship with my whole heart, in a way that pleases You.

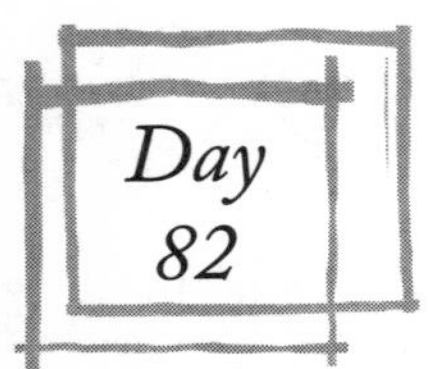

ONE CHAPTER

"In the future, when your children ask you, 'What do these stones mean?' tell them that the flow of the Jordan was cut off before the ark of the covenant of the LORD*. . . . These stones are to be a memorial to the people of Israel forever."*
JOSHUA 4:6–7 NIV

Faith boils down to a willingness to trust God without knowing the end of the story. It means we trust the promises of God even though we don't know how He's going to work them out.

Centuries ago, Joshua faced that very issue of trusting God without knowing the outcome. God told him to march the Israelite soldiers around the city of Jericho in complete silence, once a day for six days. On the seventh day, they were to march around the city seven times. Then the priests were to blow their rams' horns and the soldiers to shout.

That's all the information Joshua had to conquer Jericho. But that's not the only chapter in this story. Joshua had a long history with God's interventions. He had seen God part the Red Sea for the wandering Israelites and had just witnessed another watery miracle as the Israelites walked through the Jordan River to reach Jericho. Joshua knew, by experience, that God was trustworthy.

When his army did what God had instructed, Joshua saw Jericho's walls come tumblin' down.

It's easy to focus on a single chapter in our story, and to forget God's many provisions. But the Lord wants us to keep the big picture in mind, remembering His answered prayers.

Is it worth starting a journal, like Joshua's stone monument, that will remind you and your kids of God's trustworthiness?

Lord, Your compassion has never failed me or my family.
May I remember to praise You and thank You all the days of my life.

Dream Big

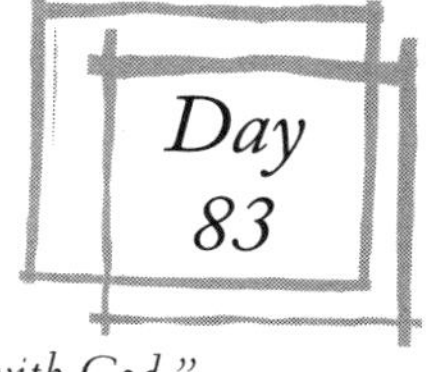

Jesus replied, "What is impossible with men is possible with God."
Luke 18:27 NIV

Society has stereotyped us single moms in a not-so-pleasant way. Unfortunately, we often fit into it well. We have little financial security, an unreliable vehicle always in need of something, few close friends to call upon, and little patience. We are worn out and disappointed. We barely allow ourselves to set personal goals or dream of a better future, because those ideas seem like impossibilities.

But the Bible says what we see as impossible is possible with God. Think of those familiar Bible stories: The Israelites crossing the Red Sea. . .Moses speaking with a burning bush that was never consumed. . . Lazarus receiving his life back again—after four days in the grave. Those were impossible things to man—but completely possible with God.

Now think of the things you need in your own life. You might even want to write them down. Do they seem like impossibilities? In human hands, they very well may be beyond hope. But we have God's hands—and God's heart—and with Him, even the impossible becomes doable.

Dear Father, You know what I need and You know what I dream of. I have goals with no way to achieve them, but I know You can make the impossible a reality. So I pray for You to work in my home and my life, and give me tenacity to hold on to those impossible dreams until You make them a reality.

Microwave Faith?

And so after waiting patiently,
Abraham received what was promised.
Hebrews 6:15 NIV

Pop a little bag into the microwave, and in two minutes you have hot, delicious popcorn. Unfortunately, faith doesn't always work the same way.

Imagine what Abraham wondered nine months after his conversation with God. He had been promised a son. Abraham believed God. His faith was credited to him as righteousness (Genesis 15:6). Nine months later, he was still waiting. Even nine years later, there was no sign of the promised child. Each passing day brought an opportunity for doubt. But Abraham "*considered him faithful who had made the promise*" (Hebrews 11:11 NIV). Abraham looked past the facts. He was not swayed by the circumstances. He simply believed God and many years later, received his son.

How many times have you given up on the promises of God because circumstances told you something different? It's not too late. Pick up your faith. Determine to see those promises come to pass.

Heavenly Father, I thank You that You are faithful. Your Word does not return void. I ask You to forgive me for doubting You. I believe Your Word. I praise You and glorify You in advance for the promises You are bringing into my life.

WEATHER "MOM"

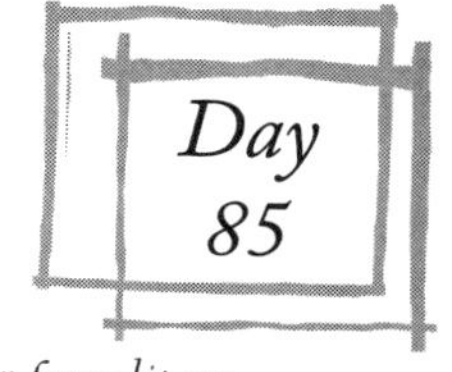

"When I smiled at them, they could hardly believe it; their faces lit up, their troubles took wing! I was their leader, establishing the mood and setting the pace by which they lived."
JOB 29:24 MSG

A dark and gloomy sky in the morning may set the tone for an unproductive and disappointing day. But a bright sunny sky can add hope and promise to the day's outlook.

So it is in the home.

Mom's face is the forecast for the day—and the children's radar is always ready to take a reading. A gloomy mom indicates hopelessness and an expectation of failure, but a cheerful mom brings joy and eagerness to the day's outlook.

Attitude alone may not change our circumstances. But it can affect how we perceive things—and completely alter our final results. When we meet tough times with a cheerful, positive attitude, we can expect success and growth rather than failure and loss.

Perhaps we should examine our own habits. Do we mope around our homes with the "storm clouds" of long faces and gloomy dispositions? Or do we face each new day (and each new challenge) brightly with a sunshiny, eager confidence?

We set the forecast. May we reflect in our faces the kind of day that honors ourselves, our families, and our God.

Heavenly Father, please help me to control my mood so that I can cheerfully lead my family through the day. Let my face reveal the hope and expectation I have in Your promises. Amen.

Day 86 Nap Time for Moms

And on the seventh day God ended His work which He had done; and He rested on the seventh day from all His work which He had done.
Genesis 2:2 AMP

It was the first time they had left their baby for an evening of "adult time." They dropped her off with Grandma and Grandpa and drove back down the road in an unusually quiet car. But the couple didn't head out for dinner and a movie. They returned home to take a nap.

If rest is important for couples, it's especially so for single parents. But it's so hard to find time simply to rest—physically, emotionally, and spiritually. When our children are infants, they wake up for feedings. As the kids grow, play dates, school, and other activities keep us busy. The never-ending cycle of activity can run us ragged.

Remember, though, that even God "rested." No, He wasn't tired after creating the universe and everything in it. But He was giving us an example—because *we* do get tired! When the daily routine becomes all-consuming, take some time out for yourself. Be it five minutes before bed or a couple hours when the kids are at a babysitter's, consciously pursue some quiet time to rest your mind and body.

Dear Lord, remind me daily that even You took time to rest after Your work. Help me to find a few minutes daily to sit quietly and rest my mind and body so that I may be a better servant for You in all that I do.

God's Foolishness Is Man's Wisdom

For the foolishness of God is wiser than man's wisdom,
and the weakness of God is stronger than man's strength.
1 Corinthians 1:25 NIV

Cindy reached a fork in the road, facing a troubling decision about her child. Which was the right path? She felt a vagueness and an uncertainty about what to do.

Finally, after time in prayer, she felt the Holy Spirit's prompting to move forward. The choice she felt led to make didn't entirely make sense—but she decided to follow the prompting anyway. Only afterward, as she looked back, did she realize God had mysteriously guided her to the right decision.

This is faith in God. Sometimes, He'll lead us to act contrary to common sense. Did it "make sense" to have Jesus Christ die for our sins? How could a man, hanging on a cross outside Jerusalem, take away our sins? It's foolishness. Impossible!

But with God, all things are possible. He asks us to simply take Him at His Word—and we have plenty of evidence, both biblical and in our own lives, that shows us we can believe Him.

Believing God can seem like foolishness—at least in the world's eyes—but we know the deep peace that comes with that decision.

Lord, teach me to pray and to listen for Your guidance. I thank You
that You go before me in every choice, even the confusing ones!
I can move forward with confidence, knowing You are with me.

Letting Go

Am I a God at hand, saith the Lord,
and not a God afar off?
Jeremiah 23:23 KJV

Mothers let go all the time.

For most of us single moms, leaving our children with a caregiver is a regular workday occurrence. But we vividly remember the first time we left our precious babies in someone else's care. We gave the babysitter detailed instructions in case of emergencies. We cried as our children did when we had to leave them behind.

We let go on other occasions, too. There's the first day of school, the first sleepover at a friend's house, the first time at camp. Or we send our children off to visit their dads, watch them leave for their first dates, and eventually, wave good-bye as they venture into adulthood.

As long as our children are in our sight, we feel that we can somehow protect them. We feel more confident in their safety. And we relish their company.

God knows how hard it is to say good-bye. So He gives us a promise: He is the God at hand— in our homes and schools and churches. He is also the God who is far off—at camp, in another state, with people who may not honor Him. Even when *we* can't be present with our children, *He* is. No matter how far they roam, they cannot travel to a place where God is not.

As we say good-bye to our children today, let's take courage in the fact that God goes with them—wherever they may roam.

Lord, You are the omnipresent God. I thank You for Your ever-present watchfulness of my precious children. I commit them to Your care.

Nobody's Fool

He who trusts in his own heart is a fool.
Proverbs 28:26 NKJV

Ever heard one of these lines? "Follow your heart." "What's your heart telling you?" "Let your heart be your guide."

Today's world—including many of the movies our children watch—gives a clear message to look to our own hearts for direction. But are our hearts the best guide for making important life decisions? The Bible says our hearts are not to be trusted. In fact, God calls us *fools* when we trust our own hearts. Those are mighty strong words.

Think about it: As single parents, we may so deeply desire a companion to share the joys and challenges of life that we allow our desperate feelings to lead us into hasty decisions—decisions we may later regret. Our hearts might persuade us to rationalize, "He'll be a good provider—he only needs help finding a job." Or worse, "He really *is* a Christian—he just doesn't like church."

Making choices based on heart leanings can lead us into a world of trouble, even danger. Though feelings are important, they should never be the sole basis of a choice we make.

Let's not be anyone's fool.

*Heavenly Father, I am often tempted to allow my heart—
rather than You through Your Word and Your people—to guide me.
Teach me to trust You more than my own feelings.*

Faith Eyes

Now faith is being sure of what we hope
for and certain of what we do not see.
Hebrews 11:1 NIV

Think for a moment of things we can't see, but we know are there.

There's the wind, for one. Its effects are obvious, as golden grain sways to and fro or fall leaves blow into the sky. And there's gravity, which pulls our kids' cups—full of red Kool-Aid, usually—right to the floor.

It's the same with faith, as we simply believe in what we do not see. God *says* He is faithful, and so His faithfulness exists. He gives us the signs of His unseen presence, and its effects surround us.

We read how the Israelites walked to the sea and, at Moses' command, the sea parted. They could have been killed—by the pursuing Egyptians or by the sea itself—but God made a safe way of escape for them.

What signs surround you, showing you God is real? Perhaps someone blessed you with money to pay a bill or purchase school supplies. Maybe your "guardian angel" caught your attention and helped you avoid a serious accident. Or perhaps your child prayed to accept the Lord.

Those are all signs of the faithfulness of God. Look around with your "faith eyes" and see the signs surrounding you.

God, I struggle to have faith. Show me where You have been faithful so my faith can be strengthened. I know You are faithful, but today I'm asking for a special sign that You have not forgotten me. Thank You, Father.

BUDGETS

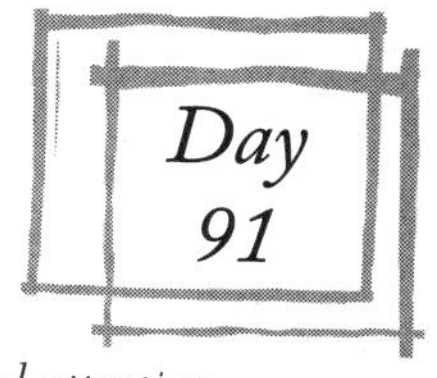

Be sure you know the condition of your flocks, give careful attention to your herds; for riches do not endure forever, and a crown is not secure for all generations.
PROVERBS 27:23–24 NIV

Budgets are good things. But some of us prefer not to see our financial situation in such black-and-white terms. That can be a problem because, as we're told in Proverbs 27, riches don't last forever.

It's important to know our true financial state so we can best determine where to allocate funds for life' s necessities—*before* we spend frivolously on things we don't need. Our own retirement, the kids' college education, home repairs, even an inheritance for the children—they are all things to consider when budgeting and establishing a family financial plan.

Of course, life is unpredictable, and even a careful budget can't guarantee financial success. But everything is in God's hands. He recommends that we know the state of our finances then surrender them all to Him. He leads and guides, even in the realm of our personal money matters.

Pray that the Holy Spirit would guide you into sound financial decisions and prepare you for a secure life that honors Him.

Lord, I want to be a good steward of the resources You've given me. Teach me good financial practices so that I may honor You in my choices. And help me to trust You for my future so that I can make wise choices today.

Swing and Miss

And though she spoke to Joseph day after day,
he refused to go to bed with her or even be with her.
Genesis 39:10 NIV

Hardships? Joseph knew them.

Sold into slavery by his brothers, he was carried off to a foreign land. By God's grace, Joseph gained an opportunity to manage the household of an Egyptian official named Potiphar. He was still a slave, but he had impressed Potiphar tremendously.

Joseph also impressed Potiphar's wife. She had a lusty eye for the "well-built and handsome" young man (Genesis 39:6 NIV), and she was determined to seduce him.

Was God tempting Joseph? Had the Lord set Joseph up to test his mettle? Maybe God was giving Joseph a chance to practice with temptation so he'd be more skilled at saying no when bigger temptations came later. You know—like a baseball player taking batting practice, hitting some balls, but occasionally swinging and missing.

That may seem logical, but scripture tells us God would *never* entice us to sin or fail. Since doing so would be contrary to His nature, He allows situations into our lives only for good. He wants us to succeed, each and every time. He wants us to hit a home run, by faith, every time we come to bat.

Joseph did. He told the woman, "How then could I do such a wicked thing and sin against God?" (Genesis 39:9). Then he ran!

Let's learn from Joseph's example.

Lord, help me to see every circumstance in my life as ordained
by You for my welfare. Teach me to respond in faith, every time.

Mom's and Grandma's Faith

I call to remembrance the unfeigned faith that is in thee, which dwelt first in thy grandmother Lois, and thy mother Eunice; and I am persuaded that in thee also.
2 Timothy 1:5 KJV

When Amy read yet another magazine article emphasizing a father's powerful spiritual impact on his children, she felt like throwing in the towel. Her ex was not a Christian. And if a mother's faith made little difference, why bother with wiggly, jiggly devotions at night, when she felt ready to fall over? Why drag children out of bed every Sunday morning and spend time, energy, and gasoline to attend church? Why live a moral life and say no to temptation when following her lonely heart would have made much more sense?

Maybe I should just quit trying. Even as the thought tried to sink its talons into her mind, Amy knew better. She yanked it out and tried to focus on God's love for her and her family. Chad had left them, but God would not.

Timothy, a young pastor in the first-century church, grew up rooted in the deep faith of his mother, Eunice, and grandmother Lois. Although his father, a Greek, did not love Jesus, Timothy chose to follow in the footsteps of the women in his life. His decision made a huge difference not only in Timothy's personal life, but also in those of thousands of people down through the centuries.

Lord, Your wonderful love sows seeds of grace in all generations, despite less-than-perfect conditions. I praise You for Your faithfulness!

Simplicity

So if we have enough food and clothing,
let us be content.
1 Timothy 6:8 NLT

You've probably seen the advertisement that promises more free time if you'll simply use "just one skillet" to make tasty, home-cooked meals. The idea behind the ad is, simply, *simplify.* One box, one pan, one happily fed family. Sounds great! But what about the rest of life? Is there a way to simplify that, too?

Single mothers often try hard to entertain their children, or find themselves striving relentlessly to win the undeclared popularity contest against other parents. We may work tirelessly to buy the latest fashions, or put in the extra mile to be that super-terrific-mom-of-the-year. In the process, we can find ourselves overwhelmed and exhausted, even resentful of all we feel is required of us. But is all that activity necessary?

Though we might think our kids have to have the newest fashions or the fastest Internet connection, what they really need is simple: You. Your time, your love. Sharing a bag of microwave popcorn over a board game creates a lasting memory for kids and forges a bond far beyond any new cell phone we may labor to give them.

As our verse reminds us, shelter, food, and clothing are the essentials. Start with the simplicity of those needs. Anything above and beyond is an unnecessary bonus.

Father God, free me to live in simplicity. Show me where I have needlessly burdened myself, and open my eyes to the simple joys of just being a mom.

FILL 'ER UP— WITH JOY

We also pray that you will be strengthened with all his glorious power so you will have all the endurance and patience you need. May you be filled with joy.
COLOSSIANS 1:11 NLT

We've all had days when we feel exhausted on every level, when we've drained our emotional gas tanks bone dry. As Paul prayed for the Christians of Colosse, we need a filling of God's strength so we can keep going—and rediscover *joy*.

But when can we find time to refill our tank in a life of constant work and worry? We don't have enough time for the rat race itself, let alone a pit stop. But if we don't refuel, we'll stall out—and be of no use to anyone.

That means we have to learn to make time for ourselves. We can explore things that give us a lift. Some things, like listening to a favorite CD as we drift off to sleep, take no extra time. Others, like a bubble bath, may require minor adjustments to our schedule. Maybe we'll want to spend time in the garden or call a friend. There are any number of ways to recharge our spiritual batteries.

Every week—perhaps every day—we must set aside time to refill our tanks. The joy of the Lord will be our reward.

Lord of joy, we confess that we are tempted to work until we fall apart. We pray that You will show us the things that will give us the strength to go on.

Whose Purpose?

For it is God who works in you to will and to act according to his good purpose.
Philippians 2:13 NIV

Exhausted—the word that best describes single moms. We are tired nearly all the time. Simply worn out.

After Jesse spills his milk for the second time, and Brady falls off his chair and bangs his head, there's no time to clean up the table before rushing off to the hockey rink. In our world, it can be difficult to act according to God's purposes. We want to respond in frustration and weariness. We want to lie on the couch, send the kids to Grandma's house, and simply crash for a week.

The only way to make it through days like these is to realize it's not *our* will or *our* purpose or strength. It's all God's. *He* works in us, giving us the will and the strength to act according to *His* purpose—and His purpose is good.

When we come to this realization, life becomes less frustrating and easier to accept. When we become His workmanship, the crazy pieces of our lives begin to come together. And our children benefit, too.

God, sometimes my life becomes so hectic I can hardly breathe. I know Your purposes for my children and me are good. I need You to continue to give me what I need to will and act according to those good purposes.

Tucking an Octopus into Bed

"Do not worry about your life, what you will eat or drink; or about your body, what you will wear. . . . Who of you by worrying can add a single hour to his life? . . . God clothes the grass of the field. . .will he not much more clothe you, O you of little faith?"
Matthew 6:25, 27, 30 NIV

Who among us doesn't struggle with anxiety?

Compare worry with trying to tuck an octopus into bed. One tentacle or another keeps popping out from under the covers. If we're not worried about one child, it's the other. If we're not worried about our kids, it's our aging parents. Or the orthodontist's bill. Or the funny sound under the hood of the car.

In the Bible, Jesus spoke much about worry. In a nutshell, He told us not to! Jesus never dismissed the untidy realities of daily life—He knew those troubles firsthand, having spent years as a carpenter in Nazareth, probably living hand-to-mouth as He helped to support His family.

But Jesus also knew that, without looking to God in faith, worry would leave us stuck in a wrestling match with the octopus. Only when we look to God to provide for our needs are we released from worry's grip. "Seek first his kingdom and his righteousness, and all these things will be given to you as well," Jesus promised (Matthew 6:33 NIV).

At that point, worry no longer has a hold on us. It is replaced by a liberating confidence in the power of God.

Lord, with Your help we can live our daily life free from the grasp of worry.

Letting Go, Letting God

"This is the word of the God of Israel: 'The jar of flour will not run out and the bottle of oil will not become empty before God sends rain on the land and ends this drought.' "

1 Kings 17:14 MSG

Too many times, the only peaceful moments in the day are when the children are asleep. Tucked away at last, curled beautifully beneath the covers, their faces relax and their cares melt away. Mom's worries, however, are not so easily set aside.

Being a mother means worrying about the children's health, their success in school, and their wisdom in picking friends. Will they make the right choices?

In the Bible, the widow of Zarephath had an even sharper concern. She had only enough flour to make one more meal for herself and her son. After that, only starvation awaited. Yet Elijah asked the woman to make that flour into a biscuit for *him*—with God's promise that, if she did, her food would never run out. She chose to trust, to turn her life and the life of her son over to the Lord.

Turning *our* children over to God—truly trusting Him—is undoubtedly one of the hardest steps a mom can take. Yet God is ever faithful and never changing. The Lord who helped a desperate widow three thousand years ago remains by our side today.

Father God, help us remember Your steadfast love and support, and that You care for our children intimately and eternally. Remind us that You will not let us fall.

Status Symbols

"You meant evil against me, but God meant it for good in order to bring about this present result."
Genesis 50:20 NASB

Single-mother status may have come to us by careful choice, through adoption. Or maybe it was thrust upon us by divorce or a relationship outside the bonds of marriage. However we arrived at this place is of less importance than how we respond to it.

For many, "single parent status" represents a crushing blow to future plans, and the hopes and dreams of what might have been. For others, though the joy of parenthood is incalculable, the challenges may be more than anticipated.

So what do we do? Look for the good in your situation, as the young man Joseph did in ancient times. In Genesis 50, Joseph tells his brothers (who had sold him into slavery!) that though they meant evil against him, God meant the circumstance for good, to bring about a good result.

Refuse to harbor bitterness toward those who may have put you in such a difficult situation. Recognize that God can and will bring good out of your parenting. Nothing catches Him by surprise.

Whatever your status, the heavenly Father has it all under control.

Father God, in Jesus' mighty name, I thank You for the promise You've given me to bring good out of all that comes my way. Your sovereignty gives me courage and hope.

ANSWERED PRAYER

Delight yourself in the LORD;
and He will give you the desires of your heart.
PSALM 37:4 NASB

Sometimes our heartfelt prayers receive a "yes" from God. Sometimes, it's a "no." At other times, we get back only a "not yet."

Have you heard anyone quote today's scripture, saying that God will give us the desires of our hearts? Some believe the verse means that a Christian can ask for anything—health, money, possessions, you name it—and get exactly what she wants. But this passage actually teaches something much deeper.

Note the first part of Psalm 37:4: "Delight yourself in the Lord." A woman who truly delights herself in the Lord will naturally have the desires of her heart—because her heart desires only God and His will. Our Father takes no pleasure in the things of this world—things that will all wither and die. Neither should we.

So what pleases God? He loves it when we witness for Him, live right, and raise our children in His Word. If those are things that we also truly desire, won't He grant us the "desires of our heart" and let us see people brought into the kingdom? Won't we have a life rich in spiritual growth and children who honor His name?

Lord, please help me see where my desires are not in line with Your will—so that the things that I pursue are only and always according to Your own desires.

Learning to Say No

"Why do you not judge for yourselves what is right?"
Luke 12:57 ESV

A wise preacher once said that a *need* is not a *call*.

We do well to remember his words when constant needs bombard us from every side. Our children's school wants us for the PTA. Our parents want us for family get-togethers. Our children want us at games and special events. Our churches invite us to meetings almost every day of the week. Each invitation represents a worthwhile activity. How do we decide?

Too often we cave in and agree to do more than we can handle. It's easier to say yes than to deal with the guilt of saying no.

Jesus challenges us to judge what is right for ourselves when it comes to daily choices. A good rule of thumb to determine our priorities is the acronym JOY: Jesus, Others, You. We have to nurture our primary relationship, with the Lord. We can define the "others" who have priority in our lives: our children, certainly; our extended families to a lesser extent; and only those others whom God leads us to include. We also need to plan on time for ourselves, or else we can't take care of the first two priorities.

JOY—Judge for yourself what God wants you to do.

Lord and Master, I pray that I will learn to judge for myself what is right, and how I should spend my time. Make me strong against the claims of others.

TAKE YOUR MEDICINE

A happy heart is good medicine and a cheerful mind works healing, but a broken spirit dries up the bones.
PROVERBS 17:22 AMP

As the young mother entered her daughter's hospital room she heard laughter. She rounded the corner to see the girl who'd been diagnosed with cancer, smiling and laughing at a clown building her a balloon animal. With tears in her eyes and a smile on her face, the mother thought, *We'll make it through this.*

Even science recognizes that laughter is one of the best forms of medicine available. Studies have shown that many diseases are directly related to stress. Laughter displaces stress. Laughter gives hope. Laughter brings joy. Joy is our strength.

So go ahead, laugh at that joke. Tickle your kids. Play with them. Push the swing higher and take joy in their squeals of happiness. Not only are you connecting with your children, you are relieving stress in your lives. And you're teaching your kids, in a very practical way, the joy of the Lord.

We all have jobs and responsibilities, things that need to be done in a timely manner. But we can't forget the importance of laughter and fun in our homes.

Take a big dose of your medicine today. Do your body some good. Find—and share—a good, hearty, belly-shakin' laugh.

Father, help me always to take time to laugh. I choose today to operate in Your joy. As I do, I know I am strengthened and health comes to my body.

Near Misses

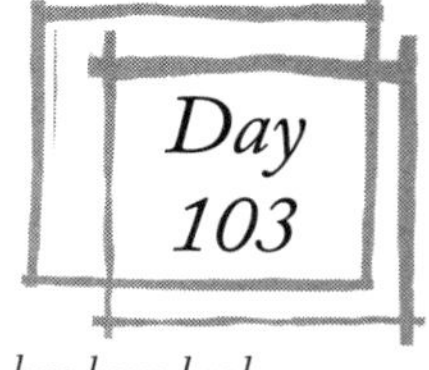

We have escaped like a bird out of the fowler's snare; the snare has been broken, and we have escaped. Our help is in the name of the Lord, the Maker of heaven and earth.
Psalm 124:7–8 niv

Near misses in the car always serve as wake-up calls. With a sigh of relief, we whisper a quick prayer of thanks. Hearts pounding, we're reminded how fragile life can be. With that narrow escape from potential disaster, we become more attentive drivers. . .at least for the rest of that particular trip.

Thousands of years ago, King David wrote Psalm 124 to praise God for deliverance from a near miss. "If the Lord had not been on our side. . .if the Lord had not been on our side!" he wrote (Psalm 124:1, 2), filled with the confidence of knowing the Lord *was* on his side. David was protected from the wrath of his enemies, from a flood that should have swept over him, from a trap that could have led to his death.

In the course of a day, a week, a month, or a year, our families face potential disasters. Bad drivers, preoccupied babysitters, broken bones, high fevers, damaging divorces, disappointing church experiences. . . if God were not on our side, we would be done in! The torrent of troubles would have overtaken us. But they don't! Our help comes in the name of the Lord, the Maker of heaven and earth.

Great God, You are on my family's side! You are our refuge and our shield. Thank You for Your faithfulness, Lord of heaven and earth.

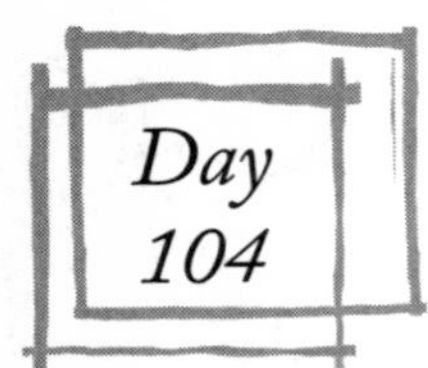

QUIET REFLECTION

Stand in silence in the presence of the Sovereign LORD.
ZEPHANIAH 1:7 NLT

As parents, we teach our children to enter a room with their ears, not their mouths—to listen before speaking. Though we are not always successful, we try to instill in them this important lesson in conversation etiquette. Because someone else may already be talking, our kids must learn to stop and listen before speaking.

This truth applies to our devotional life with God, as well. How often do we race into our "quiet time" with a laundry list of needs? Do we inform God of all that is wrong—of all we'd like Him to do—then declare our "amen" and leave the room? If we aren't careful, "quiet time" can become not an opportunity to linger in God's presence, but a whirlwind of quickly stated prayers.

When walking into our special time with God, let's make it a habit to relax for a bit. Listen for His voice, read a few verses from the Bible, and simply rest in His presence. It need not be a lengthy process—time is often in short supply for busy moms. But it is a matter of listening before speaking—a lesson in good manners that we, as well as our children, need to learn.

Holy Father, teach me to enter my time alone with You, listening rather than speaking. Enable me to pour out my heart to You, then rest in Your care.

The Gift

Sons are a heritage from the Lord, children a reward from him.
Like arrows in the hands of a warrior are sons born in one's youth.
Blessed is the man whose quiver is full of them.
Psalm 127:3–5 NIV

Riley. . . Jesse. . . Brady. . .sit down and be quiet for five minutes! Give me a minute's peace!"

Sound familiar?

Children are demanding, loud, selfish, and messy. That's not new. When they're young, they need diaper changes, naps, blankies, and, most importantly, *Mommy*. As they get older, they need help with homework, transportation to everywhere, skates tied, lunch money dispensed, and, a bit less importantly, *Mom*. They get still older and need even less from their mother and more from their friends. At that point, we might exhale a sigh of relief, enjoying the quiet for just a moment.

Children are a bunch of fun, and endless work. They're exhausting no matter the age—and no matter how big they get, they are forever our babies. Through our children, God says, we are blessed. Our little ones are a reward from Him!

Imagine that—the toothless, red-cheeked, goopy-nosed little man with the ruffled hair and smelly shirt is actually a gift, directly from God's hand to our heart. If you have children, you are blessed—and the more you have, the more blessed you are. Try to remember that the next time you hear, "Mommy. . .I need you!"

Lord, I thank You for my precious children. I often get frustrated and forget they are gifts from You. Help me to remember they are a blessing—and my life would be incomplete without them. Thank You for blessing me with such an irreplaceable gift.

Does God Speak to Children?

And the Lord *said to Samuel: "See, I am about to do something in Israel that will make the ears of everyone who hears of it tingle."*
1 Samuel 3:11 niv

The child Samuel heard God's voice because he was both serving and seeking God. His mother had brought him to the temple to grow in spirit and find the Lord. She knew that God speaks even to little children, impressing His Word and His will on their young hearts.

If we as parents desire God to speak to our children, we should ask Him to. We should pray for our children to grow in God's grace and to feel the power and presence of the Holy Spirit in their lives. We should, both by word and deed, teach them to respect God's commands and show Him reverence.

We can tell our kids about times when we have heard God's voice. We can relate our personal experiences and share stories from scripture about times when people have felt God moving in their hearts.

And we can take our kids to church, where those various messages can be reinforced and modeled before them.

Does God speak to children? Of course. And we can help them hear His voice.

Heavenly Father, please speak to my children today and help me to be a guide and a model who always points toward Your presence in their lives.

But Everybody Does It!

"I am God, your God. Don't live like the people of Egypt where you used to live, and don't live like the people of Canaan where I'm bringing you."
Leviticus 18:2–3 MSG

As teenagers, we wanted to copy the popular kids. We wanted to dress, act, even think like them. When our parents gave us the old argument "If everybody jumped off a building, would you jump off, too?" we rolled our eyes.

God's people displayed the same immaturity. Wherever the Israelites lived, they tended to adopt the morality—or lack thereof—of the people around them. God may have used their disobedience and subsequent forty-year punishment of wandering in the wilderness to protect them from bad influences. He wanted His children to learn to love Him and His ways. So God emphasized they were to forget the gods of Egypt. When they would finally reach the Promised Land, He wanted them to avoid the destructive ways of the Canaanites. But Israel turned away from the Lord—and suffered the consequences.

God wants us to forget the ugliness and pain of the past. But His plans for us do not include new evils that may tempt us. Will we roll our eyes at Him like adolescents, crashing and burning once more? Or will we accept the healthy boundaries He defines for us in love?

Dear Jesus, You have healed me of my past and filled my future with promise. Please give me the maturity to welcome Your plans with open arms.

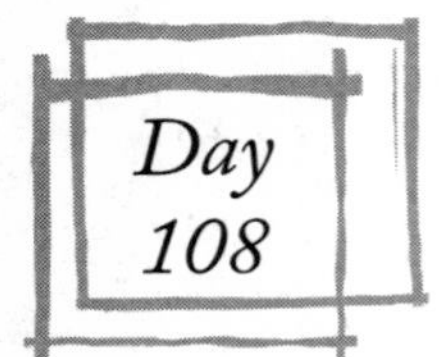

TESTED NERVES

It was about that time that the mother of the Zebedee brothers came with her two sons and knelt before Jesus with a request.
"What do you want?" Jesus asked.
She said, "Give your word that these two sons of mine will be awarded the highest places of honor in your kingdom, one at your right hand, one at your left hand."
Jesus responded, "You have no idea what you're asking." . . .
When the ten others heard about this, they lost their tempers, thoroughly disgusted with the two brothers. So Jesus got them together to settle things down.
MATTHEW 20:20–22, 24–25 MSG

Jesus' patience must have been tested often. Through parables, He would illustrate the ways of God's kingdom, only to have His disciples look at Him blankly. They saw Jesus' miracle of feeding the crowds, then worried about their next meal. Breakthrough moments—like that of Peter's stepping out of the boat to walk on water—were followed by faltering, sinking faith. Even the disciples' mothers had issues! But Jesus proved Himself a patient and compassionate teacher, slow to anger, abounding in love.

Through those thickheaded, stubborn disciples, Jesus gave us a wonderful example of good parenting. He knew the disciples were just being disciples—people in training. Just like the disciples, our children complain, disobey, drag their feet, respond in foolishness. Our kids are just being kids—people in training.

Like Jesus with His disciples, may we bear with our children in love and instruct them gently.

Lord, when my nerves are tested today,
help me to keep my head cool and my heart warm.

Way of Escape

No temptation has overtaken you except what is common to humanity. God is faithful and He will not allow you to be tempted beyond what you are able, but with the temptation He will also provide a way of escape, so that you are able to bear it.

1 Corinthians 10:13 HCSB

Single motherhood can easily become a daunting responsibility. Occasionally, we'll enjoy some serene peacefulness on a Saturday morning, lounging under the covers while the children sleep. More often, life is like the weekdays, with the frenzy of packing lunches, scrounging for bus fare, locating lost homework, and finding a run in our pantyhose as we race to our cars.

Whether quiet or overwhelming, our time as single mothers often features one prominent feeling—loneliness. We treasure our children, yet we sometimes find ourselves weighed down by the continual isolation of our singleness. That can be a dangerous feeling.

But in 1 Corinthians, God promises to keep us from temptation or testing that goes beyond our ability to endure. He says He'll always be faithful to provide a "way of escape" so we can endure the challenges of life. The escape plan could include our female friends, who can keep us on track emotionally and spiritually. Or it could be as simple as a hot shower that melts away the tensions of the day.Whatever we face, we can be certain that God will provide the release we need to move forward in righteousness.

Father, I do not always recognize the way of escape You have provided. Help me to see it and take it! I thank You for Your constant care.

Wish List

But they cried the more, saying, Have mercy on us, O Lord, thou Son of David. And Jesus stood still, and called them, and said, What will ye that I shall do unto you?
Matthew 20:31–32 KJV

The two blind men heard that Jesus was passing by. They called out a generic plea. "Have mercy on us!"

The man they addressed as Lord and Son of David stopped in His tracks. He responded with a simple question: "What do you want?"

Wasn't it obvious? Jesus knew their thoughts and what their hearts desired. But that wasn't enough. They had to verbalize their request: "We want our *sight*"—the one thing they could not receive without divine intervention. Jesus answered their prayer by opening their eyes—and they responded by following Him.

God wants us to bring specific needs to Him. Do you need a job? Tell Him how much salary you need, what kind of work you like to do, and where you want to commute. Do you need a new home? Tell Him exactly what you'd like.

God doesn't *need* us to tell Him our desires. He already knows them. But He delights in going above and beyond what we can ask for. He loves to demonstrate His lavish love. Even if He doesn't give us what we want, it's because He has something better in store.

God wants us to bring the wishes of our hearts to Him in prayer.

Heavenly Father, I thank You that You care about the smallest details of my life. Teach me the joy of specific prayer.

My Steps

"His eyes are on the ways of men;
he sees their every step."
Job 34:21 NIV

Tammy watched her son intently. She had been working with him over the past month, teaching him not to walk into the street without her. It had been a daunting lesson, but Tammy felt it was extremely valuable.

Today, the inevitable presented itself to Josh. He stood on the sidewalk, arms stretched toward the ball, his favorite, that had rolled into the street. Not for a second did Tammy's eyes wander from her son, watching for any quick movement toward the dangerous street. She held her breath and moved within arm's reach, lest he step out to retrieve his toy.

In the same way, our Father watches His children intently. Life sometimes feels as though *we* are wandering on a busy street with dangerous traffic zipping all around. But all the while, God keeps His eyes on us. He intently watches our every step, lest we fall. And when we do stumble, He is always within arm's reach—ready to catch us, love us, and teach us once again His perfect ways.

Father, I may not know what direction my life will take or where my path may lead. I do know, though, that You never take Your eyes off me; You see every step I take, guiding me and directing me and catching me when I stumble. Thank You for loving me enough to keep Your eyes on me in this journey.

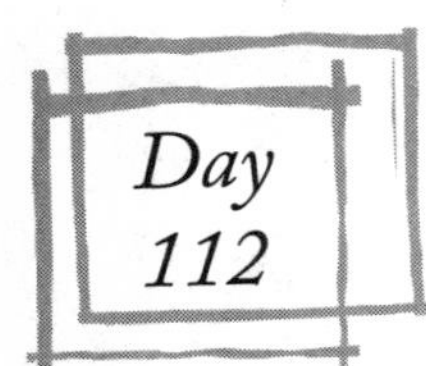

I Want That!

My Christian brothers, our Lord Jesus Christ is the Lord of shining-greatness. Since your trust is in Him, do not look on one person as more important than another. . . . God has chosen those who are poor in the things of this world to be rich in faith.

James 2:1, 5 NLV

"Mom," fourteen-year-old David said with a slight whine in his voice, "all the other kids wear this brand. Why can't you buy these jeans for me? They're only eighty-five dollars."

In our consumer-driven society, children and parents alike are bombarded with images of things we "must have." It's not always easy to tell kids—or even ourselves—no. But sometimes that's exactly what the Bible would suggest.

God has told us that we should never think more highly of others who have more stuff than we do. Nor should we look down on anyone—including ourselves—who has less. Every person is equally a creation of God Himself—and the important thing is to be rich in faith.

Here's a lesson we must pass along to our children: Don't store up treasures on earth. God loves us whether we're dressed in designer clothing or tattered rags.

Dear God, remind us to tune out the world's message that having "stuff" is important. Help us to remember that our treasure is truly in heaven—and that we should not judge ourselves or others by the standard of possessions.

A Satisfied Tummy

"The wolf and the lamb will feed together, and the lion will eat straw like the ox, but dust will be the serpent's food. They will neither harm nor destroy on all my holy mountain," says the LORD.
ISAIAH 65:25 NIV

During the summer in Alaska, it's not uncommon to see grizzly bears at the mouths of rivers, feeding on salmon. The bears need all that protein to fatten up for a long winter's hibernation.

Grizzlies are solitary animals. Normally, they'd fight over food. But at the rivers' mouth, there are plenty of salmon for all. With the bears' tummies satisfied, they can live in peace with their neighbors.

What a glimpse into heaven! Our basic needs will be filled. We'll live in perfect peace. In the complete absence of sin, our doors won't need padlocks. Our windows can be left open. We won't hear an endless recital of problems and disasters on the evening news. We won't worry over our kids' future, because their future is secure!

Our lives as single moms can be stressful. But it's good to remember what we can look forward to as children of God: One day, we'll live in perfect safety and peace, satisfied to be in the presence of God. Our tummies will be full.

Thank You for the promise of heaven, my God.

What Is Your Request?

And pray in the Spirit on all occasions with all kinds of prayers and requests. With this in mind, be alert and always keep on praying.
Ephesians 6:18 NIV

What burdens your heart today? Is there a trial that engulfs you or someone you love? Present your request to your heavenly Father with the assurance that He will act on your behalf—either by changing your circumstances or by changing you. He is always concerned for you.

But be patient. What we may view as a nonanswer may simply be God saying, "Wait" or "I have something better for you." He *will* answer. Keep in mind that His ways are not our ways, nor are His thoughts our thoughts.

God knows what He's doing, even when He allows trials in our lives. We might think that saving a loved one from difficulty is a great idea—but God, in His wisdom, may decide that would be keeping them (or us) from an opportunity for spiritual growth. Since we don't know all of God's plans, we must simply lay our requests before Him and trust Him to do what is right. He will never fail us!

Father God, here are my needs. I lay them at Your feet, walking away unburdened and assured that You have it all under control. Thank You!

POWERFUL PRAYER

The prayer of a righteous man is powerful and effective.
JAMES 5:16 NIV

"Never underestimate the power of prayer." We hear those words time and time again—especially when we find ourselves in obvious and desperate need. Often, well-meaning Christian friends or acquaintances, who don't really know what to say, come up with the handy, pat answers given to them in their last crisis. It's easy to quickly dismiss these common sayings as silly and unhelpful.

But whether we dismiss it or not, this particular saying is true. Prayer *is* unmistakably powerful and effective.

When it comes to the best interests of our own children, we mothers have a remarkable ability to seek God with all our hearts. This scripture promises us that God considers the prayers of a righteous man (or *mother*) powerful and effective.

While we may not see immediate results, there is no doubt that God pays attention to our prayers. They may not bring the results we thought we needed, but we can be confident that our prayers are bringing what God has planned for us.

Lord, Your Word says You consider my prayer to be powerful and effective. You know the burden I am carrying on my tired shoulders and I give it to You to work out. Thank You, Father.

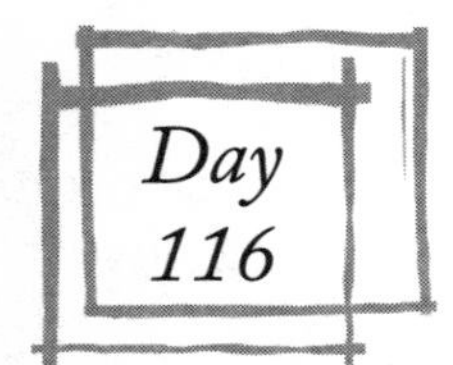

An Hour Apart

And he cometh unto the disciples, and findeth them asleep,
and saith unto Peter, What, could ye not watch with me one hour?
Matthew 26:40 KJV

An old hymn describes a "sweet hour of prayer," but let's be honest: Few of us have an hour to spend with the Lord every day. When those rare opportunities come, we don't even know how to handle them. But simply trying to fill an hour with spiritual things can be a real blessing.

Picture yourself sitting at a table, Bible in hand. You have an hour in front of you. What do you do?

First, choose a passage to study. Read through it at least five times, in different translations, if possible. Use a dictionary—both an English and a Bible dictionary—to check the meaning of any unusual words. Use a concordance to find other places where key words appear in the Bible. Check out the cross-references found in many Bibles.

Ask the five W's (*who*, *what*, *when*, *where*, and *why*) about the passage, and summarize what you've learned. List any lessons you can apply to your life.

Ask God to make you a doer of His word, not only a hearer. Then, as a final step, share what God has taught you with someone else.

Lord and Savior, show me when and how to carve out an hour with You.
Make me hungry for that intimate time.

Defective Lions

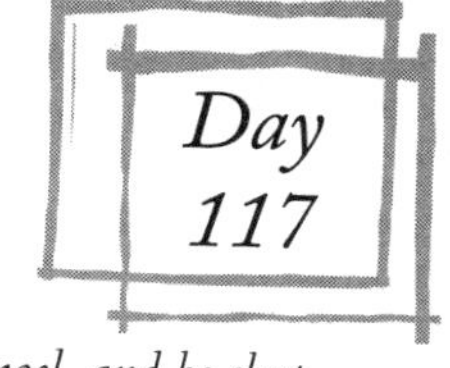

Daniel answered, "O king, live forever! My God sent his angel, and he shut the mouths of the lions. They have not hurt me, because I was found innocent in his sight. Nor have I ever done any wrong before you, O king."
Daniel 6:21–22 NIV

Daniel had lived most of his life as an exile in Babylon. Dragged from Jerusalem, probably around age fifteen, he kept his faith intact and uncompromised. Now, at about age eighty, Daniel had refused to comply with a decree to pray only to King Darius. The punishment for this rule-breaking? Daniel would be thrown into a den of hungry lions. King Darius ordered a stone to be placed over the mouth of the den and sealed it with his own signet ring so that "Daniel's situation might not be changed" (Daniel 6:17 NIV). The old prophet's fate was sealed. Or was it?

Maybe those lions weren't so hungry after all. Or maybe they were defective. Vegetarians, perhaps?

Or maybe those who sought to harm Daniel underestimated the power of the almighty God, sovereign over even the most basic instincts of hungry, ferocious cats.

Somehow, even in a hostile foreign environment, Daniel never compromised his beliefs or trust in God. And God never disappointed Daniel.

Few of us will become lions' lunch for compromising our faith, but we all face situations that are hostile to our trust in God. Daniel reminds us how to respond: firmly, boldly, trusting that God will never disappoint us.

King and Lord of my home, I want Your holy presence to shine in my family's life. Reign here today!

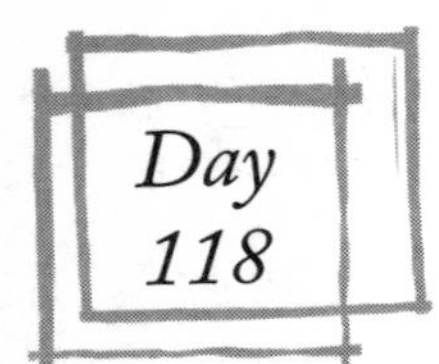

Not My Will

Jesus walked on a little way. Then he knelt down on the ground and prayed, "Father, if it is possible, don't let this happen to me! Father, you can do anything. Don't make me suffer by having me drink from this cup. But do what you want, and not what I want."
Mark 14:35–36 CEV

It's easy to believe that our righteousness would determine whether or not our prayers will be answered. Often, people think that unanswered prayers signify unconfessed sin. But there once was a great and godly man who prayed with deep conviction without receiving the answer He most desired. In case you hadn't already guessed it, that Man was Jesus.

The Lord faced a cup of suffering from which He was to drink. In His humanity, Jesus didn't want to endure the trial ahead, and He asked His Father, if it were possible, to take the cup away. But we all know how the prayer was answered. From His own Father, Jesus received an answer of "not yet." God proceeded with His plan of Jesus' arrest, trial, and crucifixion, before the suffering was ultimately overcome by Jesus' resurrection.

In faith, we can boldly take our needs before God's throne of grace. But, like our Lord Jesus Christ, we must delight ourselves in the will of our almighty God, subjecting our own desires completely to His.

We pray in obedience; we surrender in obedience. Blessed be the name of the Lord!

Blessed be Your name, Lord. I will come to You with my needs and I will trust in You. Please work in my life according to Your perfect will.

Beauty for Ashes

Get wisdom, get understanding;
do not forget my words or swerve from them.
Proverbs 4:5 niv

The decadent, triple chocolate fudge cookie recipe called for real butter, but the young mother could only find a container of lard. Hoping it would make little difference, she went on gathering ingredients. Then, another item missing. . .no baking powder. *Could baking soda be that different?* Mouth watering, proud of her ability to improvise, she mixed, scooped, and baked the ingredients with great anticipation.

As she watched the cookies bake through the oven window, they didn't look quite as she had expected. Actually, they appeared rather flat. *Well,* she thought, *at least they'll taste good.* As the cookies were removed from the oven and cool enough to bite into, she gingerly nibbled one of her creations. Though she had expected a delicious chocolate cookie, she ended up with a worthless glob of goo—and an embarrassing lesson. The right ingredients make all the difference.

We've all made embarrassing messes by trying to "substitute" our human insight for God's infinite wisdom. When His Word said "no," we've countered with "well, maybe." And the results were, predictably, poor.

But God is completely faithful to us. As we acknowledge our errors of judgment in "substitution," He will graciously offer us perfect chocolate chip cookies—rather than the tasteless mess we should have received.

Father, please help me to trust in Your wisdom rather than rely on my own brand of human reasoning. I appreciate Your faithfulness to me.

Who, Me?

Have not I commanded thee? Be strong and of a good courage; be not afraid, neither be thou dismayed: for the Lord thy God is with thee whithersoever thou goest.
Joshua 1:9 KJV

When God tabbed Joshua to succeed Moses as Israel's leader, the new chief must have felt inadequate. After all, Moses met God "face to face" (Exodus 33:11 KJV). He led Israel more than forty years, keeping them alive physically and spiritually in the desert. While the people knew Joshua as his right-hand man, this new generation never had experienced life without Moses. Would they trust Joshua as they risked their lives and families entering the Promised Land? Canaan's fortified cities teemed with fierce inhabitants who often worshipped evil gods with human sacrifice. Who could blame the Israelites if they wondered whether Joshua could handle the job?

Before thousands of families with livestock began the impossible task of crossing the Jordan River, God reminded Joshua He had handpicked him for this purpose. God's presence would more than compensate for Joshua's faults and mistakes.

We may not lead nations, but often feel very alone as we lead our families. "What if. . . ?" "How can I. . . ?" and "No way!" cloud our thinking. But God's presence is still as strong and capable as ever. He will guide us across whatever Jordan we face.

Father, sometimes I don't know how my family and I will make it. But You do. Please help me hear Your voice and follow You to accomplish the impossible.

Light My Path

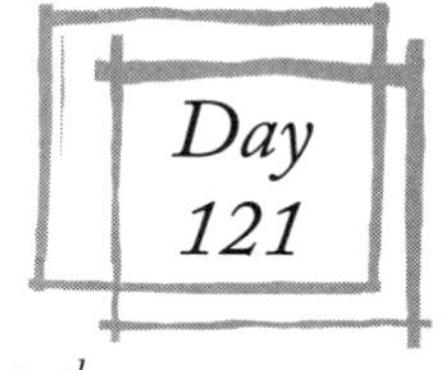

Your word is a lamp to my feet and a light for my path.
Psalm 119:105 NIV

Amy was walking a usually well-lit path around the lake. But tonight, the streetlamps had not come on—and the moon, though large and full, was covered by thick clouds. She had often walked around the lake, but this night, Amy stumbled over unnoticed tree limbs and half-buried rocks. Then the streetlamps flickered to life and a golden light illuminated the path. Amy could speed her pace, easily avoiding the dangerous obstructions.

God's Word is like a streetlamp. Often, we *think* we know where we're going and where the stumbling blocks are. We believe we can avoid pitfalls and maneuver the path successfully on our own. But the truth is that without God's Word, we are walking in darkness, stumbling and tripping.

When we sincerely begin to search God's Word, we find the path becomes clear. We see everything in a new light, a light that makes it obvious which way to turn and what choices to make. God's light allows us to live our lives in the most fulfilling way possible, a way planned out from the very beginning by God Himself.

Jesus, shine Your light upon my path. I have spent too long wandering through the darkness, looking for my way. As I search Your Word, I ask You to make it a lamp to my feet so that I can avoid the pitfalls of the world and walk safely along the path You have created specifically for me.

Creating Margin

"My Presence will go with you,
and I will give you rest."
Exodus 33:14 NIV

From the very first chapter of Genesis, God teaches us to take rest. He rested on the seventh day of creation and declared it good. Later, as the Israelites entered the Promised Land, God ordered the people to give the *soil* a rest every seven years.

When we short ourselves on rest, illness can result. That's our body's way of saying "Slow down! I can't keep up! If you won't listen to me, then I'm going to force you to."

God believes in rest! But most of us live lives that are packed to the brim with activities and obligations. We're overwhelmed. With such a fragile balance, unexpected occurrences, like a dead car battery, can wreck us emotionally, spiritually, and physically.

That's not the lifestyle God wants us to have. "He grants sleep to those he loves," wrote the psalmist (Psalm 127:2 NIV). God wants us to create a margin for the unexpected: a neighbor in need, a grandparent who requires extra attention, a friend who needs encouragement, our own kids as they grow and mature.

Life is busy. But in God's presence we find rest.

Help me, Father, to listen to Your instruction and heed Your words.

What's for Dinner?

Who provides the raven's food when its young cry out to God and wander about for lack of food?
Job 38:41 HCSB

What's the first question you hear when you get home at night? Isn't it often, "Mom, what's for dinner?"

Our children don't ask *whether* we have food for dinner. They may not know that our cupboards are bare of all but the most essential items. They might not realize that we're wondering how we can stretch the food we have until our next paycheck. No, the kids ask in confidence that we will provide. They trust us.

God wants us to come to Him in the same way. He loves to hear our cries, even a desperate, "God, I need food! I need You!" He loves for us to live in total dependence on Him. He provides food for the birds, as He told Job; He'll also provide basic necessities for us and for our children.

The next time our children cry out to us about their needs, we, in turn, can cry out to our Father God. It's such a relief to know He's always listening.

Heavenly Father, we trust You for our daily bread as the Israelites trusted You for daily manna. We trust You to supply our physical needs.

Say What You Mean

*"But let your 'Yes' be 'Yes,' and your 'No,' 'No.'
For whatever is more than these is from the evil one."*
MATTHEW 5:37 NKJV

In today's world, too often a person's word has little value. Our signature may be worth thousands or millions—but our word counts for less and less in the business world and even in many personal lives. Prenuptial agreements are signed before some people will make a marriage vow. Employment contracts are demanded from workplaces. The list goes on and on.

As Christians, when we give a person our word we should stand on it. Others should know they can count on our word as if it were gold in their hands. So should our children.

When we tell our kids the rules, we should demand that they follow them. It's a big mistake to give in to their tears or whining.

The best way to teach our kids the value and importance of their own word is to back up our words with consistent action. Let the children see we really mean what we say and only say what we mean.

Jesus stated, very simply and clearly, "Let your 'Yes' be 'Yes' and your 'No,' 'No.'" Consistency and commitment are not choices, they are commands.

Dear Jesus, help me follow Your command and always back up my words with supporting actions. Help me be consistent with my children, teaching them the value of their own words.

Making Memories

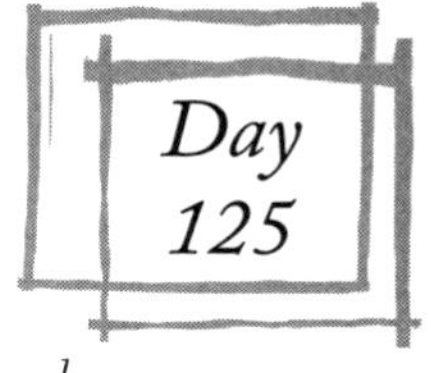

*They shall abundantly utter the memory of thy great goodness,
and shall sing of thy righteousness.*
Psalm 145:7 KJV

Scrapbooking has become a popular pastime for many American families. You take an ordinary, unstaged photo and create a page of memories to be enjoyed long after the moment has passed. Something as simple as a trip to the ice cream shop can be transformed into a beautiful keepsake memory page. Everyday events become cherished lifelong memories to be enjoyed over and over again.

As the scrapbook pages turn, we move from potty training to the first day of school—then first dates. We reminisce over day trips to the park or living room campouts. We remember visits to the pet store and trips to the library. Those commonplace events that shape our children's memories become the cherished "good old days" to be shared with future generations.

The scrapbook, though, is only a vehicle. The essential thing is forming those memories! Let's purposefully create "snapshots" of our family times, bringing smiles to our kids' faces as they recall sweet memories of bike rides, homemade pancakes, or pillow fights in the living room.

May our little ones "abundantly utter the memory" of their childhood's goodness—and call to mind "the good old days" with their own children.

*Father God, show me how to create memories for my children.
I long for them to treasure their childhood years.*

Take a Poll

The fear of human opinion disables;
trusting in God protects you from that.
Proverbs 29:25 MSG

Ever experienced "mom paralysis"?

It happens when we need to make a tough decision—and we just can't decide what to do. Often, we'll take a poll of our friends and acquaintances to see what they would do in a given situation. Somehow, that advice gives us comfort, absolving us of personal responsibility if the outcome disappoints.

Rather than polling other people, though, why not seek the scriptures' advice?

God is very clear on what He expects from us. His advice is sound. Many life issues are specifically addressed in the Bible. And for those that aren't, we can ask the Holy Spirit for guidance. He'll always answer that prayer, speaking to us and guiding us through the Word to lead us to God's will. Of course, there are times when the Lord uses other people to give us wise counsel. But that godly counsel will always center on the scripture.

Today, let's put God's advice first. Led by Him, we'll never lose.

Lord, help me to seek You first when I'm in doubt and in need of direction. I know that You will help me to obey Your good guidance. Please lead me to people who will give me godly counsel based only on Your Word.

EAT YOUR FILL

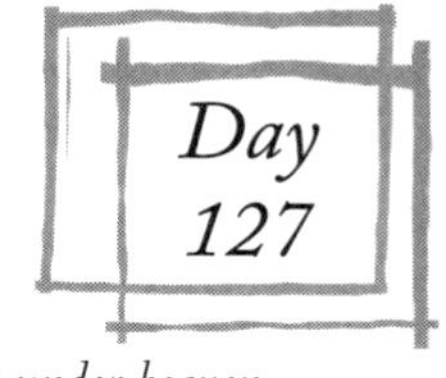

There is a time for everything, and a season for every activity under heaven. . .
a time to embrace and a time to refrain.
ECCLESIASTES 3:1, 5 NIV

Author Carol Kuykendall tells a story of stopping at a roadside fruit stand after dropping her son off at college. As she filled a bag with peaches, the cashier commented, "Better eat your fill of those peaches. When they're gone, you won't miss them so much."

Carol felt the cashier had given her wisdom that applied to more than peaches. She went home, cleared her calendar of all but necessities for the year and became more available for her daughter still living at home.

Rather than resist or ignore the changing season of her life, Carol embraced and savored it. When her daughter left for college, they were closer than ever—and Carol felt a deep peace that she had "eaten her fill." She wasn't burdened by regret over missed moments.

Wise old Solomon observed a certain pattern that God Himself had set into motion: seasons of nature, seasons of change in our lives. Solomon could see the big picture, understanding that we have little control over many things. Things like growing older or facing an empty nest. Instead of fighting that rhythm, we can embrace it, acknowledging that seasons are part of God's plan for our lives.

Lord, help us to see our lives with a long view.
Give us Your peace as we face our future,
knowing You are in control.

Marvelous Thunder

"God's voice thunders in marvelous ways;
he does great things beyond our understanding."
Job 37:5 NIV

Have you ever reflected deeply on the power that God is? Not that He *has,* but that He is.

The ailing woman who simply touched Jesus' garment was healed. That's power. Lazarus walked out of the tomb alive. That's power. Jesus could walk on water and calm a storm with His words. That's power.

Only a God who *is* power could do such things.

Job's friend Elihu made some false assumptions about his suffering companion, but he certainly understood God's power. Elihu described God as telling lightning where to strike (Job 36:32), and generating thunder with His own voice (Job 37:2–4). That's power—full-blown, mind-boggling, earthshaking power.

Now, consider this: The One who controls nature also holds every one of our tears in His hand. He is our Father, and He works on our behalf. He is more than enough to meet our needs; He does things far beyond what our human minds can understand.

This One who is power loves you. He looks at you and says, "I delight in you, my daughter." Wow! His ways are marvelous and beyond understanding.

Lord God, You are power. You hold all things in Your hand and You chose to love me. You see my actions, hear my thoughts, watch my heartbreak. . . and You still love me. Please help me trust in Your power, never my own.

UNCONDITIONAL LOVE

"If you then, being evil, know how to give good gifts to your children, how much more will your Father who is in heaven give what is good to those who ask Him!"
MATTHEW 7:11 NASB

Whether you gave birth or adopted, do you remember the first time you laid eyes on your child? The chubby round cheeks or slender fingers instantly enraptured your heart. Right there, on the spot, you were hooked.

Love and devotion for this little one coursed through your veins. Immediately, you would have instinctively and willingly given up your life for the child's. This parent-child bond, so powerful to forever alter your life, also gave you a glimpse of unconditional love.

What happens to that bond when this little bundle of joy gets a few years older—and breaks your treasured vase or gets mud on your new beige carpet? What becomes of the profound and unconditional love when your not-so-little one, perhaps now a teenager, shatters your heart with hurtful words and rebellious acts?

Do we tell our children, "You've crossed the line one too many times. I don't love you anymore. In fact, you're no longer my child." The idea is absurd, isn't it?

Yet how often do we fear that our heavenly Father will react that way with *His* children? If we—imperfect as we are—have the capacity to show compassion, love, and mercy to our children, why would our Father in heaven show us any less?

Father, please open my eyes to the love and devotion You have for me. Thank You!

Help Line

What will you do on the day of reckoning, when disaster comes from afar? To whom will you run for help?
Isaiah 10:3 NIV

Darcy didn't know where to turn for help. She had scheduled a move from the expensive apartment she'd shared with her former husband to a less expensive place across town. She had already submitted her thirty-day notice to the landlord.

But Darcy encountered a problem: The weekend she had to move from one place to the other, she found herself in the hospital with appendicitis. She couldn't move. And she didn't know who to ask. She was a newcomer to the area and hadn't yet made friends.

God—through the single adult class of the church she had recently joined—stepped in. Total strangers moved six rooms of furniture and belongings. Throughout the upcoming months, single parents from that class became her safety net, celebrating holidays with her and easing the unique challenges she faced as a new single mother.

A support system. Like Darcy, single moms need a deeply rooted support system to be able to manage well. For some, our families provide that safety net. Others lack that option. But whatever our situation, we can run to God in our time of need. He'll lead us to the right people.

Dear Lord our Helper, we praise You for the people who cross our paths, those who help us in our times of need.

MISSION POSSIBLE

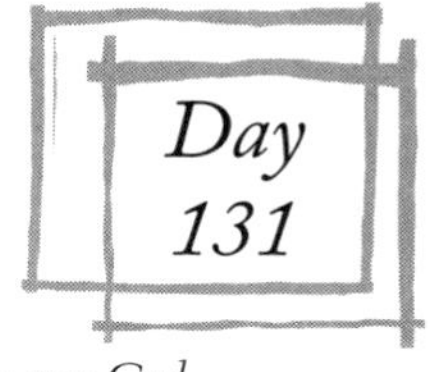

I announced we would all fast and deny ourselves before our God.
We would ask God for a safe trip for ourselves,
our children, and all our possessions.
EZRA 8:21 NCV

Kelli's preschoolers only knew Grandma and Grandpa by their pictures. Ever since Matt left six months earlier, Kelli had longed to visit her parents. She needed their love and faith to help her through tough times. Finally she scraped together enough money to make the thousand-mile trip—if they ate peanut butter and jelly on the way.

A hundred details tormented Kelli. How would she supervise her kids while driving solo? What if a tire went flat? Her stomach churned at the thought of staying alone in a cheap motel, with small children. What scary people might lurk next door?

During another night of tossing and turning, Kelli turned on her bedside light and reached for her Bible. She read, then bowed her head. "I'm sorry, Lord. I forgot You never leave me or forsake me."

Kelli folded her arms. Satan might try to intimidate her, but she and her family needed this trip. Kelli decided to fast during lunch hour the next day, praying in a nearby park.

Not only did Kelli and her children enjoy a safe, wonderful visit, but years later, she looked back at her decision as the turning point in her life journey.

Loving Lord, forgive me when I act as if You aren't there.
Thank You for Your faithfulness. Help me turn to You whenever I feel afraid.

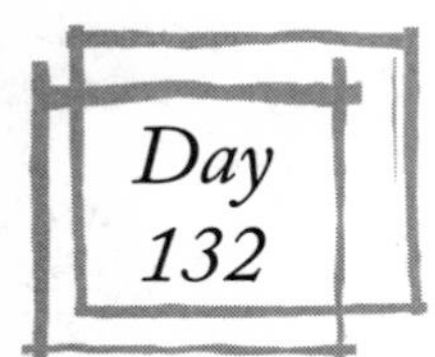

Rachel's Saddlebags

Rachel had taken the household gods and put them inside her camel's saddlebag and was sitting on them. Laban searched through everything in the tent, but found nothing.
Genesis 31:34 TNIV

Why did Rachel feel a compulsion to steal her father's household idols and hide them in her saddlebags? The idols were probably little statues of gods common to the time and culture. She risked the wrath of the true God and jeopardized the safety of her family. Didn't she know better, as the wife of Jacob—the great patriarch of God's nation of Israel?

From our twenty-first-century vantage point, it's easy to wag a finger at Rachel. Living in a western culture, we find such idols, of sexualized bulls and multi-breasted women, to be grotesque. But in Rachel's day, those little idols were pervasive, part of the culture. She didn't dismiss Jacob's God—she just added to Him. Naive, ignorant, or sinful, she allowed idols to replace God's primary position in her life.

Household idols probably don't tempt us. But we can all identify with Rachel. Think of the importance we place on material things, financial security, the achievements of our children—those ambitions can easily consume us! They can occupy our thought life, fill our spare time, and become our life's focus.

Let's take care to keep God exactly where He belongs, in first place.

Lord, clean my house!
Open my eyes to the worthless idols in my life.
Teach me to desire only You.

Free to Be Me

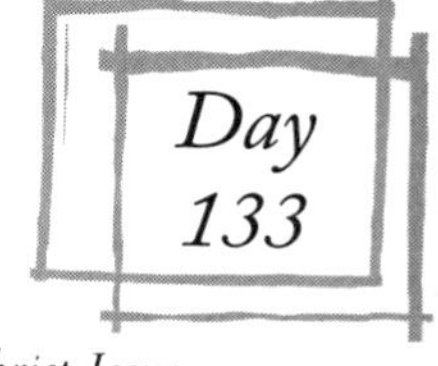

There is now no condemnation for those who are in Christ Jesus.
Romans 8:1 NIV

The world is full of self-righteous people who love to judge the actions of others. Why? Probably because judging others can make us feel just a bit better about ourselves.

"Well, at least my children have their father. . . ." "I wonder what she did to drive him away. . . ." We've all heard such comments, and they burn to the core. Whatever the circumstance that led us to parent our children alone, we as mothers feel guilty—for somehow robbing our children of their other parent. Although we may have had little say in the matter, society and our own self-accusation heap guilt upon us.

But the truth is this: If we have come into a relationship with Christ Jesus, we are no longer condemned. The world may try to tell us differently, but God's Word is the standard—and it tells us we are free. We can hold our heads up high and walk in victory with our children because we are free of guilt and condemnation.

If God the Father, maker of heaven and earth, doesn't condemn us, why should we let anyone else? We are free to be ourselves, loved by God Almighty.

Father, sometimes I feel like everyone is looking at me with judgment and condemnation. They don't know my heart—nor do they care. But I believe You care, Lord, and You don't condemn me. Your Word says so. Help me choose today—and every day—to live in Your truth.

Because I Love You. . .

"Because he loves me," says the Lord, "I will rescue him; I will protect him, for he acknowledges my name."
Psalm 91:14 NIV

A brother and sister were arguing over the last piece of pizza.

"But you had more slices than I had!"

"Yeah, well, you had bigger pieces than I did!"

That's when Mom saved the day by revealing a second "last" piece.

"Where did that come from?" one of the children asked. "I thought we only had one slice left."

"I'd held this one out as my dinner," the mom answered.

Puzzled, the other child asked, "Why would you do that? Then you won't have *any* dinner."

"Because I love you, sweetheart. Now you can both have another slice—go ahead and enjoy it."

Scenes like this are replayed countless times by countless mothers all over the world. Why? Because we love our kids. Not because of their academic successes, their performance on the football field, or their mastery of fractions. Just because we love them.

God wants us to love Him, too, and He reminds us in the psalms that He will protect and rescue those who love and acknowledge Him. Our love for Him is a key that opens the door of His provision. It's not our accomplishment or achievement that God wants—He longs for us to love Him.

Father, if I love my children sacrificially, how much more do You care for me? Wow! I love You, Lord.

Full of Hope

Thy servant my husband is dead; and thou knowest that thy servant did fear the *Lord: and the creditor is come to take unto him my two sons to be bondmen.*
2 Kings 4:1 kjv

The woman had never flagged in her support for her husband's studies with Elisha the prophet. But her husband became ill and died. For their boys' sake, she made herself face each day. The widow struggled to feed them. When a creditor threatened to take the children as slaves, she fell at Elisha's feet, weeping.

"My husband loved God!" she cried. "But he is dead. We cannot pay our debts, and I may lose my sons!"

"What do you have in the house?" Elisha asked.

"Nothing, except one pot of oil."

"Borrow pots from your neighbors." His eyes held hers. "Lots of empty pots. Then shut your door and pour oil into them."

"What is she *doing*?" The widow's neighbors stared at her.

The boys didn't get it either, but they helped her borrow every pot on the block. She took her one pot of oil and began to pour. And pour. The woman filled all the borrowed pots to the brim. Dizzy with excitement, she ran to tell Elisha.

He smiled as if expecting her. "Sell the oil to pay your debt; you and your children can live on the rest."

The widow ran home, thanking God from the bottom of her heart.

Loving Lord, You provided for a mother with no hope for her children.
I know You can still do it today.

I Take It Back

He who guards his mouth and his tongue keeps himself from troubles.
Proverbs 21:23 AMP

Angry words spoken with malicious intent are bad—and scripture clearly identifies them as wrong.

But Proverbs 21:23 speaks of those words that slip carelessly from an unguarded mouth. Even though there is no hurtful intent, loose words and careless speech can leave lasting wounds.

We've all heard of someone who asked a woman when her baby was due, only to learn that the woman was not, in fact, pregnant. Those stories may seem funny at first, but such careless words can really cause pain. Even if a quick apology is offered, those words can never be taken back—and that woman is probably ashamed of her appearance.

Loosely spoken, unguarded words can be extremely painful to children, especially when they come from the person those kids trust most in the world: Mom. Today, let's be very careful in the way we speak to our children. Rather than pouring failure, disappointment, and anger into their young, impressionable lives, let's speak hope, joy, and grace.

As we guard our mouths, we save ourselves—and our children—from trouble.

Father, help me to guard my tongue and rein in the speech that might carelessly escape my lips. Let me speak the light of Your love into the lives of my children, and let my words be a beacon of Your hope to them.

A Shadow of the Past

"Only Rahab the prostitute and all who are with her in her house shall be spared, because she hid the spies we sent."
Joshua 6:17 TNIV

Rahab lived in the city of Jericho. When Israelite spies came to her home, she hid them under flax on the roof until they could make a fast getaway. In return, they promised her safety during the coming siege of the city. True to their word, the spies saved Rahab and her family from Jericho's doom. Rahab apparently converted to Judaism, married an Israelite, and became part of the lineage of King David—and, eventually, of Jesus Christ.

And Rahab had been a prostitute in Jericho.

That fact was part of her story. But Rahab wasn't trapped by her past. Her past didn't hold her back. It may have hurt her, but it didn't shape her. She was used by God. Her name has come down to us centuries later because of her bold faith.

We all have to deal with a past. All of us! Disappointments, poor choices, dysfunctional families, parents who failed us, husbands who harmed us. God is able to bring good from even those years that were painful. By the grace and power of God we can make choices in the present that can affect our future.

There is transforming power with God. We have hope, no matter what lies behind us.

Holy Spirit, You are always at work. Don't ever stop! Show me a new way, Lord. Help me to make healthier choices for myself and my family. Thank You for Your renewing presence in my life.

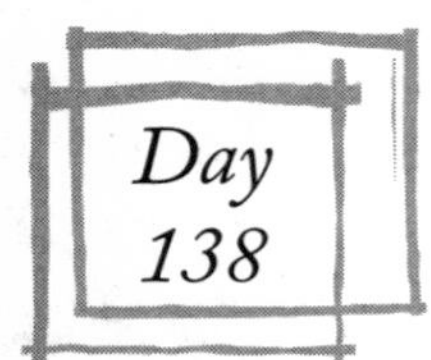

Pinching Pennies

"Suppose one of you wants to build a tower. Will he not first sit down and estimate the cost to see if he has enough money to complete it?"
LUKE 14:28 NIV

Most single mothers skate by financially. We juggle money to pay bills, put food on the table, and keep a roof over our heads.

The problem is that we want more than just to "get by." We want our children to take music lessons and play sports. We want a better, more reliable car. We want to take a family vacation. We want to buy a house, not rent. We want the American dream.

Jesus gives us the first rule of realizing those dreams: Count the cost. How can we raise that kind of money?

Financial wizards tell us to save 10 percent of each paycheck in addition to the tithe. Some of us manage that. Many more struggle with saving.

But if we're serious about those goals, we have to count the cost. Determine how much you'll need for that car or vacation. Set up a place to save, whether it's a coffee can or a bank account. Have money deducted from your paycheck to eliminate the temptation to spend those dollars. Set aside any extra money that comes in—the extra paycheck you get every few months, the income tax refund, or even money found on the ground. Have your children fill a jar with pennies.

With creative planning, we can count the cost—and see what dreams God will help come true.

O God our Father, You want only the best for us. Teach us to manage the resources that You give us, and not to let them dribble away.

Rock of Ages

You will guard him and keep him in perfect and constant peace whose mind [both its inclination and its character] is stayed on You, because he commits himself to You, leans on You, and hopes confidently in You. So trust in the LORD (commit yourself to Him, lean on Him, hope confidently in Him) forever; for the LORD God is an everlasting Rock [the Rock of Ages].

Isaiah 26:3–4 AMP

You and I can have peace. Authentic peace. God-breathed peace. Not because we live in some make-believe world, repeating positive-thinking statements in an attempt to alter reality. Not because we've been able to avoid adversity or opposition. No, we can have peace simply and only because we trust our heavenly Father.

It's not our incredible faith or extraordinary, over-the-top godly lives that brings us peace. God simply wants our complete trust. He calls us to lean confidently on Him and His faithfulness, rather than fretting over, and focusing on, our circumstances.

This doesn't imply that we'll live without difficulties. All single moms have those! But when we make the commitment to trust our heavenly Father, come what may, He guards us and keeps us in His peace.

No matter what we see with our eyes, no matter what the hardship, God is our solid rock. . .our Rock of Ages.

Father God, grant me the ability to trust You, come what may. Cause my eyes to focus on You, not the challenges I face.

More Faith

We live by faith, not by sight.
2 Corinthians 5:7 NIV

Faith is a word often carelessly used. People—rich and poor, single and married, content and miserable—randomly toss the mysterious term around. But what is faith, really? It's believing in something without first having to prove it.

Imagine the scene: At a family barbeque, you watch in mock horror, trying desperately to contain a giggle, as Aunt Sally plops herself onto an unsteady lawn chair—only to have it fold in on itself, spewing the red-faced woman onto the lawn. Amazingly, after she peels herself off the ground and finds some composure, she snaps open *another* chair and sits right down, trusting this one will support her. We live by faith, not by sight.

Faith is what we have in Christ. Our daily circumstances may point to failure and frustration, but faith says God has all things under control—and He never fails. God is the object of our faith. He will never fail, even when it seems like we are drowning. He will lift us up, keep us strong, and put a song in our heart. We live by faith, not by sight.

Lord, I need more faith. I know You will never leave me or forget about my troubles. Life seems overwhelming at times, so I ask You to increase my faith in You.

PRAYER CHANGES THINGS

"The LORD says you won't ever get well. You are going to die, so you had better start doing what needs to be done." Hezekiah turned toward the wall and prayed. . . . The LORD sent [Isaiah] back to Hezekiah with this message. . . . I heard you pray, and I saw you cry. I will heal you.

2 KINGS 20:1–2, 4–5 CEV

Had Hezekiah not prayed to God for healing, he would have certainly died. It was God's plan for the king to die, and the Lord even gave Hezekiah advance warning of his coming demise.

But Hezekiah cried out to God and prayed for healing. He begged for more time, reminding God of the life he had lived and the kind of man he was. And, graciously, God agreed to give Hezekiah fifteen more years.

Sometimes, somehow, the Lord will allow our prayers to effect changes in our circumstances—even in His own plans. As His children, we are in such a close relationship with our Father that He knows our every need and responds to our heartfelt prayers.

When we pray out of obedience, with faith, we can be sure that God hears our prayers. And we can know that He will always answer in the best way, whatever the answer may be.

Thank You, Father, for hearing and answering my prayers according to Your will. Remind me to present my petitions before You as an act of obedience—and then to accept Your will and walk in it.

Love Is Patient

Love. . .is patient and kind.
1 Corinthians 13:4 amp

Why does the apostle Paul start his list of biblical characteristics of love with *patience*?

For most of us moms, that's the hardest quality of all. What mother doesn't get exasperated when her kids dawdle, drag their feet, and make her late? Who hasn't become irritated as we tucked a child into bed for the third or fourth time in one night? Who hasn't struggled with their children's lack of initiative with schoolwork?

But Paul says that love and patience are related. The root word used in this biblical text refers to patience with people, rather than patience with circumstances. By emphasizing the characteristics of love, Paul taught us how love behaves: Love suffers long. Love never gives up. Love is patient.

What happens when we are impatient with others? We view ourselves as more important than them. The Bible tells us that impatience is ultimately caused by pride (Ecclesiastes 7:8). And pride is the opposite of godly love.

God is patient with us, and expects us, in turn, to be patient with others. We don't give up on a child who frustrates or disappoints us. We hope for the best; we're quick to forgive; we don't keep a running list of petty wrongs; we work to keep our tongue reined in.

This is how true love behaves, Paul says. This love reflects the very Author of love.

Lord, remind me to turn ordinary annoyances into opportunities in which I may honor and exalt You.

AIDING THE ENEMY

Would God my lord were with the prophet that is in Samaria! for he would recover him of his leprosy.
2 KINGS 5:3 KJV

The young girl screamed as the burly Syrian soldier hauled her onto his shoulder like a sack of grain, far away from the only home she had known. She never saw her parents or baby brother again.

Still, the girl prayed every night to the God of Israel, as her parents taught her. She found herself a slave in the household of Naaman, the scary captain of the soldiers who kidnapped her. But his lovely wife talked to her kindly. Little by little, the girl's fears subsided. She even pitied her master. Despite his great victories, Naaman suffered from leprosy, a sad fact that dimmed her mistress's smile.

"Elisha, the prophet in Israel, could make him well!" the girl told her.

Naaman's wife gave him her maid's strange advice; the desperate soldier traveled to see Elisha, who told him to wash in the Jordan River. After Naaman swallowed his initial stubbornness, he found, to his amazement, that the God of Israel had healed him.

The Lord did not forget the young girl, alone in a difficult world. And the lessons her parents had taught her made a difference not only in her life, but also in the lives of unbelievers around her.

Father, I do not know the paths my children will take, whether happy or sad. But please let the truths I have tried to teach them glorify You.

Rip That Bandage Off!

He has torn us, but He will heal us.
Hosea 6:1 NASB

The young mother knew the old dressing needed to be removed—but her son just wouldn't cooperate. Though the dirty bandage had to go, the child couldn't possibly understand why—and he vehemently protested her attempts to remove the covering.

Finally, after all other attempts had failed, the mother saw an opportunity and quickly ripped the bandage off. One moment of pain for the boy, and it was all over. Then she washed the wound, reapplied ointment and a fresh bandage, and set the boy on a path to full recovery.

Of course, the son didn't see the situation in quite the same way. In his eyes, his mother had callously caused him needless pain. Unconcerned for his feelings and ignoring his frightened cries, she ripped off the stuck-on bandage. He couldn't yet comprehend that the pain his mother inflicted was for his *good*. . .it was in his best interest.

So, too, our heavenly Father often allows pain as He seeks to bring healing to our lives. As He moves to heal our wounds, He may even cause pain that defies our understanding. But, as He reminds us through the prophet Hosea, there are times when God must tear in order to heal.

Lord, I haven't always recognized Your healing hand in my life.
At times, I've only seen the tearing and screamed for it to stop. . .
yet it was ultimately for my good. Thank You for healing me, Father.

SEX EDUCATION

Who told thee that thou wast naked?
GENESIS 3:11 KJV

Many of us have pictures of our naked, or near naked, children. Small children have no sense of modesty—nor do they need it. Their nakedness is pure and innocent.

At some point between birth and adulthood, sexual modesty sets in. The child who used to run about happily without so much as a diaper tells you, "Don't come in! I'm not dressed yet."

Who told you that you were naked?

One of the great privileges of parenting our children is teaching them the facts of life. Our own attitude will strongly affect whether they view their awakening sexual desires as something shameful or a gift from God.

We start when we teach them the words for their body parts—reproductive organs as well as fingers and toes—and we continue by answering their questions. We can look for natural opportunities to share the wonders of conception: Perhaps a friend or a family member is having a baby, or maybe our pet is giving birth. If we're uncomfortable discussing the subject, we can search a Christian bookstore for helpful resources. One thing is certain—we want our children to learn about their "nakedness" from *us*, not their peers.

Dear Lord and Creator, You made us beautiful. I pray for guidance as I look for opportunities to teach the wonder of Your creation to my children.

The Finest Jewels

Preserve sound judgment and discernment, do not let them out of your sight; they will be life for you, an ornament to grace your neck.
Proverbs 3:21–22 NIV

According to the dictionary, *judgment* is the ability to form opinions and have good common sense. *Discernment* refers to insight and the ability to see things clearly in a shrewd way. God instructs us, as His precious daughters, to keep these two specific qualities very close to us. So close, in fact, that we display them like fine jewelry.

When we are lonely, we risk overlooking our judgment and discernment. Every day, we pour our lives wholeheartedly into our children, rarely finding any time for ourselves. With few of our adult needs being met, it can be tempting to take off our beautiful ornaments of judgment and discernment, lay them neatly on our nightstand, and make bad choices in an attempt to fill the void within us.

All of us carry unmet needs—but God will fill every one if we look to Him and seek His answers.

Ladies, let's always wear these fine ornaments of judgment and discernment, keeping them front and center, because there are little ones watching, learning from both our wise and unwise behaviors.

Father, please give me more discernment and sound judgment. I want to avoid falling into painful and dangerous traps. Please help me avoid unwise decisions that will lead me to places that are unhealthy for me and my children.

KEEPING A PROMISE

"I prayed for this child, and the LORD has granted me what I asked of him. So now I give him to the LORD. For his whole life he will be given over to the LORD."
1 SAMUEL 1:27–28 NIV

How did Hannah feel as she handed Samuel over to Eli, the priest, to raise? Scholars think Samuel was about three years old at the time. Did Hannah have doubts as she packed up her son's favorite books and blanket? Did she lie in bed at night, staring at the ceiling, worrying over what kind of surrogate parent Eli would be for her boy? Eli had a terrible reputation as a father! His sons, also priests, were labeled as "wicked men" who "had no regard for the Lord" (1 Samuel 2:12 NIV). Harsh words!

Years before, Hannah had begged God to bless her with a child. In return, she relinquished the child to the Lord's service. Hannah seemed to know that Samuel belonged to God. Amazingly, as she left the temple with empty arms, Hannah sang a song of praise and thanksgiving to God (1 Samuel 2:1–10). The source of her joy was the God who answered her prayer. She trusted God with Samuel's life, even with the influences he would encounter living among Eli's wicked sons. And Samuel came out just fine—in fact more than fine! He was the spiritual leader for Israel for many years!

Our kids will encounter bad influences, too—even in good places. Can we trust God confidently, like Hannah did, resting assured that they belong to Him?

Lord, when situations are out of my control, I thank You that You are always in control.

Be with Jesus

The officials were amazed to see how brave Peter and John were, and they knew that these two apostles were only ordinary men and not well educated. The officials were certain that these men had been with Jesus.
Acts 4:13 CEV

The third grader needs help with his multiplication tables, the spaghetti is boiling over, the phone is ringing, and the baby just threw applesauce on the wall.

With all the concerns and distractions of motherhood, it's easy to get so busy that we overlook our need to spend time with Jesus—reading His word, praying, praising, and worshipping Him.

Don't let your time with Jesus slide! The "officials" of Acts 4:13 were amazed not by Peter and John's education, wealth, or status, but simply because it was obvious they had been with Jesus.

Others can tell when we've made time for Jesus. He'll give us bravery for our tasks, but also love, joy, peace, patience, kindness, goodness, faithfulness, gentleness, and self-control.

Each morning as we seek Jesus, let's not just give Him a list of our needs for the day. Let's listen to what He wants to tell us, and praise Him for who He is. The results will be amazing!

Dear Jesus, help me not to be so busy that I push You aside. I love You for who You are. Shine through me today so others can be amazed by You.

TIME IS FLEETING

Teach us to realize the brevity of life, so that we may grow in wisdom.
PSALM 90:12 NLT

"They grow up so fast."

We've all heard it, probably even said it ourselves. It's oft repeated, because it's so true. Our children's childhood is fleeting. Our opportunity to influence them is moving at breakneck speed. Yet many of us are so absorbed in day-to-day parenting that we don't recognize that time is escaping quickly.

We rush little Johnny to school. Hurry little Sarah to day care. Speed through the workweek to spend Saturday and Sunday doing extra chores around the house. Maybe we'll occasionally take a week's vacation just to catch our breath. But then we're off to the races again.

What if we determined to enjoy the moment? To drink in the aroma of our morning cup of coffee? To savor the innocence of our child's kindergarten graduation performance? Maybe we should sit back and really listen to our teenage daughter as she describes her favorite band. Perhaps we could enjoy a Saturday morning breakfast of cold pizza with the kids—in our pajamas.

Life is brief. So is our opportunity to influence our children.

Father, help me to see how fleeting is the
time with the little ones You've given me.
And please help me make the most of that time.

The Little Things

He blesses her with [children], and she is happy.
Shout praises to the LORD!
PSALM 113:9 CEV

She had been up all night. Her six-month-old baby had recently stopped sleeping through the night, which meant that mom had been attending to crying for several hours now. She felt she'd reached her limit when something beautiful happened: The baby stopped wailing and, after a few minutes of rocking, both mother and child drifted off to sleep together.

Sometimes it feels as if this thing called "parenting" is the hardest, most thankless job around. But God reminds us in Psalm 113 that children are truly a blessing. They are His gift to us. The salvation of all humanity arrived in the form of a child—God's Son, Jesus Christ—who would grow up to pay the price for all our sins.

In the midst of the struggle, the little things—a smile, a laugh, a present from our children—can remind us how worthwhile this job of motherhood really is and how happy our children make us. Rejoice in these moments each day. Remember, with the psalm writer, the continual blessings of children, the gift of parenthood, and the joy of both.

Dear heavenly Father, thank You for the gift of children. Help me to rejoice in each moment of their lives and remember the good when parenthood seems like a difficult task. I praise You, Lord!

Wedding Ring

For thy Maker is thine husband; the LORD of hosts is his name; and thy Redeemer the Holy One of Israel; the God of the whole earth shall he be called.
ISAIAH 54:5 KJV

Alice was the mother of a teenager and had been single for most of her child's life. She struggled with loneliness, fearing that she'd been condemned to a lifetime of singleness. Alice dreaded the empty nest and growing old on her own.

But the Lord directed Alice's attention to Isaiah 54. His promise to be her husband resonated deep within her soul, and she decided on a symbolic act: She purchased a ring of pure white gold and planned a wedding ceremony. With her daughter and sister as witnesses, Alice read Isaiah 54:5 and claimed God's promise to be her husband.

From that point forward, whenever loneliness threatened to overwhelm Alice, she let the wedding ring remind her of God's promise.

We know that God has deep compassion for widows and orphans (see Psalm 146:9)—and He has those same feelings for us as single mothers. Perhaps, like Alice, we'll choose a visible reminder of His promises. Or perhaps we can simply meditate on one of the several names of God mentioned in Isaiah 54:5.

God is the answer to a lonely mother's heart.

Oh God, our husband, we thank You that we are the bride of Christ. Whenever we feel alone, overwhelm us with Your love.

Support Staff

Pile your troubles on God's shoulders—
he'll carry your load, he'll help you out.
Psalm 55:22 msg

Moms are the unsung heroes, the support staff, the ones everyone depends on. Our purses hold everything from bandages for skinned knees to granola bars for hungry tummies to tissues for runny noses. If you need it, we'll find it. But there are days when we tire of carrying the weight of the world. Sometimes, we run ragged, taking care of everyone—everyone, that is, except for ourselves.

There came a time when Elijah grew tired of caring for Israel. Worn out, he ran for the hills, contemplating early retirement. In fact, he hoped God would give him a break and end it all. "Just kill me," Elijah begged God. He was *that* exhausted. *That* depressed.

Was God angry with Elijah for seeking an escape? Did God stand over Elijah, wagging a finger, telling him to pull it together?

Just the opposite! Tenderly, oh so tenderly, God sent angels to care for Elijah. They provided food and rest and encouragement.

Sometimes, we're so busy and tired we have nothing left to give. During those times, remember Elijah. Rest, eat, nourish yourself. Just let God be in charge for a while.

Dear Lord, teach me to ask for help. Prod me to take better care of myself.
Thank You for Your gentle response to my low periods.
Remind me that things will get better again! They always do.

FINDING STRENGTH IN SILENCE

For thus says the LORD God, the Holy One of Israel: "In returning and rest you shall be saved; in quietness and confidence shall be your strength."
ISAIAH 30:15 NKJV

Long days, frantic schedules, and the ever-increasing demands of work and home can crowd God completely out of our minds—and weary us to the bone.

We plan and anticipate troubles with money, work, and our children. . .yet we are never quite prepared enough. Something always comes up, making our lives a touch more difficult and exhausting. Too many times, there is just not enough Mom to go around.

That's when we need to remember that our true strength never comes from our own efforts. Our sure rest isn't something that we create. According to Bible scholars, "quietness and confidence" in this verse can also mean "utter trust." Only when we rely on God and spend time with Him does comfort find a way into our everyday world. Trusting in God's strength is the only way to true rest and success.

Father God, You care for us so much! When we let the whirlwinds of life crowd You out, help us remember that only by trusting in Your love and grace do we find true strength and rest.

Of Lasting Value

Not that I speak in respect of want; for I have learned, in whatsoever state I am, therewith to be content.
PHILIPPIANS 4:11 KJV

Bigger isn't always better." We've heard that maxim and perhaps even quoted it, but how many of us display it in our lives?

What do we model for our little ones if we're striving for a newer car, a bigger house, a larger-screen television, or a newer and better wardrobe? What would they learn if we complained about having to eat hamburger *again*, or wished away our days because we dreaded our work? What would they pick up? Discontentment.

The way we live our lives teaches either contentment or discontentment. For single moms, of course, there's always something that could make us unhappy. Many lack the little extras that others may take for granted—like pizza on a Friday night, money for new school clothes, or a decent vacation each year.

We may not have all the benefits of this world, but we do have something very special to offer our children: We have the opportunity to teach them how to be content with what they have. Not with what they *will* have, but what they *do* have, right now. Today's scripture reminds us that we need to *learn* contentment—it's not our natural state.

Sure, our lives can be difficult. But let's turn them into opportunities to impart a vital life lesson. If we teach our kids to be satisfied with or without an iPod or pizza twice a week, they'll gain something of lasting value.

Father God, how do I teach contentment when all around I see such excess? Teach me to impart to my children the things of real value.

Faithful One

Let us hold unswervingly to the hope we profess, for he who promised is faithful. And let us consider how we may spur one another on toward love and good deeds.
Hebrews 10:23–24 NIV

When we have painful questions, therapists and counselors often have answers. Their offices overflow with hurting people looking for those answers.

But the people who offer the most practical and beneficial advice are those who have walked in our shoes—and who kept walking even when their soles wore through.

Such people have helped us—and we, in turn, can help others. We may feel as if we have nothing to offer, but that's simply not so. As single moms who have traveled the potholed road of instability and loneliness, we can be a blessing to others just lacing up their sneakers for the journey.

By holding tightly to the hope we have, we can benefit those around us who are struggling to find hope of their own. We can spur another hurting mom on to love and goodness and, in so doing, help ourselves better understand the God in whom our hope lies.

Dear Jesus, I know You are faithful—but I often forget that. Sometimes I wander in a direction that does not encourage others to love or do good. Please forgive me and help me to hold tighter to that which I know is true. Show me how to live every minute today to spur others toward Your love tomorrow.

An Apple a Day

"Everything that lives and moves will be food for you. Just as I gave you the green plants, I now give you everything."
Genesis 9:3 NIV

It was a typical weekday morning. The kids were washed, dressed, fed, and off to the bus. Natalie pulled herself together and took a few minutes to grab some coffee and a bite of breakfast before heading to the office.

"I don't have time for a hot breakfast," she told herself as she eyed the one prepackaged item left in the pantry. With that, she grabbed the candy bar and headed out the door.

It's easy to put the kids first and eat whatever is left over—but in the long run, staying healthy is just as important as reaching work on time. God gave us all the green plants and animals as food, but we must choose those foods and preparations that will keep us in good health.

Tough as it might be, try to plan an extra five minutes to simply choose healthful foods for yourself. Stock the pantry with whole grains and snacks like dried fruit or trail mix. Not only will you be giving your body the fuel it needs, you'll also model healthy habits for your children.

Dear God, remind me that making healthy choices now will be better for me and my children in the long run. Help me to pick healthful foods and to take care of the body You gave me.

On the Back Burner

Based on the gift they have received, everyone should use it to serve others, as good managers of the varied grace of God.
1 Peter 4:10 HCSB

"I used to love to garden," Tracy explained, "but since I had children, that hobby had to go on the back burner." What a mistake!

There is a season for everything in our lives. But shelving that haven of creativity that fills and reenergizes us isn't what God intended. He wants us to use our gifts and share them with others. We might even miss an opportunity by leaving some of our talents out of our motherhood—our art or music, cooking or gardening, writing or playing a sport.

Pursue creativity with your children. Cook with them. Pick up a crayon and color with them. Grow a garden with them. Learn a new skill together. Let your kids see that you value your own creative spark. It doesn't have to be an enormous endeavor or result in a masterpiece. But pursuing our God-given creativity sets an example—of taking pleasure in God's gifts.

God observed His own work of creation and declared it was "very good." Creativity is a wonderful gift that reflects God's image to our kids and our world.

Lord of all, You gave me a creative spark to use! Show me how to keep that flame alive and nourished, to benefit myself and my family.

Taking Care of Ourselves

When Jesus saw him lying there and knew that he had already been there a long time, he said to him, "Do you want to be healed?"
John 5:6 ESV

A paralyzed man had lain by the pool of Bethesda for thirty-eight years, waiting for an opportunity to get in the water and experience its miraculous powers.

When Jesus passed him one day, the Lord asked what sounds like a silly question: "Do you want to be healed?" The Divine Healer probed deeply into the man's desires. "Do you *really* want healing, after all this time?" The poor man explained his plight: He had had no one to carry him into the pool. After that answer, Jesus healed him.

Like the paralyzed man, single moms often don't make it to the healing water. We put our family's health before our own. We take our children to the doctor, buy them medicine, make sure they're vaccinated, and stay home with them when they're sick. By the time we've spent our sick days (and much of our money) on our children, we feel we can't afford to take care of ourselves. Is it any wonder that we often struggle to shake colds, headaches, and other maladies?

Jesus' question should resonate with us: *Do you want to be healed?* We must learn to care for ourselves as well as we do our children.

Dear Lord my Healer, I pray that You will give me wisdom regarding my health. Teach me how to take care of myself.

Still Waters

"They will lie down on good grazing ground and feed in rich pasture. . . . I will feed My flock and I will lead them to rest," declares the L*ORD God.*
EZEKIEL 34:14–15 NASB

"I have to get this house clean." "The last load of laundry has to be done before I go to bed." "If I miss that meeting at work, how will I ever get that promotion?" "I can't forget the kids' school play—they've had enough disappointment." "We have to be at church by 10:00." "I need to get the oil changed soon." "Where's that dry cleaning?" Whew. . . one gets tired just reading a single mom's to-do list.

How do we rest? By simply stopping. The laundry can wait. The house doesn't have to be squeaky clean. You can push the oil change out to 5,000 miles. Maybe we can ask a friend to help with the dry cleaning, or go to an occasional Sunday evening service so the family can sleep in.

When do we rest? It won't find us, so we'll have to pursue it. Schedule it, pencil it in, do what needs to be done—just get some rest. Physical, mental, and emotional rest is paramount. If we miss it, we'll burn out, stress out, or just plain give out.

God promises to lead us to lush, green pastures, while restoring our soul. Let's take Him up on the offer!

Heavenly Father, I need to learn to simply rest and relax. I see so much to do and have so much responsibility—so please enable me to lie down in the pastures You have provided.

Lacking Nothing

Consider it pure joy, my brothers, whenever you face trials of many kinds, because you know that the testing of your faith develops perseverance. Perseverance must finish its work so that you may be mature and complete, not lacking anything.

James 1:2–4 NIV

Trials are never fun. Nor are they pain-free. But they're still necessary.

When people speak of trials, they might mean anything from sleep deprivation to the loss of a loved one—or anything in between. How can we "consider it pure joy" when we face such trials? It's not the trial itself that we celebrate, but the personal growth and expansion of our faith that can lead to joy. Unfortunately, our attitude in the midst of the trial often leaves us empty and hurting.

Trials don't get easier from one to the next. But when we get through one—battered but not broken—we can look back to see growth and strength, which we can take into the next. We have become better equipped to face the next trial with perseverance, comfort, and hope. And we can walk straight ahead, knowing that in the end we will be mature and complete, lacking absolutely nothing in Christ Jesus.

Abba Father, I know You go with me through these trials. I know that any perseverance or strength I have is only because of You and Your faithfulness to me. Increase my joy through these trials and help me remember the purpose of them—that I may not lack any good thing.

Day 161

Peanut Butter and Jelly

A meal of bread and water in contented peace
is better than a banquet spiced with quarrels.
Proverbs 17:1 MSG

A beautifully seasoned pot roast with potatoes, carrots, and onions. . . a salad with croutons, cheese, and choice of dressings. . .warm bread, fresh out of the oven with plenty of butter. . . It's the perfect meal.

But the kids come to the table, bickering and pushing each other. One accuses the other of breaking a toy; someone pulls some hair. You settle things down momentarily, then hear an under-the-table kick followed by a scream.

At this point, do you even feel like eating that wonderful meal? Proverbs 17 says it would be better for a family to dine on bread and water, in peace, than on a huge feast, when everyone is unhappy and fighting.

If you find yourself in the latter situation more often than not, maybe it's time for the bread and water. Instead of devoting time to an elaborate meal, just sit at the table together with a loaf of bread and jars of peanut butter and jelly. Talk, share, and prepare the evening meal together.

Your family will live through the night without a three-course dinner. And, just maybe, the extra time together around more simple fare will reap bountiful rewards of contented peace.

Heavenly Father, Prince of Peace, please bring peace to my home. Calm the bickering and the strife. Soothe the tempers that flare and the rough edges of our speech. Unite us in You so that we can enjoy one another.

He's Watching!

The eyes of the Lord are on the righteous
and his ears are attentive to their cry.
Psalm 34:15 NIV

Does it seem strange to think that God is watching everything we do? As if He's a traffic cop, hiding behind a billboard, waiting to catch us doing something wrong, more than ready to give us a big, fat ticket. Just waiting for us to slip up and fail.

Cancel that mental image.

Instead, replace it with the memory of the first time you held your baby in your arms. Or when you watched your child participate in a sport or play on a playground. Or act in a school play. Or sing in the church choir. Your eyes scanned the crowd, searching for that familiar little face. What wonder! What joy! We couldn't keep our eyes off our kid. We gazed at him, amazed and proud. *That child belongs to me!* we thought.

God's ability to be near us every moment is no threat—it's a promise. A guarantee! His Word tells us that He is near to everyone who calls out His name. "Come near to God and he will come near to you" (James 4:8 NIV).

God is watching each one of us with the same intense love with which we watch our children. We belong to him! He can't keep His eyes off us.

Lord, why is it so hard to believe that You love me? Your Word reassures me, over and over, yet still, I doubt. Remind me again, Lord. Convince me! Draw close! Open my eyes to Your presence.

Me Do It

"If then you are not able to do as small a thing as that, why are you anxious about the rest?"
Luke 12:26 ESV

Toddlers try a mother's patience in many ways. When we're trying to get them ready in the morning, they insist on doing things themselves. "Me do it!" they say as they struggle into their coats, hold their own cups, and waddle about—usually where we don't want them to go. We watch, sigh, and think how much easier it would be if they would only let us do it for them.

God must feel that way about us. He waits, letting us struggle and even fail, until we reach the point that we acknowledge our limitations.

Do we worry about food and clothing? God provides for the ravens of the air and the lilies of the field (Luke 12:24, 27).

Do we struggle to be good Christians and role models? God is pleased to give us the kingdom (Luke 12:32).

Do we cram as much as possible into each day, trying to add an hour to our lives? Forget it (Luke 12:25).

Jesus reminds us that we can't do something as simple (to Him, that is) as adding an hour to our lives. Why do we think we can carry the world on our shoulders?

Instead, the Lord invites us to seek Him first. To take our worries to God in prayer and make that relationship our primary focus. Prayer is the treasure we should seek.

Almighty Lord, You can and do provide everything we need. Teach me to take my worries to You in prayer.

A Spirit of Unity

May the God who gives endurance and encouragement give you a spirit of unity among yourselves as you follow Christ Jesus.
Romans 15:5 NIV

Our single-parent status can give us a built-in ministry.

Many single moms find themselves feeling alone in the church setting. From "couples meetings" and marriage seminars to family potlucks—clearly designed for the classic "two parents, three kids" family—the church is appropriately a family-focused environment. So it's easy for us as single moms to feel isolated and different at church, especially if we focus on our obvious differences rather than what we have in common—our faith.

In the church, God has graciously given us a ready-made platform from which to minister. We have an automatic legitimacy with other single moms due to our similar circumstances.

The next time we see a single mom, children in tow, slip in the back door and sneak into the back row, we could offer a hand—or just a knowing smile. Maybe we could suggest a Sunday lunch together, or invite her to meet for coffee some weeknight.

Knowing the aloneness associated with single motherhood, let's use what could have been a discouragement as an instrument of encouragement for others.

Lord God, I offer You my position as a single mom.
Use it as an instrument of comfort and encouragement to those around me.

Not Like Father, Like Son

Go ye, enquire of the Lord *for me, and for the people, and for all Judah, concerning the words of this book that is found.*
2 Kings 22:13 KJV

Josiah became king of Judah at the age of eight after the assassination of his father, Amon. Eight years old! Most boys that age worry about striking out in Little League. Few encounter the national concerns Josiah faced.

No one expected Josiah to become a godly leader. Both his father and grandfather Manasseh worshipped idols. How could a little boy with so many strikes against him go against the flow? Yet he did. At age twenty, Josiah began destroying the idol worship that had ensnared his people, including an altar where children were offered as sacrifices to the god Molech. Josiah instigated a celebration of the Passover matched by none, including King David. And when one of his servants discovered God's long-lost book of the Law in the temple and read His instructions, the young king tore his clothes in grief at his own sin and the sin of his people.

Why did Josiah pursue God with such passion? Perhaps his mother, Jedidah, or another godly relative played a vital role in leading him away from the ways of his father and grandfather.

That person made all the difference.

Father, sometimes my children seem to let Your truths go in one ear and out the other. But I know You are with them. Please let negative influences only serve to make them run to You.

Devoted

Devote yourselves to prayer, being watchful and thankful.
Colossians 4:2 NIV

When we are devoted to something, we pour ourselves into it. We'll be faithful in that pursuit and work to ensure its success.

As mothers, we're devoted to our children—and we anxiously watch over every area of their lives. We do whatever it takes to feed, clothe, and house them. We happily give all we have to fill their emotional tanks.

Are we so committed to prayer? God wants us to be. Devoting ourselves to prayer indicates a deep involvement, firm faith, and the outpouring of our hearts toward Christ. As we pray, we should watch with expectation for God's faithful answers to our requests. Then we should show Him our sincere thanks.

Ultimate devotion in prayer will bring about powerful results, both in our attitudes and our circumstances. It's really a commitment to Christ—and there's nothing better we can be devoted to.

Lord, You are the mighty God—and there is nothing better for me to devote myself to. Help me to be totally committed to prayer as I grow closer to You. In Jesus' name I come into Your presence, my heart in hand.

One Home Run after Another

But Daniel resolved not to defile himself.
Daniel 1:8 NIV

Whenever Daniel came to bat, he never missed! He hit a home run off every pitch thrown to him. The big, slow beach balls, like his decision not to eat food that had been offered to idols. The fastballs, like Daniel's guilt-by-association death sentence when Nebuchadnezzar demanded the killing of all wise men because they could not interpret the king's dream. The curveballs, like the one Daniel's jealous colleagues threw to him when they tricked the king into making a law that sent people to the lion's den for bowing and praying to anyone but the king. Did that prevent Daniel from praying to God? No. Not our star player.

If only we had a batting record like Daniel's. Parenting is hard for us. Sometimes we foul out. At other times, we just watch the pitches whiz by. We strike out a lot.

What made Daniel a home run hitter? The secret is tucked into that first glimpse of his heart: He "resolved." Daniel wholeheartedly loved God. He sought God's wisdom and discernment, and he had a habit of prayer. He knew that God—not some earthly king—was in control of this world.

We may not be home run hitters, but we can improve our batting average—by resolving to love God wholeheartedly.

Lord, I pray that each member of my household will be like Daniel—loving You devotedly and with his or her whole being.

You Are an Answer to Prayer

Praise God, the Father of our Lord Jesus Christ! The Father is a merciful God, who always gives us comfort. He comforts us when we are in trouble, so that we can share that same comfort with others in trouble.
2 Corinthians 1:3–4 CEV

It's part of our maturing process. At some point, as Christians, we should arrive at a place where we are comfortable using our own past experiences and current circumstances as tools to reach out to others in need. A maturing believer is one who is beginning to look back on the things she has gone through with gratitude, as her purpose in the body of Christ begins to unfold.

For various reasons, it can be difficult to move past that point of being ministered to, in order to minister to others in need. But, according to the apostle Paul, one of the reasons God comforts us is so we can share that comfort with others when they need it.

We might say, "I'm just a new Christian," or "I wouldn't know what to say," or "I'm only a single mom." But as members of the body of Christ, we are an extension of the Holy Spirit.

So when someone is praying for comfort, be ready—it might just be you God will send to minister to that hurting soul.

Jesus, please help me open my heart and eyes to see the needs around me. Give me the grace and wisdom to comfort others with the comfort You have shown me time and time again.

JANITOR OR JUDGE

The Lord says this to you:
Be not afraid or dismayed at this great multitude;
for the battle is not yours, but God's.
2 CHRONICLES 20:15 AMP

We want what's best for our children. It motivates us—drives us, really. We push them to excel academically. We fret over which school they should attend, how to discipline properly, even their diet and vitamin intake. And why not? There is so much at stake. Their future rests in our hands, with our choices.

Though we very much want our kids to have a good life—not having to struggle financially or socially as we may have—that particular objective may be a bit shortsighted. Will those things bring genuine happiness and contentment? Haven't we all seen celebrities who "have everything" yet are riddled with discontentment, even depression?

What then should our goal for our children be? Our highest aim is to raise children who genuinely love God and want to serve Him. And they can do that whether they become judges or janitors, press operators, or presidents.

God is the only One worthy of our kids' devotion, and the only One able to lead and guide them through this life. The battle is His, not ours—so trust Him with your family.

Father, what a relief to know I don't fight this battle alone. I've felt such pressure to be the "perfect" parent. I acknowledge my need for Your guidance and wisdom as I raise my children.

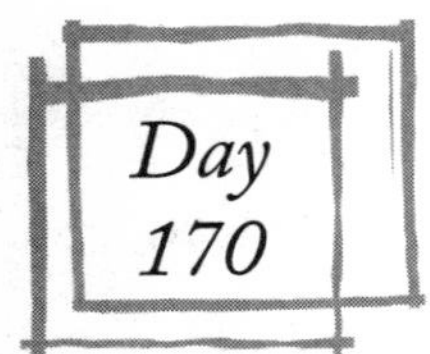

Inside Out

"Don't you understand either?" he asked. "Can't you see that the food you put into your body cannot defile you?. . . It is what comes from inside that defiles you."
MARK 7:18, 20 NLT

People have generally focused on keeping the outside clean. The Jews of Jesus' day made sure they washed the same hand first each time. In keeping with the law, they refused to eat certain foods, declaring them "unclean."

We act in much the same way today. Some foods turn our stomach and become "unclean" to us. Americans consider daily baths the norm.

If only we exercised the same care in keeping our *minds* clean. Jesus listed some of the unclean things that flow from our minds: lust, pride, envy, and slander, among others. Unfortunately, once we have allowed images or thoughts into our minds, we can't "scrub" them away the way soap washes away dirt.

Safeguarding our thought-life starts with what we allow into our minds. As much as possible, we should "see no evil" and "hear no evil." Music, television, movies, books, even our friendships must be filtered.

We can't erase bad thoughts from our minds, but we can crowd them out—by filling our minds with noble, lovely, and true thoughts. "How can a [single mom] stay pure? By obeying your word" (Psalm 119:9 NLT).

The blood of Christ cleanses us and the Bible helps to keep us clean.

Lord, search my thoughts, and show me my impurities. Fill me with Your Word.

The House of Babel

"Let Us go down there and confuse their language so that they will not understand one another's speech." So the LORD *scattered them from there over the face of the whole earth, and they stopped building the city. Therefore its name is called Babylon.*

GENESIS 11:7–9 HCSB

Early in biblical history, the world's people spoke only one language. They wandered about, came to a plain in Babylonia, and settled there. Then they had an idea: to build a tower, a religious symbol, to reach the sky. On top of this tower, or ziggurat, there was probably an altar on which human sacrifices were offered to the gods. Ruins of such ziggurats can still be seen today.

Those people were deaf to the Almighty God. They didn't seek Him, listen to Him, or follow His instructions. Finally, God responded by confounding their language.

Communication is a powerful tool. But it's often confounded, even in our homes. There are times when it seems as if parents speak a totally different language than their children! Oftentimes, parents and children each hear only what they want to hear. Thankfully, God can cut through all the miscommunication. He hears and understands what we're saying, and He speaks to us, too. God says, "I will instruct you and show you the way to go; . . . I will give counsel" (Psalm 32:8 HCSB). But that requires listening as much as talking.

May our homes not be places like Babel!

Lord, unstuff my ears and those of my children!
Help us to listen carefully to Your voice and to each other.

But Even If

"If we are thrown into the blazing furnace, the God whom we serve is able to save us. He will rescue us from your power, Your Majesty. But even if he doesn't, we want to make it clear to you, Your Majesty, that we will never serve your gods or worship the gold statue you have set up."
Daniel 3:17–18 NLT

Shadrach, Meshach, and Abednego were men of faith who stood on their belief in God's power. They trusted God to take care of them, no matter what King Nebuchadnezzar did.

These three faithful men said, "But even if he doesn't [rescue us], it wouldn't make a bit of difference" (Daniel 3:18 msg). Even in the face of earthly consequences—like a blazing furnace—they were committed to obeying God.

Every day, our faith is tested by fiery furnaces of one sort or another. The baby needs a coat; do we tithe? The boss gave us cash; do we report it as income and pay the tax?

We need to be so grounded in the Word of God that we know His truth and trust Him above all else. Regardless of the circumstances or the temptations to disobey, we can stand firm in our faith in God's ability to rescue us from all situations. That's a faith that says, "But even if God doesn't rescue me, I'll obey Him no matter what."

Is our faith like that of Shadrach, Meshach, and Abednego?

Heavenly Father, I trust You no matter what and will obey Your Word. Help me stand in faith and face any fiery furnace that comes my way. Please give me total confidence in You.

Who I Am

The unfolding of your words gives light;
it gives understanding to the simple.
Psalm 119:130 NIV

Who are you? If you were to describe yourself, what words might you use?

For many of us, one of the first phrases to come to mind is *single mom*. Any mother loses part of her identity to children, but those women with husbands still have a more defined role as wife and mother. Single moms, though, pulled in so many different directions, often find their identity blurring into an almost unrecognizable form.

But God's Word shines a clear light on who we are: His own daughters. When we open His Word and search wholeheartedly, we find understanding and uncover our true identity.

According to the Bible, we are more than conquerors (Romans 8:37); we are complete and whole in Him (1 John 2:5); we can do all things through Him who gives us strength (Philippians 4:13). We are His delight (Psalm 18:19) and the apple of His eye (Psalm 17:8).

When we know who God says we are, we can lift our heads high—and pursue all He has for us. If we find our identity in Christ, we will never fall short or be led astray. As single moms, we are exactly who God created us to be at this moment. Never lose sight of that fact!

Lord God, I want to become all that You created me to be. I ask that You would shine Your light on me, that I would find my identity only in You.

You Look Just Like. . .

For those whom He foreknew [of whom He was aware and loved beforehand], He also destined from the beginning [foreordaining them] to be molded into the image of His Son [and share inwardly His likeness], that He might become the firstborn among many brethren.
Romans 8:29 AMP

"You look just like your mother." "You have your father's eyes." "You have your grandma's talent for art." "You're tall like your Uncle David."

Family resemblance. We all have some resemblance to our parents. Even if we never saw them—due to death or adoption—there will be some resemblance. It could be physical, like the shape of our nose, or it could be in our mannerisms, like the way we walk or laugh.

When others tell us how much our children look like us or act like us, we generally respond by saying, "Thank you." For some reason, such comments elicit pride in us.

It's much the same in our Christian experience. Once we've been brought into the family of God through Jesus Christ, we begin to take on the family characteristics. Through God's Holy Spirit living within us, we are changed, molded into the image of Christ, sharing His mind-set and traits. Patience, kindness, compassion, and the desire to please God become part of who we are.

But it's a gradual process of change. Few of us instantly resemble our Father. Little by little, we are "molded" into Christ's image.

Just as we enjoy the resemblance our own children bear toward us, our heavenly Father wants His children to "look like" Him.

Lord, please have Your way with me.
Cause me to bear the family resemblance.

From Pasture to Palace

Then King David went in and sat before the Lord; and he said: "Who am I, O Lord God? And what is my house, that You have brought me this far?"
1 Chronicles 17:16 NKJV

When Samuel the prophet asked Jesse, the father of eight sons, to introduce his family, Jesse almost forgot David! He was the youngest, who looked after the sheep. But God made special plans for this low man on the totem pole. David killed the Philistine giant Goliath and became a great warrior, winning King Saul's daughter for his wife. Unfortunately, he then spent years trying to escape his insanely jealous father-in-law. After more than a decade of danger, intrigue, and battle, David finally was crowned king and achieved the stable regime God desired for His people.

Like most kings, David built himself a beautiful royal palace. Unlike them, he began to think of ways he could say thanks to God for His goodness. David decided to build Him a large, ornate temple.

To the king's surprise, God objected because David was a man of war. David's son Solomon, a man of peace, would build the temple. But God told David his family would possess the kingdom forever if they followed God's ways. David, the ex-shepherd, could only sit and marvel. David had wanted to give to God; instead, God had given the unthinkable to him!

Lord Jesus, how good You have been to my family and me!
We can never out-give Your generosity.

A New Day

God, treat us kindly. You're our only hope. First thing in the morning, be there for us! When things go bad, help us out!
Isaiah 33:2 msg

There are days that start off wrong and finish worse. Days in which we feel out of sorts, like a tire out of balance, clumsy and inefficient. We say things we shouldn't say to our children, using a voice that is too harsh, too loud. We experience days full of failure, tinged by sin. Wouldn't it be great to redo our bad days?

We have that opportunity. It's called *tomorrow*. Lamentations 3:22–23 tells us that by God's mercies, He gives us a fresh canvas every twenty-four hours. Anger, grudges, irritations, and pain don't have to be part of it. No matter how stormy the day before, each new day starts fresh. And He is there for us first thing in the morning and every step of the way in our day, even if things begin to go wrong—again.

Every day in parenting is a new day, a new beginning, a new chance to enjoy our children. Tomorrow, we can do it better.

Each day is a new day with God, too. We can focus on the things that matter most: worshipping Him, listening to Him, and being in His presence. No matter what happened the day before, we have a fresh start to enjoy a deeper relationship with Him. A fresh canvas, every twenty-four hours.

Before I get out of bed in the morning, let me say these words and mean them: "This is the day the Lord has made; let us rejoice and be glad in it" (Psalm 118:24 niv).

SMALL BEGINNINGS

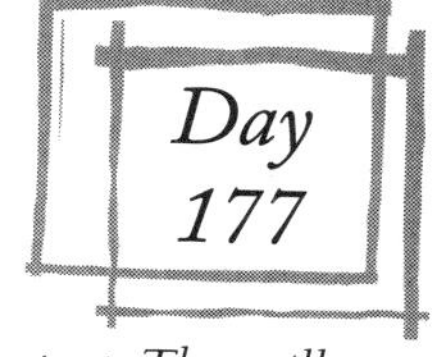

"The people should not think that small beginnings are unimportant. They will be happy when they see Zerubbabel with tools, building the Temple."
ZECHARIAH 4:10 NCV

Babies grow from the merger of a tiny egg and an even smaller sperm. Magnificent sequoias start as a single seed. The world of Narnia began in the mind of C. S. Lewis, with the image of a faun carrying parcels and an umbrella.

The Israelites discovered that small beginnings are important, too—when Zerubbabel arrived with tools to start building the second temple.

As single moms, it's easy for us to put off family vacations or other adventures until we can afford something "big." We'd love to take our children to Disney World or to Washington, D.C. But until we can pull off that "big" event, we stay too busy to take advantage of the many smaller things around us.

We'd like to take our children to a professional ball game. They just want us to show up for their practices and games.

We'd like to go to a fancy restaurant. Our children enjoy grilling hot dogs and toasting marshmallows.

We'd like a weekend alone. But somehow, we don't enjoy the quiet that descends on the house once the children are in bed.

When we add up the small things, they become something big.

Dear Lord, teach us to add up the minutes and not seek out the hours. You are present in every moment of our lives.

Steady Hands

I have set the Lord always before me.
Because he is at my right hand, I will not be shaken.
Psalm 16:8 NIV

What shakes you? For single moms, the list can be unending. The illness of a child, a behavioral problem, or a pending eviction can shake the foundation of any mother, especially the one who lacks someone to turn to for help or encouragement.

Whatever the circumstances, remember that the Lord is at your right hand! In the Bible, the "right hand" symbolizes the kingship of God. He's the King of all kings, the ruler and ultimate authority over everything. And you know what? He holds your right hand and steadies your foundation.

Since God knows the beginning from the end, He's acutely aware of what we can handle. And He'll never allow even a smidgen more than we can take.

The Lord never said He'd take our hard times away. But at just the perfect time, He'll supply exactly what we need to get through the earthquakes of life. He'll lead us safely to a place that's solid and firm.

With Christ at our right hand we need never be shaken.

Jesus, please take my hand and steady my walk.
When my circumstances are shaky, be my firm foundation, Lord.

Money + Time = Achieved Goals

Easy come, easy go, but steady diligence pays off.
Proverbs 13:11 MSG

When Julia's children were little, she lived in the Seattle area. She often read in the newspaper about a little computer company that seemed to be going somewhere. When the company went public, she bought ten shares of stock for each child—all she could afford to spend comfortably.

Julia let the stock sit. And sit. And sit. It multiplied and divided, many times, over the years. Sixteen years later, Julia sold the stock. That small investment funded her children's college education.

God wants us to prepare for our future with wise planning. There are major costs ahead that we know we will be facing: orthodontics, college tuition, weddings. Planning for the future by saving diligently, combined with the benefit of time, will help us reach those goals. Julia was very fortunate to have accomplished that goal with one stock; most of us will require more planning and more saving.

Someone asked Julia if she wished she had bought more stock—that she had put everything she had into that company. But, she explained, it wasn't her intention to get rich quick. Her goal was simply to prepare for the funding of her children's college education—and the Lord blessed her efforts.

Lord, give me wisdom in how I spend my money and how I save my money. Bless my efforts to prepare for my children's future.

Finding Balance

But the LORD said to her, "My dear Martha, you are worried and upset over all these details! There is only one thing worth being concerned about. Mary has discovered it, and it will not be taken away from her."
LUKE 10:41–42 NLT

With people in the house, needing to be fed, Martha jumped in to accomplish her tasks. Mary, on the other hand, chose to spend time in the presence of Jesus.

Because of Mary's choice, Martha had to do all the work by herself. She was even chastised for criticizing Mary. But if Martha hadn't done that work, who would have?

The two sisters from Bethany are a perfect example of the inner struggle that most women face daily. On one hand, we want to please people, entertain, multitask, and control the many facets of our lives at one time—because we believe those are marks of a strong woman. On the other hand, we crave rest, spiritual growth, and peace. The challenge is to blend the two into a healthy whole.

Each of us should consider our own role. Am I the person who is always working in the kitchen during the worship service, or always filling in for the nursery worker who didn't show up? Or do I never take a turn, leaving others to bear the bulk of the work?

God has called us to good deeds, but not to stress and worry. Ask Him to show you the line.

Dear Lord, I want to do my part, like Martha—but, like Mary, I also need to be strong enough to say no, in order to have time with you. Please show me how to find that balance in my life.

Pick Your Battles

To these four young men God gave knowledge and understanding of all kinds of literature and learning. And Daniel could understand visions and dreams of all kinds.
DANIEL 1:17 NIV

Daniel was one of the first Hebrew exiles taken from Jerusalem into friendly captivity (if there is such a thing) in Babylon. Separated from his family, forced into servitude, given a new identity and new gods, Daniel was probably only a teenager! He was now living in Babylon, the pagan center of the earth.

Did Daniel completely reject his new lifestyle? Did he argue with his master and refuse to learn? No! Amazingly, there were only a few areas where Daniel refused to compromise: He would not bow down and worship any other god or eat food that had been offered to idols.

We live in a type of Babylon, too. We're surrounded by anti-God behavior, customs, pop culture. It's easy to be offended by just about . . .everything. Everyday language is flavored with swear words, television shows mock our faith, schools introduce curricula that make us cringe.

Surprisingly, God didn't tackle every single issue in Babylon. He picked Daniel's battles for him, and Daniel was greatly used in the midst of a pagan culture. Not indignant or antagonistic, but compassionate and seeking the best for his captors.

Can we be Daniels in our communities today?

Lord, show me how to seek Your wisdom and discernment while picking my battles. Help me to love those who oppose You.

THE MONEY FACTOR

"Whoever can be trusted with a little can also be trusted with a lot, and whoever is dishonest with a little is dishonest with a lot. If you cannot be trusted with worldly riches, then who will trust you with true riches? And if you cannot be trusted with things that belong to someone else, who will give you things of your own?"
LUKE 16:10–12 NCV

A line from the popular movie *Pirates of the Caribbean* puts it quite succinctly: "Not all treasure is silver and gold."

God has entrusted us with many treasures, including our children. God is the Creator and owner of everything we have; everything we have is a gift from Him. He provides for our needs and gives each one of us a spiritual gift. Yet with every treasure comes a responsibility to manage those gifts—time, money, talents, even our children—in a way that honors Him.

Christian stewardship is not just about money, and it must be taken seriously. We are called to trust in God, but can God trust us? Small moments of selfishness and irresponsibility now can result in great trouble later. Likewise small generosities grow into great gifts.

Our children are watching every move we make. Let us pray that, no matter how great or small our income, we remember that God's treasures make us all quite rich.

Lord, help me be grateful for the blessings You bestow, and guide me in ways that honor You. Show me how best to dedicate my time, services, and gifts to You.

Fasting for Others

"Is not this the kind of fasting I have chosen? . . . Is it not to share your food with the hungry and to provide the poor wanderer with shelter— when you see the naked, to clothe him?"
Isaiah 58:6–7 NIV

Whether you live in a large city or a small town, you've probably seen a homeless person with a sign saying something like, *Anything will help. God bless.* Maybe we look at the man with the red face and grizzled beard and think, *I'm a single mother. I have to support my family on my income. And* you're *asking* me *for help?*

Money won't solve a homeless person's mental illness or alcoholism. But does that mean we should turn our backs on the needy in our community?

God gives us clear direction: When we want to honor Him, we can begin by caring for people around us. Feed the hungry. Find shelter for the homeless. Provide clothing for those without.

Churches and community organizations offer a multitude of ways to get involved. One particular church offered these options: supplying the food bank; joining a mission trip to build a home in hurricane-stricken Louisiana; furnishing a room at a home for unwed mothers; filling boxes for Operation Christmas Child.

Whether we give through our church or a social service organization— or even if we do something more radical like housing a wayward teen— we can all be involved with helping others. That's what God asks.

Heavenly Father, You have given me so much. Teach me to give back to others.

Heart Condition

"You are like whitewashed tombs, which look beautiful on the outside but on the inside are full of dead men's bones and everything unclean."
Matthew 23:27 NIV

Ah, the infamous car salesmen. They are, fairly or not, stereotyped for making their merchandise appear to be what it isn't. Maybe that sparkling-clean engine under the hood was just power washed—and after a bit of driving, you find that what you've purchased isn't all it appeared to be.

We expect to "get what we pay for," as the old saying goes, whether we're purchasing a car, buying the latest cell phone, or even investing in our relationships. We assume people will be inside what they appear to be on the outside.

But deep down, we know that doesn't always happen. And we certainly don't want our children to fall into that trap. What good is it if our kids grow up to become lawyers, doctors, or company presidents, but have no inner character? Is that real success?

Let's be careful today to focus our parenting on the hearts of ou children, rather than outward appearances. If we lead them in the righ paths, someday they will "arise up, and call [us] blessed" (Proverb 31:28 KJV).

Father God, cause me to have a correct focus as I raise my children, looking at their heart and not what they appear to be outwardly. Please fill me with Your wisdom.

Faithful Father

Be joyful in hope, patient in affliction, faithful in prayer.
Romans 12:12 NIV

This verse gives three straightforward instructions.

First, "be joyful in hope." It sounds simple, but that often depends on what we're hoping for. Is it a bonus at work—or just a job in general? Hoping for a raise to cover a vacation is easier than hoping for a job to simply pay the rent. Can we be joyful in either circumstance?

"Patient in affliction" is even more difficult. Our level of patience largely depends on the day. Is your child's father becoming demanding? Are creditors pushing you for payments? Or is a medical situation looming? Romans 12:12 offers no escape clause for afflictions that seem unbearable. God simply says to be patient.

Finally, we're to be "faithful in prayer." That shouldn't be a problem, right? But "faithful" implies a continuing pursuit. Sometimes we start out well, but get weary and give up. If we pray with faithfulness, though, we'll see results.

Implement these three straightforward commands, and you'll begin to see changes in yourself and your circumstances. Try it—experience God's faithfulness.

Father God, some days my life seems manageable—but at other times it's more than I can handle. Help me to "be joyful in hope, patient in affliction, [and] faithful in prayer"—then show Yourself to be my faithful Father and Friend.

A Block of Marble

I praise you because I am fearfully and wonderfully made;
your works are wonderful, I know that full well.
PSALM 139:14 NIV

In 1501, Michelangelo looked at a block of marble and saw David. Michelangelo worked on the premise, an artistic discipline called *disegno*, that the image of David was already in the block of marble—in much the same way the human soul is found within the physical body. Three years later, Michelangelo had chiseled out a masterpiece. Out of a hunk of rock came the most recognizable sculpture in the world.

That's a picture of how God sees us! With His divine genius, God made us purposefully, with loving intention, as an outpouring of His joy. "For you created my inmost being; you knit me together in my mother's womb," wrote King David in Psalm 139:13 (NIV).

We look at ourselves and see the uncut sections, the rough edges, the areas that need sanding and polishing. Will we ever be considered a work of art? We seem like such a mess. But God looks at us and sees the sculpted piece, His completed masterpiece!

Do we see our children in the same way that God sees us? Or the way Michelangelo looked at a block of marble and saw David? Our children are miracles, filled with possibilities! God is accomplishing a soon-to-be revealed masterpiece.

Dear Lord, how awesome is Your artistry! Open my eyes to Your creative ways. Give me Your vision to see my children's potential.

Where Is the Miracle?

Then Peter said, "Silver or gold I do not have, but what I have I give you. In the name of Jesus Christ of Nazareth, walk."
Acts 3:6 NIV

A beggar asking for money got the surprise of his life: a complete healing. He probably realized later that he'd been asking for the wrong thing all along. A little money might have fed him for a day; a lot of money might have brought more comfort and security to his existence. But a healing? He never asked for that because he didn't dream it to be possible. The idea probably never darkened the recesses of his mind.

More money, better time management, physical healing, favor at work—they're all things we might pray for and seek with our whole hearts. But where is the miracle? Our children seek friendships, toys, security, the love of their parents. Again, where is the miracle?

The miracle is found in the spiritual transformation that Jesus Christ brings to our lives. That kind of healing causes the cares of the world to fall away to a far distant second place. In the true light of the glory of Jesus, no earthly thing can compare.

Today, let's teach our children that, though we may have little in terms of silver and gold, we have access to the greatest resource imaginable. We can show them that their deepest needs are met in the name of Jesus Christ.

Heavenly Father, I surrender my worldly views to You. I realize that You have far better things in store for me than I could ever imagine. Teach me to seek You, and help me impart those values to my children.

Help in Disguise

Strengthen ye the weak hands, and confirm the feeble knees. Say to them that are of a fearful heart, Be strong, fear not: behold, your God will come.
Isaiah 35:3–4 KJV

Work. A college class. The boys' homework. Laundry by the ton. Samantha wondered how much longer she could cope. And these weren't the only things that "dogged" her! A scroungy mutt followed Sam to her apartment door every evening. She looked even worse than Samantha felt. *Oh, no, Lord. Not another mouth to feed!*

Braden and Joel named the dog Molly and swore they would care for her forever. Sam couldn't find the energy to object.

Now Molly stayed in their apartment, tipping over garbage, eating toilet paper, and chewing Sam's shoes. Worse, her predictions about the dog's care came true. Every night while the boys were at basketball practice, Sam walked Molly. After grumping her way through a week, however, Sam found herself looking forward to the walks. Molly greeted her as if she were queen of the world. Fresh air eased the headaches that ruled Sam's life. The setting sun pulled her thoughts toward God's beauty and majesty. And she lost two pounds! With the exercise, Sam slept better instead of lying awake worrying about the next day's demands.

Sam never expected such a blessing in the form of four paws and a wagging tail. But her creative God had provided a surprising benefit.

Lord Jesus, I want balance in my life, but sometimes I feel clueless about change. Thanks for Your unique ideas!

Value Beyond Measure

"Suppose a woman has ten silver coins and loses one. Won't she light a lamp and sweep the entire house and search carefully until she finds it? And when she finds it, she will call in her friends and neighbors and say, 'Rejoice with me because I have found my lost coin.' "
Luke 15:8–9 NLT

We've all complained about the work involved in being a mom. Of course, we don't mean anything by it, but out it comes: "I can't wait until they go back to school.". . ."I can't wait for him to turn eighteen.". . . "When will I get some 'me' time?". . .

The feelings are natural. But a problem can arise if our children pick up the idea that *they* are the source of our unhappiness.

Have we inadvertently caused our kids to believe they're not worth the sacrifices we make to parent them? Or have we made every effort to show them just how valuable they are to us?

Can our kids tell by our actions that we wouldn't trade them for anything? Do we listen with suspense as they tell us the same story for the fifth time? Are we available to play dolls or wrestle or take a walk together?

Our children are certainly worth the hard work and sacrifice it takes to raise them. Let's be sure they know their value, which is truly beyond measure.

Father, help me to show my children how valuable they are. Forgive me for when I have not.

TEMPER TANTRUM

He prayed to the LORD: "Please, LORD, isn't this what I said while I was still in my own country?" . . . The LORD asked, "Is it right for you to be angry?"
JONAH 4:2, 4 HCSB

Poor Jonah. After he escaped that big fish, he obeyed God's call to preach to his nation's greatest enemy. Then Jonah waited for judgment to fall—but God spared the city of Nineveh when its people repented.

That's when Jonah threw a tantrum. He told God, basically, "You're compassionate. I knew You would spare them. I'd rather die than see that."

So God asked Jonah a rhetorical question: "Is it right for you to be angry?" Jonah had his priorities all wrong.

Like Jonah, we can be angry over the seeming injustices in our lives. Why should our friends have happy marriages and our exes enjoy a higher standard of living than we do? Why does God show compassion to others—even the people who hurt us—when our own needs are so great?

When we're tempted to grumble, God may ask, "Is it right for you to be angry?" Others need His mercy as much as we do, like the 120,000 people of Nineveh, too lost to know the difference between their left and right hands.

The next time we feel a temper tantrum coming on, we should stop and, instead of venting, praise God that His grace, compassion and love are available equally to all—including us.

Lord God, You are slow to anger.
You love us even when we fail You.
Teach us to have the same patient compassion for others.

Critic from the Crowd

"Forget the former things; do not dwell on the past.
See, I am doing a new thing!"
Isaiah 43:18–19 NIV

A sixteen-year-old boy was pitching in a high school baseball game, and doing a poor job of it. A walk with the bases loaded brought in a run for the opposing team. The crowd began to boo. And the loudest heckler of all was the pitcher's mother.

What would make a mother do that? If that behavior occurred naturally and automatically in public, what must have gone on in their home?

That true, dramatic event may seem shocking, but we all run the risk of disrespecting our kids. Report cards can be disappointing, athletic talent may be lacking, popularity can be fickle, follow-through on chores is often dismaying. How do we respond when our kids don't meet our expectations? Do we give a message, subtle or blatant, that they are disappointing us? That we had hoped for more from them?

Who hasn't made that parenting mistake? Often, we find ourselves parenting from our own past. We repeat unhealthy patterns from our own childhood. Maybe that booing mom had been raised with constant criticism, thinking it could bring about a desired change. It doesn't. Criticism just begets criticism.

God can show us a new way. We can make different, healthier choices as we respond to our children. We can learn to be encouragers, not critics.

Lord Jesus, show me a new way. Break those habits from the past.
Help me to learn from my past instead of letting it hinder
my future and that of my children.

In Whom We Have Hope

May the God of hope fill you with all joy and peace as you trust in him, so that you may overflow with hope by the power of the Holy Spirit.
ROMANS 15:13 NIV

It's surprising what trials people get through if they have hope.

Single moms endure hardships beyond society's norm. Our challenges are often long term and life altering. We know how difficult life can be when, for example, our kids come down with chicken pox: The babysitter won't take children with a contagious illness, and the boss won't allow more than two days off of work. Of course, the job is essential for feeding the kids and paying rent. Face it—in a situation like that, you're stuck.

Is it possible to have peace and joy in such circumstances? Yes! That is, if you have hope.

But not just any old hope. The power of hope arises from its Subject: Our security lies in "the God of hope," as Romans 15:13 says. Hope in our jobs, our finances, our babysitters, or even our own family members often falls flat.

But we can securely put our full hope in our heavenly Father—since He's the God of hope. And no matter what happens, He can fill us with overflowing joy and perfect peace.

God, in the midst of my circumstances, please teach me to put my hope in You. I look to You to fill me with joy and perfect peace.

An Unlikely Disciple

But I tell you to love your enemies and pray for anyone who mistreats you.
Matthew 5:44 CEV

At first glance, Peter may seem a surprising choice for a disciple. He wore his heart on his sleeve; at times he was fiercely loyal, at others surprisingly cowardly. Satan knew Peter would have a huge impact on the body of Christ, so he tried many times to use Peter's greatest weakness, his emotions, against him.

The impulsive Peter physically attacked the soldiers who came to arrest Jesus. At other times, he verbally blundered through events and situations. In his immaturity, Peter lacked self-control and godly insight. He failed to realize that, sometimes, God's plan is to allow seemingly bad things to happen to achieve a greater result.

As parents, we must occasionally allow tough things to happen in the lives of our children, even though we'd like to jump in to rescue them. Although we might want to lash out at the world pressing in on our kids, attacking those people who attack them, we need to exercise self-control and godly wisdom in the face of those worldly battles.

By doing so, God's will may be realized and others will give glory to Him.

Lord, help me to control my tongue and my actions in the face of my righteous indignation. Show me when to defend and when to allow circumstances to work Your will in the lives of my children.

Dented Vases

You have. . .made me happy despite all our troubles.
2 Corinthians 7:4 NLT

Though single parenting poses many challenges, they can never erase the overwhelming joys of motherhood.

Consider the young mother, having just paid what she could on the heating bill and setting aside the rest of her paycheck for groceries, who sinks into her chair frustrated and more than a little disheartened. Surveying her home, she sees rickety windows that let in the winter's cold, a stove in need of repair, shabby mismatched furniture, and a pile of other bills that will have to wait for a future paycheck.

Then her youngest son walks in, proudly carrying a rather dented and lopsided "vase." With a wide smile, he shouts, "Mom! Look what I made for you in art class!" Blissfully unaware of his mom's inner struggle, he continues, "Won't it look great on the coffee table, beside the picture of us?"

The mom's eyes are drawn to the picture of her and her three children. With tears beginning to well, she tells her son, "Yes, it'll look perfect there."

There is surpassing joy in being a mother, a deep love and contentment that fills us as nothing else can. Our little (or not-so-little) ones are often used by God to remind us of His hand of blessing on our lives. . .despite all our troubles.

Father God, help me to remember that whatever troubles I face,
I have my children. My children! How grateful I am.

Just Say No. . . Isn't Enough

He who walks with the wise grows wise,
but a companion of fools suffers harm.
Proverbs 13:20 niv

In 1982, the Ad Council created a public service campaign to discourage America's children from using illegal drugs. Championed by First Lady Nancy Reagan, the campaign's slogan was, "Just Say No."

Catchy? Yes. Effective? Maybe not. The message assumes that it's easy to say no, but peer pressure actually makes that quite difficult. Once a child is in the situation where he's approached to use drugs, it's often too late. In fact, in an ironic twist, some of the child actors involved in the campaign ended up being illegal drug users.

A better campaign would have encouraged thinking ahead, to avoid getting into difficult situations in the first place. Maybe the slogan should have been, "Just Stay Away."

God's Word is loud and clear on the dangers of running with the wrong crowd. "Do not join those who drink too much wine" (Proverbs 23:20 niv). "My son, if sinners entice you, do not give in to them" (Proverbs 1:10 niv).

Solomon wrote those words as warnings to his own children some three thousand years ago. They're just as relevant today. *Those* are the messages we need to give to our children—wisdom from God's Word, not wisdom from the Ad Council.

Lord God, give my children a healthy caution about the reliability of their own wisdom, or their friends' wisdom, or the world's wisdom. Teach them to seek only Yours.

Shake It Off

Then [Paul simply] shook off the small creature into the fire and suffered no evil effects.
Acts 28:5 AMP

How many times do we make a mistake and confess it to the Lord, then continue to punish ourselves with guilt and condemnation? Psalm 103:12 tells us that God will remove our transgressions as far as the east is from the west.

When we make a mistake—and we all do—we should be like the apostle Paul. Immediately shake it off. Don't worry about it or allow guilt to grow. God removed the sin and no longer thinks about it. Why should we?

By immediately shaking a snake off his hand, Paul avoided harm. The viper's intentions were to infect Paul with poison and make him ill. Paul recognized the danger and immediately went into action, shaking it off. Afterward, he didn't worry over it. Instead, he went about helping the people on the island of Malta.

Don't allow your mistakes to so worry or condemn you that you can't be helpful to others around you. The poison of stress and worry will harm us if we allow it to penetrate our hearts and minds. Follow Paul's example: Shake it off.

Dear Lord, thank You for cleansing me of my sins. I will not worry or feel condemned any longer. Thank You, Lord, for helping me to shake things off and suffer no evil effects.

Help, I'm Clueless!

"O our God, will You not exercise judgment upon them? For we have no might to stand against this great company that is coming against us. We do not know what to do, but our eyes are upon You."
2 Chronicles 20:12 amp

Clueless. Sometimes, we have no idea how to handle the predicaments before us. Yet fix them we must. We are "the man." There is no one else. So how do we handle what is so obviously beyond our abilities?

Maybe we have a car in need of repair—or maybe it's a teenager's broken heart. Perhaps it's money needed for a utility bill, or having to answer our child's hard questions about life. It could be our having to cope with betrayal, or the need of extra cash at Christmastime. Maybe it's the pain of loneliness.

First, acknowledge your need for help. Second, realize that our needs are chiefly met in and through prayer. God alone has sovereign control. He holds the answers to our difficulties, and He has the capacity to meet all our needs—abundantly.

He may have a friend drop a check in the mail. Or maybe a Christian radio program will provide wisdom beyond ourselves. Or perhaps He'll thrill us with an example of maturity on our children's part, as they draw upon God for their own answers.

We may sometimes find ourselves clueless. But, through our relationship with God, we have access to an endless supply of wisdom.

Father God, grant me a humble heart, that I may turn to You with my needs. Thank You for making a way through the wilderness of my circumstances.

Hide and Seek

"And do you seek great things for yourself? Seek them not, for behold, I am bringing disaster upon all flesh, declares the Lord."
Jeremiah 45:5 ESV

When we were little girls, we all dreamed big. Maybe we aspired to be a prima ballerina, to win an Oscar, or to own a mansion. Somewhere along the line our expectations fell into step with reality.

While the scope of our dreams may have narrowed, our desire for "great things" probably never changed. We'd like recognition for our talents, we want success at work, and we hope for more than just a minimum standard of living.

But God warns us: *Don't seek great things.* The more we seek them, the more elusive they become. As soon as we think we have them in our grasp, they disappear. If we commit to more activities than we can realistically handle, the best result is that we can't follow through. At worst, we neglect our children. If we buy more things than we can really afford, we may lose them. Worse, we might make them our god. Our God—the true God—wants to rearrange our priorities.

Jesus tells us what we should seek: the kingdom of God and His righteousness (Matthew 6:33). He won't hide from us. When we seek the right things, He'll give us every good and perfect gift (James 1:17). And that will be more than we can ask or dream.

Lord, please teach me to seek not greatness, but You.
May You be the all in all of my life.

JOYFUL SONGS

Sing joyfully to the LORD, you righteous;
it is fitting for the upright to praise him.
PSALM 33:1 NIV

Singing often reflects our mood. When we're lighthearted and happy, we may tend to sing more often than when we're feeling burdened and downtrodden. But the Word of God tells us to sing joyfully to the Lord, without prerequisites. The Bible doesn't say, "Sing if all is well and you're overjoyed." It just tells us to sing joyfully.

It's fitting for us as Christians to praise Him. Not only when our circumstances are conducive to a joyful spirit, but any time—simply because of who He is.

If our actions depend on our situations, we may never try a tune. But if we sing amid our situation, whether good or bad, joyous or painful, we will soon find our moods—and our spirits—rising from the ashes to reflect our joyful songs.

When we, like the psalmist, sing joyfully to the Lord, our spirits will follow—and we'll become deeply joyful moms, unshaken and steady.

Lord, I know I need to sing to You out of a joyful spirit. For all You have done for me, and simply because of who You are, I will choose today—whatever my circumstances—to sing songs of praise, joy, and thanksgiving.

What Concerns You?

The Lord will perfect that which concerns me.
Psalm 138:8 NKJV

What concerns you? What situations give you pause throughout the day? What circumstances crowd your mind, clamoring for attention?

As single mothers, we have so many to choose from! Money for the rent. . . Our children's futures. . . Whether the diapers will last until payday. . . Junior's unexplainable temper. . . When will the baby finally sleep through the night? . . .Where is my "prince charming"? . . . Will that work promotion come through?

God knows all your concerns, and He's working on your behalf. Think of a mom who bakes and lavishly decorates a cake for her daughter's birthday. She knows chocolate is the girl's favorite, and she puts great effort into creating the perfect birthday treat—then she enjoys presenting the masterpiece to her daughter.

God's like that, too, only better. If human mothers can and do go to such lengths over birthday cakes that lasts only a few minutes, how much more will God do for us? He will perfect that which concerns you.

Heavenly Father, I lay my concerns before You this day, knowing You will "perfect that which concerns me." What a relief!

Bear Fruit

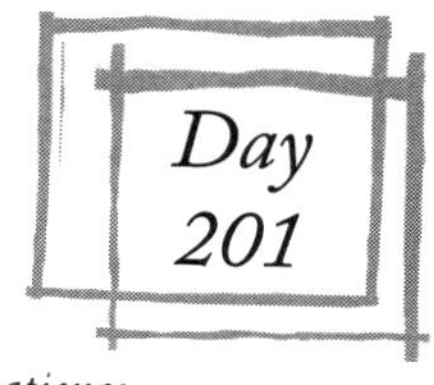

But the Spirit produces the fruit of love, joy, peace, patience, kindness, goodness, faithfulness, gentleness, self-control. There is no law that says these things are wrong.
Galatians 5:22–23 NCV

For a short time each fall, apple orchards are full of sweet, ripe fruit ready to be enjoyed. The rest of the year, though, the trees spend time growing, taking nourishment from the sun, soaking water up through their roots, and waiting for the fruit to grow and ripen. Picked too soon, apples are bitter; too late and they're overripe and mushy.

There's no season, though for the fruits of the Spirit listed in Galatians 5. Those desirable behaviors are exhibited in our own lives and toward others as we mature in Christ. None of us can master the qualities on our own, as each of us has one or more areas of weakness the Holy Spirit is addressing in our lives.

Sometimes, when we don't see immediate growth in our lives, we become impatient. But just like the apples on a tree, our own spiritual growth requires cultivation and patience. We need to soak up the light of the Father, be nourished from His Word, and be patient while the Holy Spirit works within us.

If we simply remain rooted in Christ, we'll bear fruit—to the glory of His name.

Jesus, please continue to develop Your godly traits in me.
Help me to bear good fruit and be an example of Your love toward others.

Friend or Authority Figure

Come, my children, and listen to me,
and I will teach you to fear the Lord.
Psalm 34:11 NLT

Now that Brandi is a teenager, she and her mother, Lisa, have reached the point where they can "hang out" and talk. Brandi seeks Lisa for advice, and Lisa talks to Brandi about her work and friends.

Sometimes, though, Brandi sees Lisa as more of a "buddy" than a parent. She takes advantage by staying out late or breaking house rules. At the same time, Lisa struggles to find the line between parenting and friendship with her daughter.

Mothers want to be friends with their children, but it's vitally important for them to maintain their role as an authority figure. Look to the relationship we have with God as our Father: We can speak to Him directly and bring Him our hopes and concerns. But we are also taught to treat Him with fear and reverence. The same goes for earthly relationships between parents and children.

It's okay to be friends with your children. But be sure to set boundaries, and teach those kids to treat you with respect. Don't be afraid to use discipline and don't back down from rules. You, as mom, know that boundaries are meant to protect our children.

Dear Lord, please help me find the balance between being my children's friend and being their mother. Remind me that discipline and respect are also a part of a parent-child relationship, just as they are in my relationship with You.

Smelling Like Smoke?

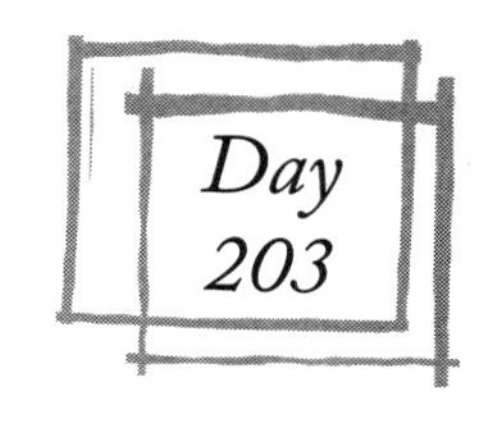

"When you pass through the waters, I will be with you; and when you pass through the rivers, they will not sweep over you. When you walk through the fire, you will not be burned; the flames will not set you ablaze."
ISAIAH 43:2 NIV

Life isn't all bouquets and teddy bears. It's tough. Even God's Word acknowledges that life can be difficult, painful, sometimes tragic.

A single mom often faces more than her share of life's nastiest storms. She struggles to keep the waves from overtaking her. She feels the heat of the flames and fears the damage the fire can cause.

Thankfully, even the scariest of storms of life must obey our God. Jesus, who calmed a storm with a few words, assures us that He's with us in every storm. We may pass through deep waters and raging rivers—but they'll never pull us under. And when we face a fire of life, He'll prevent us from being burned.

We may look like a drowned rat or smell like smoke. . .or maybe not (remember Shadrach, Meshach, and Abednego?). But we can rest peacefully, knowing that God will always bring us through.

Father God, I trust You, and I know that no matter how close I am taken to the flame or how high the storm rages around me, You will bring me safely through to the other side.

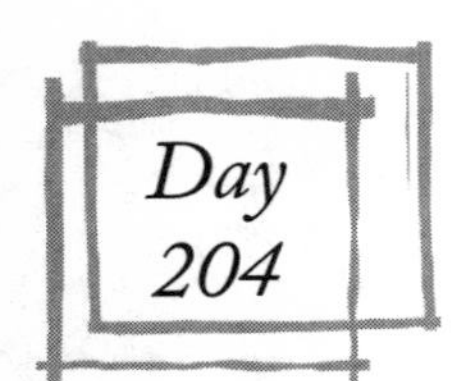

Skeptical

But God, who encourages those who are discouraged, encouraged us by the arrival of Titus. His presence was a joy.
2 Corinthians 7:6–7 NLT

A young and newly single mother cried out to the Lord: "Oh God, please help me! I feel so alone and discouraged. Will You please relieve this loneliness in my heart?" She rose from her knees and began her day, vaguely hopeful of a miracle but struggling with skepticism.

She dropped the baby off at the sitter's and drove on to work, still looking for her "miracle." While walking through her company parking lot, a friend called her cell phone to ask how things were going. "Okay," was the response. "I guess I'm just feeling a little sad today."

After a brief conversation, the friend promised to keep her in her prayers. During lunch break, she opened and read several e-mails from family and friends. One offered to take her and the little one to dinner. Another promised prayers. Yet another asked if she needed help buying groceries and diapers. *So thoughtful,* she mused.

As night approached, she retraced her day with wonder. "Father," she prayed, "it wasn't the miracle I had expected or the way I expected it—but You did it. Using my friends and family to encourage me. Thank you." She crawled into bed and drifted off to sleep—no longer skeptical.

Heavenly Father, open my eyes to the wonder of Your ways—how You might choose to answer my cries for help.

ITCHY BRAIN

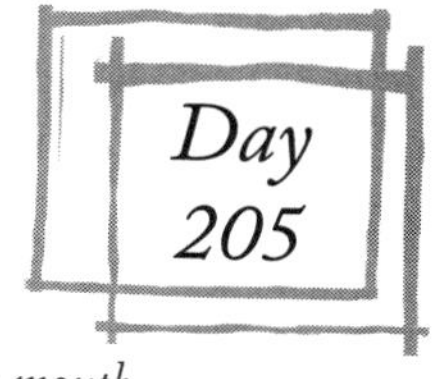

I will sing of the LORD's great love forever; with my mouth
I will make your faithfulness known through all generations.
PSALM 89:1 NIV

Some melodies have a way of getting stuck in our mind, as if somebody set the playback button on repeat. Researchers have found that certain songs create a sort of "cognitive itch"—the mental equivalent of a back that needs to be scratched. It's sort of like having an "itchy brain."

Simpler songs appear more likely to make brains itch, especially those with a repeated phrase or sequence. The brain echoes the pattern automatically. Anyone who attended Sunday school as a child can still belt out renditions of "Jesus Loves Me" or "Swing Low, Sweet Chariot."

Music has a unique ability to reach deeply into our subconscious mind. It's stored like a permanent file in our memory cache. Let's use that fact to our families' advantage.

When we memorize *scripture* set to music, we can help our children bury God's Word deep in their hearts. We can help them lay into their young minds a strong, sturdy foundation of the great truths of God's Word, knowing that it will ultimately influence and direct their every choice and desire.

Lord, may Your words of life be treasured and securely
held in my children's hearts and minds.

So Much to Do, So Little Time

But when the right time came, God sent his Son
who was born of a woman and lived under the law.
Galatians 4:4 NCV

It'd been a long day of work for Carmen. After picking up the kids from day care and stopping at the store, she headed home, stuffed groceries into cupboards, got the kids started on homework, and began cooking dinner.

Throughout the Bible, God mentions instances of how events occur at the "right time" or in their "appointed time." But for a single mom juggling work and kids and a home life, it often seems like there's no time for anything—anything fun, at least.

But a reasonable investment in organizing the house or planning meals can save a lot of time in the long run. Rather than letting household chores build up, select one room to clean or one chore to complete each day of the week. That can become a habit that keeps cleaning duties from piling up. Or instead of rushing to the store for ingredients for a single meal, make a list and shop in bulk. Then you can prepare several meals at once, saving them in freezer containers that can be easily thawed and warmed in the oven or microwave.

A few hours of preparation at the start of a week can free up time and reduce stress for the following days. Perhaps then, other tasks can be performed in that biblical "right time."

Dear heavenly Father, thank You for reminding me that everything happens at the "right time." Help me to plan ahead and take small steps to free up precious time throughout the week.

Black-Tie Affair

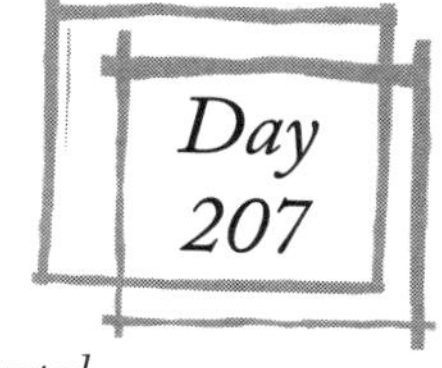

But what things were gain to me, these I have counted loss for Christ. . .for whom I have suffered the loss of all things, and count them as rubbish, that I may gain Christ.
Philippians 3:7–8 NKJV

Black Tie, Optional." Maybe the Hollywood types still get those kinds of invitations. But not us average, everyday single moms.

Maybe there was a time when we were part of the social whirl, enjoying fancy "events." But for most of us, parties now typically feature pizza and dancing mice. The hostesses don't wear slinky, strapless black chiffon numbers—they wear aprons to protect their favorite T-shirts and jeans from little hands coated with red frosting.

Do we long for a more glamorous, exciting, high society world? Those elegant parties are often full of folks who don't know or even like each other. But the guests of honor at our colorful, loud parties—complete with pinball games and animal costumes—will be forever grateful for those special times. Their names will never be forgotten, and neither will yours: Mom.

Jesus honors mothers and teaches that children have a special place in His heart. Let's embrace our roles as moms—and the crazy, messy activities that come with them—and not look longingly at some fantasy world of black ties and fancy dresses. Let's press on to our high calling of Christ.

Jesus, remind me to gladly allow my life to become what it must be, as I parent my children in Your name. Let me be to them what You want me to be, an extension of Your love.

The Forever Word

"The grass withers and the flowers fall,
but the word of our God stands forever."
Isaiah 40:8 NIV

There is nothing more powerful, more honest, more lasting, or more truthful than God's Word. Nothing else in our world stays the same. Nothing else holds such honest, hopeful power. Grass withers in the summer heat, flowers die and fall to the ground at their season's end. Even our precious children grow up, eventually leaving the nest to venture into the world without us.

The one thing that never changes—that's consistently the same yesterday, today, and for all eternity—is the Word of our God. We have it printed between worn black leather covers, or inside a slick contemporary hardback, or even on our computer. Wherever we keep God's Word—on fragile onionskinned paper or in some hard-to-understand electronic world—we find life. We find the God-inspired guidance, understanding, and wisdom we need to raise our children well. God's Word is more powerful than any storm life can bring, sharper than any double-edged sword, and brighter than all the stars in the heavens.

When we study God's Word wholeheartedly, He will illuminate it, giving us an understanding that brings perfect peace. While everything around us changes, we can rest in the one thing that stands forever—the true, unchanging Word of God.

Lord Jesus, I thank You for Your Word. I pray that You would teach me more and more how to obtain its nourishment and wisdom for my spirit. I ask You to bless me with great understanding.

Teamwork Among "Rivals"?

"Can two walk together, unless they are agreed?". . . If it is possible, as much as depends on you, live peaceably with all men.
AMOS 3:3; ROMANS 12:18 NKJV

Raising good kids as a single parent can be a daunting challenge, to say the least. The job can be even more difficult when another parent—one we may not be on the best terms with—is thrown into the mix.

Childrearing is both the most important and most difficult task we'll ever attempt. It pales in comparison to the career field we've chosen, the educational heights we've reached, or the financial security we're striving for. How can we accomplish such a vital task with someone who may not see eye-to-eye with us? Is it possible to have teamwork—to literally be coworkers with someone who may be a rival or adversary?

Our answer is tucked into verse 18 of Romans 12: "If it is possible, as much as depends on you"—*you*—"live peaceably with all men" (NKJV). We are challenged to do all we can to live at peace with those who might oppose us. We are responsible for our part only.

In a conflict over what television programs are appropriate, the right age for a cell phone, or who'll pay for the next pair of shoes, let's ask God for His flawless wisdom—then do all *we* can to be at peace. Then just let it go.

Father God, please grant me the wisdom I need to live at peace with others. And having done all I can do—help me let it rest with You.

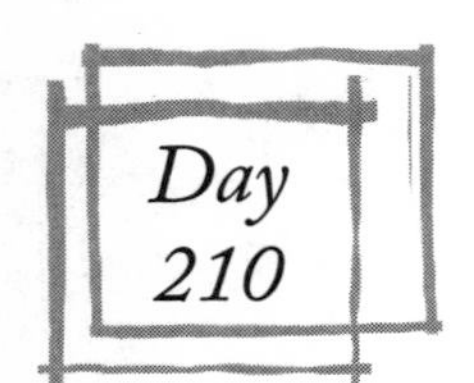

So, Talk!

No one is able to come to Me unless the Father Who sent Me attracts and draws him and gives him the desire to come to Me.
John 6:44 AMP

In some of the psalms, the writers seem to shake their fists at God, shouting, "Where are You, Lord? Why are You so slow? Are You sleeping? Wake up and help me!"

Interestingly, the psalmists never doubted God's existence, only His methods. They loved Him, they believed He would triumph over enemies, and they knew He was the One True God. But they had some strong opinions about the way He went about His business. And they had no qualms about telling Him!

Fortunately for us human beings, God isn't easily offended. He is deeply committed to holding up His end of our relationship, and He doesn't want us to hide anything from Him. He already knows every thought we have, anyway. Why not talk to Him about those thoughts? Every concern about our children, every worry for our family's future, every little thing that's good, bad, or ugly.

Our Father always wants to talk. In fact, the very impulse to pray originates in God. In his book *The Pursuit of God*, author A. W. Tozer wrote, "We pursue God because, and only because, He has first put an urge within us that spurs us to the pursuit."

So, talk!

Lord God, it boggles my mind that You want to hear from me! And often! Your Word says that I can call out Your name with confidence. That You will answer me! Today, Lord, I give You praise, honor and glory—and my heart's deepest longings.

OPPORTUNITY KNOCKS

Now is when God's people must have faith and not give up.
REVELATION 13:10 NLV

You think we have it bad?

According to Revelation 13, "the beast" will fight against God's people in the end times. Not only that, he will overcome them (Revelation 13:7). God didn't promise to protect the saints of that time. Instead, He sent them a strange message: *Don't be dismayed. This is your great opportunity.*

God works the same way today. He puts His people in situations that call for endurance. That endurance then builds confidence. Yesterday's victories help us to face today's trials.

Gail learned that lesson when her baby battled one ear infection after another for more than two years. It took a tonsillectomy to end the constant siege of illness. But then another problem arose: Poor hearing during those crucial early months had slowed her daughter's speech development. She would require therapy to keep academic pace with her peers. Because of her previous experience, though, Gail faced this new challenge with a calm assurance. God was in control.

Hope comes easy when things go our way. We only learn soul-deep confidence in the school of hard knocks. Whatever the contrast between our present sufferings and our hopes and dreams, we know that a loving God will provide what we need.

My loving, heavenly Father, train me to hope in the school of suffering. Teach me perseverance today in hope of tomorrow.

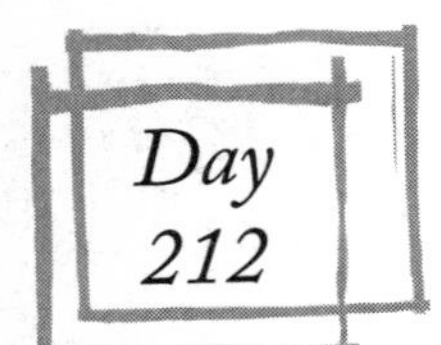

A Laugh a Day

On your feet now—applaud God!
Bring a gift of laughter, sing yourselves into his presence.
Psalm 100:1–2 MSG

There's an old saying that "laughter is the best medicine." But it's actually more than that.

The Bible tells us that laughter is a *gift*. We should rejoice in the Lord and bring our gift of laughter to Him.

Sometimes, as a single mom, you just have to laugh. Maybe you and your young son have just enjoyed a funny movie together. Or perhaps your teenage daughter thought it would be cool to dye her hair purple. In such cases, laughter can be both a song of praise and a catharsis.

It's important to find joy in the events of everyday life. But it's also wise to schedule time to pursue a good laugh after a tough week. Call some friends for a girls' night movie party, or curl up with a funny book. (A cup of hot chocolate never hurts, either.) Maybe you could listen to a Christian comedian for some good, clean humor, and worship through laughter.

Whatever the source, make time to laugh—and send those giggles up to God.

Dear God, thank You for giving us the gift of laughter. Help me to find joy in my daily life—and to make time to laugh with family and friends.

REST AND RESTORE

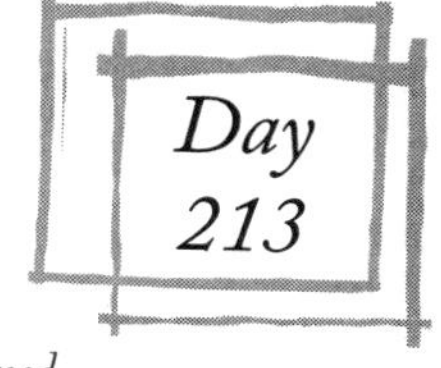

"Come to me, all you who are weary and burdened, and I will give you rest.
MATTHEW 11:28 NIV

Weary and burdened—such is the daily existence of the single mom. Weary from long hours of working, cleaning, and parenting—giving all we have to our children. Burdened from knowing we have to do it all again tomorrow and the next day and the day after that. It's a common place for single mothers.

Thankfully, we don't have to stay in this exhausting place. God offers rest to the mom whose shoulders are tired from carrying much more than her share of burdens. "Come to Me," says the Lord. "I want to give you rest."

When we bring Him our weary spirits, He lifts off the burden and exchanges it for His comfortable rest. He gives us strength to get through tomorrow and the next day and the day after that.

When we continually go to the Lord for rest, we'll find that, even though our situations don't change, we can get through our days with peace rather than exhaustion. We'll have enough left over to do it again tomorrow and the next day and the day after that.

Lord God, You are the giver of rest. I am weary and the burdens I carry are too heavy for me—but I come to You in faith, putting this heavy load in Your hands. I ask You to replace it with Your sweet rest, restoring my spirit, body, and mind for this journey.

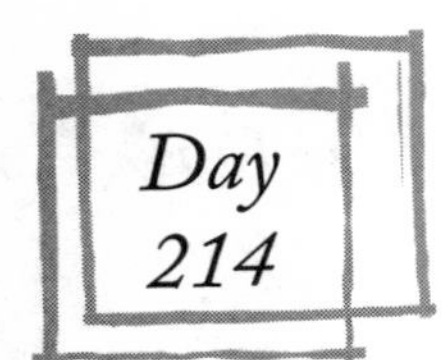

Happy Tears

My child, never forget the things I have taught you. . . .
A wise child brings joy to a father.
Proverbs 3:1, 10:1 NLT

"It's just a book report—there's no reason to cry," the confused boy said to his mother.

Embarrassed by her sudden outburst of tears, the mom quickly answered, "I know, I know. It's just that you're growing up so fast. It seems like only yesterday that you were learning to walk or tie your own shoes. And now. . .now I read your report, and I see how you've learn to write cursive and. . ." The tears started again.

"Mom, I didn't mean to make you sad," the boy said. "I only wanted you to read my book report."

"Sweetheart," Mom replied, "you didn't make me sad. I'm just so proud of you. These are tears of joy, not sadness. I'm so thankful to be your mom."

Sometimes we cry because we're sad. Other times, we'll weep tears of joy and gratitude for the overwhelming privilege of being a mom. And not just any mom—*their* mom. We'll watch them go from training wheels to Mag wheels. We'll teach them to say "please" and "thank you" as they grab a cookie from our hand and then, when they're older, watch them politely and confidently order a meal at a restaurant. Most rewarding of all, we'll teach our children about Jesus and, years later, enjoy the immense privilege of seeing them teach *their* kids about the Savior.

Yes, some tears are happy tears.

Father God, there are no words to express my thankfulness to You for the privilege of being my children's mother. Thank You!

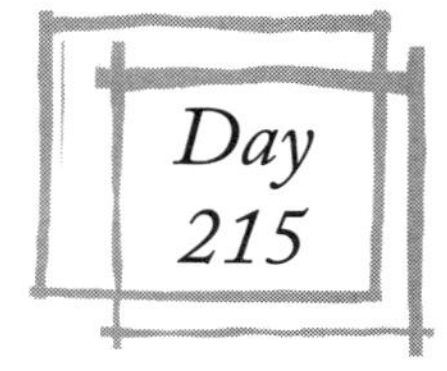

A Fleece

Then Gideon said to God, "Do not let Your anger burn against me that I may speak once more."
Judges 6:39 NASB

After seven years of judgment for doing evil in the eyes of the Lord, it was time for Israel to be freed from the Midianites. God chose Gideon, a mighty warrior, to lead the battle. He even promised Gideon that the battle would be won.

Gideon's response to this holy visit was to doubt the Lord's word! Gideon wanted proof of victory, so God gave him a sign. Audaciously, Gideon asked for another. Gideon put a wool fleece out overnight and asked God to keep it dry from the morning dew. God complied. Then Gideon asked for a reversed scenario. Again, God complied. The story of Gideon's fleece is so well known that, even today, people refer to putting a fleece before God when they try to discern His will.

Amazingly, God wasn't angry with Gideon for his disbelief. God met Gideon where he was. Gideon's faith was growing; that's what mattered to God.

When we feel inadequate about qualifications for a job God has given us—a job like single motherhood—we can take a page from Gideon's book. Gideon didn't hold back his fear of failure. He needed God's reassurance and patience in his faith walk, and God lovingly provided both.

He'll provide for us, too—if only we'll ask.

Lord, the battles I face may not be like Gideon's, but the feelings I have certainly are. Be patient with me, Lord! I need encouragement today and a reminder that You are with me.

Glory and Grace

The ransomed of the Lord shall return, and come to Zion with songs and everlasting joy upon their heads: they shall obtain joy and gladness, and sorrow and sighing shall flee away.
Isaiah 35:10 KJV

Six-winged seraphim cried, "Holy, holy, holy!" as the earth shook and smoke filled the temple. Isaiah, probably a young man of noble background, saw a vision of God's unspeakable glory. Overwhelmed, Isaiah offered himself as God's spokesman to His people. Since most of the Israelites had turned away from God, Isaiah found himself prophesying many messages that contained warnings of judgment, warfare, and suffering.

In the midst of the negative, however, Isaiah also prophesied of wonderful days when the Messiah would come to atone for Israel's sins. Isaiah predicted the people would return to their God, singing songs of praise that would last forever. The desert would blossom like a rose. The Israelites would be healed. The misery and depression they helped bring upon themselves and their families would disappear; instead, joy and gladness would become the norm.

Like Israel, we may feel no one can clean up the mess we have made of our lives. Pain has become a familiar companion. Laughter seems like a foreign language. But our merciful God longs to redeem us and teach us to smile again.

Father, I sometimes say to my children, "I've had it with you!" But You never say that to me. Please help me give others a taste of Your patient grace.

Beautiful Scars

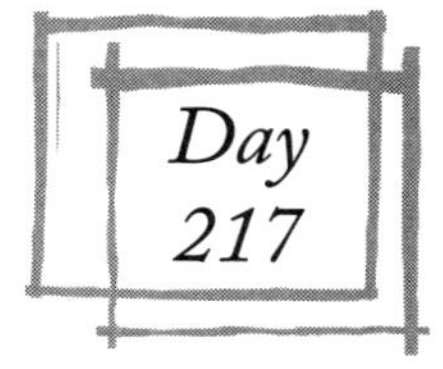

"The Spirit of the Lord is upon Me, because He has. . .
sent Me to heal the brokenhearted."
Luke 4:18 NKJV

We all have physical scars, and each tells its own story. Some of those tales might be humorous, but others conjure darker memories. Scars are caused by what has either been done to us or through us.

The most painful scars are often those that others can't see. They are the silent wounds on our hearts—the scar of rejection from an unloving father, the scar of disappointment at the loss of a child, the scar of a broken marriage—all painful reminders of the imperfect, fallen world we live in.

Whatever their cause, those injuries present us an opportunity. They are an invitation for us to share in the healing power of Jesus Christ. He can heal our open wounds and smooth over the tough, unsightly scars on our souls.

Painful memories may remain, but after we experience Jesus' healing touch, our scars can tell of His goodness. He can use even our scars for His glory.

Thank You, Lord, for Your healing power. Please help me to reveal my scars so that You can use the pain of my wounds to reach others with Your love.

Moving On

How long wilt thou mourn for Saul. . . ?
Fill thine horn with oil, and go.
1 Samuel 16:1 KJV

Samuel invested a lot of himself in Saul. He anointed Saul as Israel's first king and prophesied about him. He warned the brash leader against sinful pride. After the prophet delivered the news that God had rejected Saul as ruler of His people, the two men apparently never saw each other again. Samuel went into deep mourning.

God nudged Samuel. "How long wilt thou mourn?" In other words, God told the prophet to get moving. Samuel was to fill his horn with oil, a symbol of joy. God led the man to the village of Bethlehem and a shepherd boy named David—and we all know the rest of the story.

Like Samuel, we may mourn lost opportunities, relationships, and dreams. Whether we're single because of death, divorce, or other reasons, we're often tempted to brood on the past. Perhaps it's time for us to answer God's question: "How long will you mourn for [insert your issue here]?"

Grief is natural, and it often comes in waves. But God wants us to move forward. The end of a particular dream doesn't signal the end of hope. Let's fill our horns with the oil of gladness and reengage with life.

God will provide for us—in ways we can't even imagine.

God of love, You have so much yet in store for me.
Teach me to step forward into Your abundant joy.

The Discipline Dilemma

O Lord. . .your laws are righteous, and in faithfulness you have afflicted me. . . . Before I was afflicted I went astray, but now I obey your word.
Psalm 119:75, 67 niv

Let's face it: We want our children to rely on us, to like us, to want to be with us more than anyone else.

With that in mind, what's wrong with a little ice cream for dinner or some late night television? Nothing, really. But we will find trouble if we give in too often, simply because we want to be liked.

The I-want-my-kids-to-like-me syndrome causes some parents to recoil from even the thought of much-needed discipline. Sometimes we wrongly assume that discipline gets in the way of showing our children love. But the reality is that a lack of discipline is unkind and unloving.

"Before I was afflicted I went astray," scripture says, "but now I keep Your Word." Affliction, apparently, is one thing that created a change in this psalmist's behavior.

It's okay to "afflict" our children—with a loss of privileges or a few extra chores—to teach them a lesson. Of course, our little darlings may not like us at that moment. But, ultimately, we are showing more genuine love than any amount of "friendship parenting" ever would.

Heavenly Father, I lean on and rely on You to help me parent my child. Grant me wisdom to know when and what kind of discipline to use.

Know Love

[That you may really come] to know [practically, through experience for yourselves] the love of Christ, which far surpasses mere knowledge [without experience]; that you may be filled [through all your being] unto all the fullness of God [may have the richest measure of the divine Presence, and become a body wholly filled and flooded with God Himself]!

EPHESIANS 3:19 AMP

Love is not necessarily an emotion that gives us a warm fuzzy feeling.

God is love. It is who He is, not just something He does. To know His love is to know Him personally and intimately.

Paul desired the church at Ephesus to actually experience the love of God by knowing that love as a Person, rather than a feeling. Only then could the church become a body wholly filled and flooded with God Himself.

We, too, should seek to know love through an intimate relationship with God—not just by knowing stories about Him. We develop that relationship in the same way we get to know people—by spending time with them. Meditate on God's Word. Talk with Him in prayer. Listen to Him in the quiet moments. Obey Him.

As we do these things, we begin to experience love as a Person, not a feeling. And our families will benefit from that.

Heavenly Father, I come to You, desiring to know love in an intimate way. Reveal Yourself to me, Father. Fill me so I may have the richest measure of Your divine presence and become wholly filled and flooded with You. Help me show Your love to those around me.

Clanging Cymbals

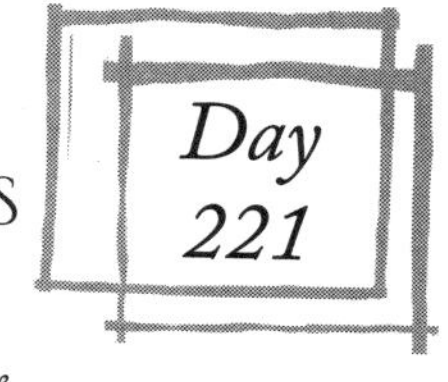

The quiet words of the wise are more effective than the ranting of a king of fools.
ECCLESIASTES 9:17 MSG

One afternoon in a crowded department store, a five-year-old boy had a temper tantrum. A loud one! The boy's mom set aside her to-do list and focused on her out-of-control child. She crouched down to quietly speak to her son, seemingly unconcerned about the disturbance her son had created—or the raised eyebrows of other shoppers. Mom only had eyes for the boy—and with a soothing voice, she calmed him down quite effectively.

That mom exhibited a wonderful model of good parenting for the wide-eyed bystanders. So often, we witness the opposite kind of parenting. Rude put-downs, sharp words, threats of punishment. Parents can sound like clanging cymbals in the ears of their kids. Too often, especially when we're tired or stressed, *we* are guilty of that kind of parenting!

God has a better way for us to parent, even in the midst of temper tantrums in public places. That wise mom in the store gave a snapshot of how God gently parents us! He is infinitely patient, speaks with a loving voice, and gives His complete attention despite our embarrassing meltdowns.

Lord of Lords, when I need to discipline my kids, help me to check my tone of voice and my expression. When I get absorbed in my own to-do lists, remind me to take the time to pay attention to my children. Bring to mind Your definition of true love: It is patient, kind, and never rude.

Puddle-Jumping

If the Lord delights in a man's way, he makes his steps firm; though he stumble, he will not fall, for the Lord upholds him with his hand.
Psalm 37:23–24 NIV

After a refreshing spring rain the night before, Jaycee couldn't wait to take her two-year-old twins outside to play. The daunting task of dressing her boys in their "puddle-jumping" outfits complete, they went outdoors.

Jaycee enjoyed watching her sons play until little Frankie suddenly cried out. Moving quickly to grab the boy before he fell face-first into a murky puddle, Mom caught Frankie by the elbow and pulled him up. His fearful face quickly calmed as he looked up to see his mom holding him safely in her grasp.

It's much the same way with our Lord. No matter how deep or murky our circumstances appear, God is there to catch us when we stumble. Jesus Christ is never caught off guard. The Lord causes our steps to be firm.

In fact, He's so close that He never needs to hurry to catch us. God simply reaches out and keeps us from falling, then puts our feet on His firm foundation.

Lord, I thank You for being so near me. You can simply reach out Your hand and catch me each time I stumble.

The Value of Simple Gifts

Then he gave her his hand and lifted her up; and when he had called the saints and widows, he presented her alive. And it became known throughout all Joppa, and many believed on the LORD.
ACTS 9:41–42 NKJV

A beautiful city on the seacoast, Joppa was home to more than its share of widows—women left behind by husbands who'd gone to sea, never to return. Many of these widows had little to rely on except God's grace and the goodness of their friends and family.

Dorcas was one of those friends who gave of herself and her talents. A devout believer, Dorcas was called a "disciple" by Luke (Acts 9:36)—the only time that word is used in reference to a woman. With her skills as a seamstress, she made clothes for the widows, which they proudly showed to Peter when he arrived. Their appreciation of Dorcas's service and their grief moved Peter, and he returned her to life. The miracle brought many in Joppa to the Lord.

In a world that often overvalues great achievements, moms can lose sight of how valuable their time, everyday talents, and service to the Lord are to friends and family. Peter's miracle was amazing—but it wouldn't have happened apart from Dorcas's quiet service.

Lord, thank You for the gifts and talents You've bestowed on me. Help me to use those gifts to show my love and faith to my children each day.

Day 224

The Kind Leading the Blind

I will bring the blind by a way that they knew not;
I will lead them in paths that they have not known;
I will make darkness light before them, and crooked things straight.
Isaiah 42:16 KJV

Natalie felt like she needed a translator to read the insurance policy. An accident was bad enough; why make everything so complicated? Tomorrow she would file a police report, then take the car to repair shops for estimates. How long would it take to fix? Would she have to walk to work? Who would take the girls to school?

Natalie could have sworn she checked both ways before pulling out. Somehow her old minivan had smacked a shiny New Yorker.

"What are you, blind?" The gray-haired owner hadn't bought her lame explanation.

"Yes!" Natalie had wanted to scream. *"I'm blind! I have no idea where I'm going or what I'm doing."* Instead, she'd muttered a vague apology, but the other driver's question stuck in her mind like an arrow. Ever since the divorce, Natalie had felt as if she were stumbling through a maze blindfolded.

Lord, I don't want to play the game. Natalie couldn't cry aloud, or she'd awaken the children. But her tears plopped onto the insurance policy.

"I am with you."

God's words seemed carved into the air. Natalie couldn't see them. But they were more real than her troubles.

Maybe she wasn't so blind, after all.

Jesus, help me remember that You specialize in giving
sight to those who have lost their vision. I love You, Lord.

Have You Looked Up?

The heavens proclaim the glory of God. The skies display his craftsmanship. Day after day they continue to speak; night after night they make him known.
PSALM 19:1–2 NLT

One afternoon, Cathy was walking around the park near her home. Her mind whirred with concerns about work and worries about her kids.

Suddenly, a man called out, "Hey lady! Have you looked up?"

She stopped and turned to see who was shouting. The voice belonged to an elderly man, seated on a bench.

"Have you looked up?" he asked her again.

She lifted her head and saw a magnificent scarlet oak tree, with leaves of crimson at the peak of their color. It was so beautiful, such a fleeting autumnal sight, that it took her breath away. She thanked the man and resumed her walk, relaxed and grateful after being reminded to "look up!"

God has placed glimpses of creation's majesty—evidence of His love—throughout our world. Sunsets, seashells, flowers, snowflakes, changing seasons, moonlit shadows. Such glories are right in front of us, every single day! But we must develop eyes to see these reminders in our daily life and not let the cares and busyness of our lives keep our heads turned down.

Have you looked up today?

Lord, open my eyes! Unstuff my ears! Teach me to see the wonders of Your creation every day and to point them out to my children.

Guide Book

"Who endowed the heart with wisdom
or gave understanding to the mind?"
Job 38:36 NIV

Edie doubted her decision-making skills. Throughout her marriage, she depended on her husband's leadership. When she did act on her own, she often felt that she had chosen impulsively. Now, as a single mom, she had to make all the decisions by herself. She agonized over each one, from which outfit to choose for work to which used car to purchase. Responsibility frightened her.

Over time, though, God spoke to Edie through the Bible. Did she have a date in court? He commanded her to stand firm. Did she wonder how to keep food on the table? He promised to provide for her as He cares for the sparrows. She drank wisdom from the pages of God's Word.

Like Edie, we may wish we were wiser and more capable of making good decisions. We may feel that we lack experience or common sense and flounder when life throws us a curveball. But both Job and Edie learned that the best thing we can do is turn to the only source of real wisdom: God.

He offers limitless wisdom in His Word and through His Holy Spirit, whenever and wherever we need it.

Heavenly Father, I acknowledge my lack of wisdom and understanding.
I come to You, believing You know everything and want what is best for me.
Guide me by Your wisdom as I immerse myself in Your Word.

Carry On

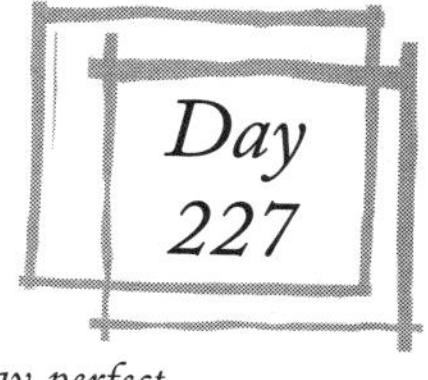

It is God who arms me with strength and makes my way perfect.
Psalm 18:32 NIV

How often do we become overwhelmed with our difficult circumstances or feel as if our strength has been sapped to rock bottom?

After a week of our little daughter's chicken pox or our baby boy's new teeth, we find ourselves sleep-deprived, our strength swirling rapidly down the drain like soapy bathwater. We become acutely aware that we can do nothing in our own strength—that raising kids alone takes enormous emotional, physical, and mental stamina.

It's at that point we realize where our real source of power lies—in God, who arms us with strength and makes our way perfect. He is the One who fills our spirit with the desire to keep praying, even when we've seen no results. He is the One who keeps our bodies moving when we are beyond exhausted. He is the One who helps us get up in the morning and face the new day, when we really want to pull the covers over our heads and sleep till next week.

It is God who arms us with strength—His amazing, mind-boggling strength.

God, I'm tired and my strength is long gone. But I believe Your Word, so I'm asking You for power for today. I thank You for making my way perfect and for arming me today with strength.

God's Exchange Policy

To appoint unto them that mourn in Zion, to give unto them beauty for ashes, the oil of joy for mourning, the garment of praise for the spirit of heaviness. . .that he might be glorified.
Isaiah 61:3 KJV

When the sale was on, the cute shoes with too-high heels seemed perfect. The coat in that odd shade of green appeared an incredible bargain. At home, however, the coat and shoes didn't look so great. Neither did the price tags. *What was I thinking?*

So you stand in a long line, hoping to exchange them over your lunch hour so you won't waste precious family time, running errands after work. But the receipt's in your other purse. Will you receive the full price back without it? Do they even accept a return on sale items? You glance at a calendar. Does the store place a time limit on returns? Whew! This exchange presents a major hassle for a single mom trying to manage alone.

God's exchange policy as recorded in Isaiah seems too good to be true. No standing in line. No hassles. For the ashes of our pasts, He offers a beautiful future. God dispels our loss and loneliness and anoints us with the oil of His Spirit as if we were royalty. We've grown accustomed to dark, depressing clothes, but He points us to dressing rooms where new outfits await: garments of praise—light, lovely dresses that fit us perfectly.

Lord Jesus, what an exchange! I want to wear this garment of praise every day, just for You.

Intimacy with God

He is intimate with the upright. . . . He blesses the dwelling of the righteous. . . . He gives grace to the afflicted.
Proverbs 3:32–34 NASB

Single parenthood—talk about an oxymoron.

Parenting by its very nature seems to beckon a couple, a team to handle the daunting challenges or to relish the choice victories. From late-night feedings to late-night dates, from potty training to drivers ed, we long to share the load. Often we yearn for someone to come alongside and share our parenting struggles and joys.

Whether we're single parents by choice or we've been thrust into it by some other circumstance, going it alone is difficult, to say the least. But—and this is a big but—as followers of Christ, we are *never* alone. In fact, in the psalms God says that He's "intimate with the upright." *Intimate.* With us!

God is with us as we read over the report cards and the nutrition labels. He is with us as we rock the little ones to sleep—or fall into bed exhausted after a long day at work, only to find our real work is just beginning as we later rise up in the wee hours, responding to a child's cry.

We have a close companion as we raise our children. . .it's God Himself.

Heavenly Father, though I may feel alone at times, cause me to be ever aware of Your intimate presence in my life. You share my parenting struggles and joys—what a privilege!

Nebuchadnezzar's Sabbatical

"This is the verdict on you, King Nebuchadnezzar: Your kingdom is taken from you. You will be driven out of human company and live with the wild animals. You will eat grass like an ox. The sentence is for seven seasons, enough time to learn that the High God rules human kingdoms and puts whomever he wishes in charge."
Daniel 4:31–32 msg

Nebuchadnezzar, king of Babylon, ruled the first known world empire. An idol worshipper as well as a man who idolized himself, Nebuchadnezzar was given multiple opportunities to acknowledge the one true God. Through interactions with Daniel, a tiny little light would begin to glow inside Nebuchadnezzar, and he would accept Daniel's God into his assortment of deities. But then the light would dim. Finally, as Nebuchadnezzar's reign stretched into its final lap, God gave him one more chance to repent—or else.

But Daniel reminded him it didn't *have* to be "or else"! God's warnings were intended to bring repentance, not wrath. Did Nebuchadnezzar heed God's warning? Sadly, no.

The king of Babylon didn't take God's Word seriously, but God took him seriously. Nebuchadnezzar spent seven years living like a beast in a field, until he looked to heaven.

What warnings has God given us—warnings that we haven't taken seriously? What habits or attitudes or influences need to be pruned out of our life? Gossip? One drink too many at a party? An attraction to the wrong man? We need to take God at His Word and heed those warnings. They're intended to draw us closer to Him.

Show me, Lord, the areas that steal my affections and turn my heart away from You. You and You alone are worthy of my worship.

WAITING

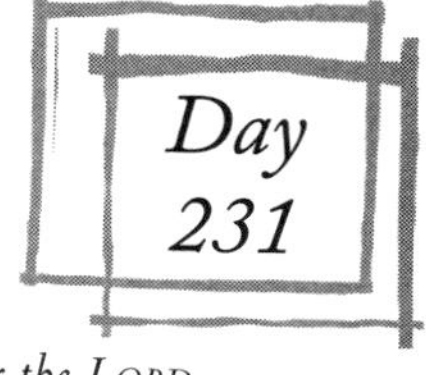

Wait for the LORD; be strong and take heart and wait for the LORD.
PSALM 27:14 NIV

"Just wait!"

Ever blurted those harsh word at your children? They're hungry for lunch, but you're in the middle of helping Jesse with a school project or urging Brady to organize his hockey equipment for tonight's practice. Riley needs his library books, but Mom is desperately trying to tame Jill's hair before the bus starts honking—again.

We want our children to wait patiently for us. . .but how do we wait for the Lord? Ever get impatient? Demand that the Lord help you "right now"?

Ideally, we should wait quietly, knowing God's timing is perfect—far beyond what we can understand. Of course, that's not easy—it takes strength and endurance to wait patiently, especially when we believe our need is desperate.

But before you try to take matters into your own hands, remember this: The Lord knows our needs and He never forgets us. He'll meet each and every need in His time, if only we'll wait on Him.

Take heart, single mom. God *will* meet your needs—every single one.

Dear Father, remind me that You know my needs. You'll meet them in Your time and by Your hand. Help me to be patient, to know that You have my best interest at heart.

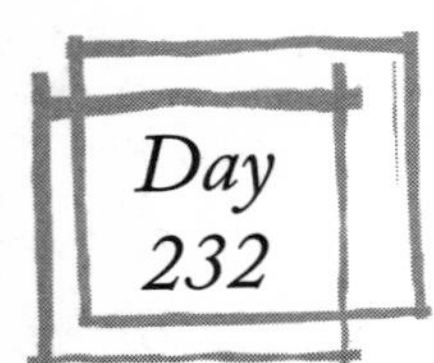

For His Own Good

And we know that to them that love God all things work together for good, even to them that are called according to his purpose.
Romans 8:28 ASV

One day, as Jesus walked down the dusty roads of Jerusalem, He came upon a blind man. Jesus spat in the dust, made a clay paste, and rubbed it on the man's eyes. When the man washed the mud from his eyes, he could see!

Many people thought the sightless man was blind because of sin in his parents' lives. In response, Jesus said, "Neither this man nor his parents sinned. . .but this happened so that the work of God might be displayed in his life" (John 9:3 NIV).

It wasn't the dirt that held the healing power—we never find healing in the dirt of our lives. The miracle was in how Jesus used the dirt. And so it is in our own lives. The dirt and pain of life are simply tools that God uses.

Sometimes life's circumstances cause us to cry out, "Why, Lord? Why?" And God's response is always the same: so that His good work might be displayed in our lives. And like the blind man's story, our stories—our testimonies of God's involvement in our lives—could be the light that points someone else to true faith.

Father, help me to trust You more. Help me to see Your hand at work and to let go of my desire for control. May Your glory be displayed in my life for all to see.

A Time to Give

"Is it right for you to be living in fancy houses while the Temple is still in ruins?"
HAGGAI 1:4 NCV

Requests for donations bombard us. Feed the hungry, save those endangered animals, support a political candidate—so many appeals are made that we run the danger of developing calluses on our hearts. And, of course, our local churches need our giving to continue their important work.

We may think, *I can barely afford to provide for my family. How can I give? I'll worry about that when I get our finances straightened out.*

God once sent a message to the ancient Israelites through the prophet Haggai. Describing that experience of never having enough to go around, Haggai said, "Your wages disappear as though you were putting them in pockets filled with holes!" (Haggai 1:6 NLT). Through His prophet, God didn't say that work, food, and clothing were unimportant. But He did stress that God's house—in our day, His work—needs to be a priority for us. The Israelites responded, and God poured out His blessing.

Do we need to examine our own spending habits? Are there times when we seek luxury at the expense of God's work? Do we set aside money to support "the Temple," or do we just say, "Someday"?

God has chosen to use us to carry out His work in the world. When we're faithful to that calling, we can be sure He'll provide for our needs.

God of all, may we make You the Lord of our financial and physical resources. Show us how much, when, and where to give.

A Labor of Love

Therefore, my beloved brethren, be firm (steadfast), immovable. . . knowing and being continually aware that your labor in the Lord is not futile [it is never wasted or to no purpose].
1 Corinthians 15:58 AMP

"Cover your mouth!"

"Did you brush your teeth?"

"Don't talk with your mouth full!"

"No, you can*not* eat candy for breakfast."

"How many times do I have to tell you to stop slamming the door?"

It seems never ending, doesn't it? To the casual observer, it may appear that our labor of love—with all of its dos, don'ts, and did yous—has been for naught. Really, now—how many times should one have to say, "Don't kick your sister!" before Bobby finally gets it? Apparently ninety-eight and counting.

And then there are the deeper issues of life. We teach our kids to treat mean people with kindness, to pray for people they actually dislike, to forgive when they would rather hold a grudge. They're hard lessons to learn, so we must keep at it, never giving up. Keep forging ahead, teaching, training, and modeling what God's Word has taught you. Our labor is not in vain. We have His Word on it.

Raising children to love and honor the Lord is tough work, especially for single parents. The key is never to give in to discouragement. Nothing we do for the Lord is ever wasted. . .even reminding little Johnny to stop hitting his sister!

Father God, as I raise my children to honor and respect You, You've promised that my labor is never wasted. What a promise to count on!

David's Diary

God, God, save me! I'm in over my head, quicksand under me, swamp water over me; I'm going down for the third time. I'm hoarse from calling for help, bleary-eyed from searching the sky for God.
Psalm 69:1–3 msg

We think of the Book of Psalms as poetry, or even a peek into King David's private diary—over half of the psalms are credited to him. But they were originally verses set to music, compiled as a hymnbook for corporate worship in the temple. Unfortunately, we have no known record of their tunes.

There is a psalm to match every emotion and mood experienced by human beings: joy, anger, frustration, discouragement, loneliness, doubt. Thousands of years after they were written, they still speak to our needs and desires.

But the psalms are much more than beautiful words that parallel our emotions: God is their central focus. Psalms often begin as a heart cry of pain from the psalmist—but they invariably end with a focus on God.

The psalm writers had a very real, genuine relationship with God. They sang praises to God, they got angry with God, they felt abandoned by God, they didn't understand God's slow response. . .and yet they continued to live by faith, deeply convicted that God would overcome.

These ancient prayers remind us that nothing can shock God's ears. We can tell Him anything and everything. He won't forsake us—His love endures forever.

Oh Lord, You know the secrets of my family's hearts. Teach us to talk to You through every emotion and every circumstance. Our focus belongs on You.

What Am I Dwelling On?

Finally. . .whatever is true, whatever is noble, whatever is right, whatever is pure, whatever is lovely, whatever is admirable—if anything is excellent or praiseworthy—think about such things.
Philippians 4:8 NIV

Moms who raise kids alone have one of the most challenging jobs in society. We are bombarded by negative thoughts, countless worries, exhausting days, and unhealed wounds. Since we have children, there is undoubtedly a man in our past—a man who abandoned us, misused us, or perhaps died too soon—and we're reminded of the pain every time we look into our children's eyes. We bear the hurt of our children who miss out on a daily "daddy" in their lives.

God's Word is clear on dealing with these painful feelings. If we allow our minds to dwell on the ugly, hurtful, and depressing, we'll never get past the pain. Those scars will cover our emotional lives. But if we follow the scripture and dwell on that which is noble, pure, admirable, and praiseworthy, our attitudes will transform—and we'll find our spirits being controlled by uplifting thoughts. Our hearts will overflow with unspeakable joy and peace beyond all human understanding.

Father, You know the hurts and fears of my past and present circumstances. Remind me to dwell on those things that are pure, noble, and right.

He Keeps His Promises

"For I know the plans I have for you," declares the LORD, "plans to prosper you and not to harm you, plans to give you hope and a future."
JEREMIAH 29:11 NIV

Unimaginable. That must describe the hopelessness the disciples felt as they saw their Master die on the cross. All the promises they held dear—all their feelings of hopeful expectation—were shot down with those final words: "It is finished."

Some of Jesus' followers may have remembered His earlier words assuring them of His return. But in the face of certain death, those words of victorious life must have been hard to accept.

We all experience moments of hopelessness in our earthly journeys. The death of our dreams, the crashing down of our hopes, the promises of God seemingly unfulfilled. . .we are no more immune to disappointment than Jesus' disciples were.

In the end, though, Jesus' promises held true—He did prevail no matter how dark that first Good Friday looked. We can always trust the words of our Lord. He knows the plans He has for us, and He has the power to see them through.

Hope and a future, prosperity and peace—we can trust that, even when things seem hopeless, God is still at work, carrying out His promises.

Thank You, Jesus, for being at work in my life. Thank You for having a perfect plan and for keeping Your promises. Give me faith to believe in You even when it seems like everything is going wrong.

Not Now, God!

The end of a matter is better than its beginning,
and patience is better than pride.
Ecclesiastes 7:8 NIV

Sarah's pastor told a story that really hit home.

"The other day I was driving," he told the congregation. "And I began to talk to God. I prayed that He would give me patience, and at that very moment, a slow-moving tractor pulled out in front of my car, blocking the road. At that moment, I thought, 'I didn't mean *now*, God!' "

Patience may be a virtue. But it's a virtue that many of us struggle with on a daily basis—particularly when kids are involved. Though we may *pray* for patience, it's hard to actually *be* patient in every situation.

So beyond praying for patience, we ought to *practice* the patience we seek. Really. Maybe you could choose the longest line at the checkout counter or allow other shoppers to go ahead of you. Perhaps you could slow down a bit and drive the posted speed limit. (And don't be angry when others drive even a bit slower.) Maybe you could even allow your kids five extra minutes to chat with their friends before rushing home after an event.

It will probably be difficult. But gaining patience will be worth all the trials.

Dear Lord, please give me patience. Remind me to be patient not just when I want to be, but in all situations. Help me to practice that virtue and model it for my children.

Dance in Your PJs!

David, ceremonially dressed in priest's linen,
danced with great abandon before God.
2 Samuel 6:14 MSG

Is it really a matter of national importance if there are dirty clothes on the bedroom floor? Or if we allow the kids to eat corn flakes for dinner? Is it necessary to talk in our stern "mother voice" all the time—as if parenthood has drained the zest for life right out of us?

King David had the audacity to be so happy, so full of joy, that he danced in public. . .in his underclothes! Certainly, he had his share of troubles and a plate full of responsibility—yet he found a way to enjoy himself as he worshipped God.

We'll probably encounter plenty of well-meaning people who remind us, "Raising children is not fun and games—this is serious business." And there's truth in that.

But parenting can be fun and games *sometimes.* Try this—as the kids sit down for dinner, pull out a Monopoly game and pop a bowl of popcorn. Plan a family pajama party or a living room campout, complete with a bedsheet tent.

Let's lighten up and enjoy this ride. It'll be over before we know it.

Father God, please help my children and me to relax—to enjoy the life You've given us. Grant me creative ideas to simply have fun and actually take pleasure in my family.

The Babylonian Brain Trust

When the magicians, enchanters, astrologers and diviners came,
I told them the dream, but they could not interpret it for me.
Finally, Daniel came into my presence and I told him the dream.
Daniel 4:7–8 NIV

Dreams were important in the ancient Babylonian culture. It was believed that they revealed the future or relayed a message that a god was angry. Dreams were not to be ignored.

So when King Nebuchadnezzar had a troubling dream, he nearly executed his entire brain trust in trying to have it interpreted. That was when Daniel intervened, praying to God for divine wisdom to figure out the king's vision.

Why, then, when faced with another troubling dream, did Nebuchadnezzar immediately turn back to his incompetent magicians for answers? Again, the brain trust failed him. Again, Daniel intervened. How could a brilliant man like Nebuchadnezzar make the same mistake twice?

When a troubling circumstance intrudes into our life, do we "get it"? Do we hit our knees and take the problem to God for wisdom and guidance? Or do we return to ineffective habits—like anxiety, despair, or anger?

Habits are hard to break, even the ones that have failed us before. Let's learn from old King Nebuchadnezzar. The next time trouble hits, forgo old habits and turn instead to the God who never fails.

Reveal my tendencies, Lord, to respond to problems in the wrong ways.
Show me a better way—Your way.

Who Am I?

Then he asked them, "But who do you say I am?"
Peter replied, "You are the Messiah."
Mark 8:29 NLT

Mom, Mama, Mother—whatever our children call us, it's the most precious sound on earth. We remember the first time our babies called us "Mama," and noted the occasion in their baby books.

For the first years of our children's lives, they see us only as "mother." We exist for them solely in our role as their parent. Only as time passes do they recognize our other roles: Christian. . .employee. . . daughter. . .church member. . .friend.

In a similar way, we see God first as a Father—and when we lisp "Daddy" to Him, it's as precious in His ears as "Mama" is to ours. But while God is a loving heavenly Father, He is also much more.

When we pray, let's stop to consider Jesus' question, "Who do you say that I am?"

Perhaps, with Peter, we'll affirm, "You are the promised Messiah, my Savior." Or like Hagar in her struggles, maybe we'll call Him "The God who sees." When we can't imagine how our topsy-turvy circumstances will work out, we'll call Him "Alpha and Omega," the One who began everything and will still be there throughout eternity.

Who is God to us today? We can't go wrong meditating on His many names.

Lord God, teach me to recognize that everything I want or need, I find in You.
Thank You for revealing Yourself to me.

What Am I Sowing?

Do not be deceived: God cannot be mocked.
A man reaps what he sows.
Galatians 6:7 NIV

What a concept: reaping what we sow. This verse is often applied to money, finances, and giving, though that's far from the full story. Here we have a godly principle that should be applied to everyday thoughts, attitudes, choices, and actions.

As single moms, it might be wise to take a good, hard (possibly painful) look into our hearts to see how we're doing with this sowing-reaping business. As we raise our children, those precious little sponges who soak up everything, do we need to find a new kind of "seed" to plant? We can't sow anger and bitterness, expecting to reap joy and blessing. We can't sow bad attitudes and disrespect, hoping to reap healthy emotions and relationships.

Moms sow with their children every day. If we want the kids to be truthful, we must tell the truth. If we want them to be respectful, we must show respect. The principle is simple, though living it can be difficult. But there's just no way around it. Don't be deceived. We reap exactly what we have sown.

Lord Jesus, please help me remember this principle and apply it to my life. Let me sow good seed that I might reap a harvest of goodness and Christlikeness in my children.

Be Still and Know

A woman must quietly receive instruction
with entire submissiveness.
1 Timothy 2:11 NASB

Five minutes of rest. That's all she needed before studying God's Word. But the moment her head hit the pillow, sleep became the priority. Spiritual instruction would have to wait until another time.

Even in the craziness of life, we will benefit by taking a few minutes (or longer) each day to receive guidance from God's holy Word—the Bible. The apostle Paul, in 1 Timothy 2:11, reminds us that we as single mothers should receive instruction from the perfect male influence in our lives—God Himself.

It's often difficult to find five minutes to spend in God's Word or prayer. And right before bedtime—when many of us try to squeeze in our devotions—may not be the period most conducive for study.

For a few days, watch for breaks in your schedule—times when you're alert and ready to receive instruction. Maybe that's first thing in the morning, or perhaps it's in your car five extra minutes before you head off to work. You could read the Word instead of the newspaper while you're drinking your coffee. Or maybe it's some other time and place.

What's important is that we make time for regular Bible reading and prayer.

Dear Lord, help me to carve out time for You today.
Remind me that Your instruction comes from Your Word—
and that I should immerse myself in that Book every day.

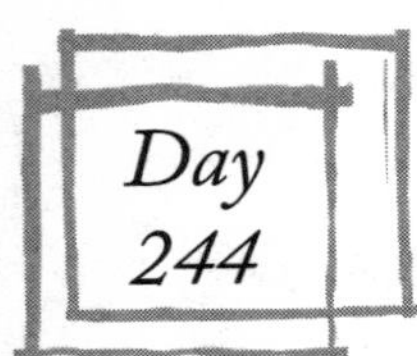

The Best

"But the father wasn't listening. He was calling to the servants, 'Quick. Bring a clean set of clothes and dress him. Put the family ring on his finger and sandals on his feet. Then get a grain-fed heifer and roast it. We're going to feast! We're going to have a wonderful time!'"
Luke 15:22–23 msg

The prodigal son had wasted his wealth. He had made mistakes—big ones. He had forgotten his position as a son and made foolish decisions based on his own selfish desires.

One phrase in this story reads, "When [the son] came to hi senses" (Luke 15:17 NIV). When the wasteful young man remembere who his father was and what he could provide, he acted differently.

In his own eyes, the prodigal son saw himself as deserving nothing He was ready to offer himself as a servant to his father. But his fathe could see his son only through the eyes of compassion. He saw a so in need of the best things a father could give him—and he lavished hi love on the young man.

In the same way, our heavenly Father sees *us* through eyes o compassion and love. When we believe in Jesus, God sees only th blood of Christ—not our mistakes, faults, and failures. He views us a worthy of the best He has to offer. If we see ourselves as less worthy we discount His amazing love for us.

Forget the past, and don't worry about the struggles of the present Our Father rejoices when we trust in Him, and promises us His ver best.

Father God, I thank You for loving me the way You do. I know You want the very best for me in all things. Help me always to remember that I am Your child—and to act accordingly.

What Fear?

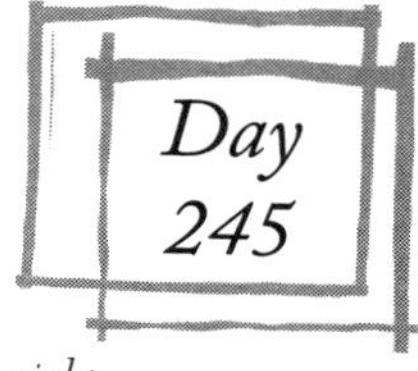

"I am the Lord, *your God, who takes hold of your right hand and says to you, Do not fear; I will help you."*
Isaiah 41:13 NIV

What are you afraid of? Single moms can quickly write a catalog of fears longer than our ten year old's Christmas list.

When we were girls, we probably had someone we trusted with our fears—whether a grandparent, or a mother or father—there was most likely someone we could go to when in crisis. From the bogeyman who appeared after the lights went out to that cute boy who might not ask us to the spring dance, we struggled with fears. But for most of us, there was someone we could go to, someone who would put a calming hand on our heads and say, "Don't worry, darling—I'm here to help you."

As adults, we calm those same kinds of fears for our little ones, even while our own fears continue. Fortunately, we have a Father who loves us beyond comprehension. God is our help. The Good Shepherd takes our hand, looks straight into our tear-filled eyes, and says, "My precious daughter, don't worry—I am here to help you."

Jehovah, You are my provider. When I am overcome with fear, remind me that You will take my hand and help me through whatever circumstances I face. I am not alone, Lord, for You are with me.

Seek Ye First. . .

"Seek first God's kingdom and what God wants.
Then all your other needs will be met as well."
Matthew 6:33 NCV

It began as a simple *yes* to her son's schoolteacher, a promise to bring cupcakes to an open house. Surely cupcakes wouldn't take long—she could work around the preparation for that major meeting the same day.

But what sounded like a simple task turned into a circus—requiring an extra trip to the grocery store (with three kids in tow) and getting up an hour earlier to deliver the treats. She spent money and time she didn't have to spare, and ended the day weak and frustrated.

This story is not unusual. With so many demands on our time—and with everyone wanting everything right this instant—it's easy to lose sight of the true priorities in life. Scripture, however, reminds us to look to *God* first. Home, workplace, and all other demands fall after Him, in that order.

Get to know yourself spiritually. Seek God's will for your life through prayer and study. Put *people* before *things*, your children before your job or church. There will be no success if the family suffers (1 Timothy 3:5; 5:8; Titus 2:4–5).

Most of all, learn to say no.

Lord, guide me through the minefield of demands on my time and energy. Help me remember that when I put You first, everything else falls into place.

Hearing with the Heart

A new heart also will I give you, and a new spirit will I put within you: and I will take away the stony heart out of your flesh, and I will give you an heart of flesh.
Ezekiel 36:26 KJV

"Mom, can I go over to Derek's?"

"Mom, I need money for the school field trip."

"Mom, would you take us to the mall? We don't have anything to do."

"Mom, you're not wearing *that*, are you?"

Mom—Mom—Mom! Have you ever counted how many times a day your children page you to serve as referee, cook, accountant, maid, social director, seamstress, taxi driver, laundress, lawyer, pastor, you name it? If asked, most mothers would estimate they answer the "Mom!" call at least a million times a day. We consider changing our names, addresses, and cell phone numbers in order to survive.

Sometimes mothers are tempted to harden their hearts into concrete. We find it much easier to respond with an immediate *"No!"* than to fully open our ears, minds, hearts, and lives to the everlasting, brain-fogging, nerve-stretching demands of "Mom!"

God, who claims millions of children who call His name, no doubt sympathizes. Even Jesus grew weary of the disciples' immaturity. But God never hardens His heart against us. He always listens. And, whenever our pleas fit into His plans, He delights to give us our hearts' desires.

Heavenly Father, by Your Spirit, please give me a generous heart like Yours. I want to say "Yes" to my children whenever I can.

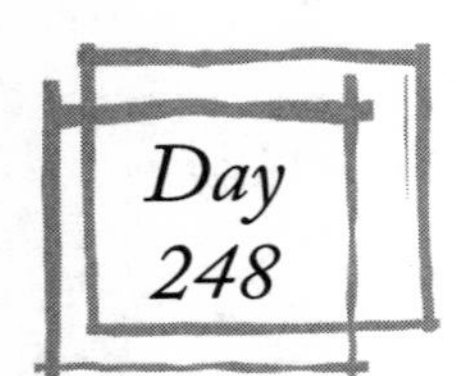

Why Pray?

"Why were you searching for Me?" He asked them.
"Didn't you know that I had to be in my Father's house?"
Luke 2:49 HCSB

Most of us have heard the story. Mary and Joseph unknowingly leave the twelve-year-old Jesus behind in Jerusalem. When they discover He's missing, they spend a frantic three days looking for him. Finally found in the temple, Jesus responds with an interesting question: "Why were you searching for Me?"

What makes us seek God out? Perhaps, like Mary and Joseph, we've missed our connection with the Lord for a few days. Often, we don't realize our mistake until an emergency arises—then we search for Him. God may seem far away, though, of course, *He* hasn't moved. Heaven is still His throne and the earth His footstool. But we seem to have lost our way.

Maybe we're rushing to God because we're worried. Then, in the presence of the Lord, who is our light and salvation, we no longer feel afraid. We trust Him to provide for us.

Or perhaps we're doubting God's goodness. We might repeat the anxious question of Mary and Joseph in our prayers: "Why have You treated us like this?" (Luke 2:48 HCSB). When we hurl anger at God, He simply absorbs it, reprimands or encourages us as needed, and renews our strength for another day.

So why do we pray? There are as many reasons as there are minutes in the day.

Heavenly Father, I know that when I seek You, I will find You.
I praise You, and pray that I will learn to come to
You with every detail of my life.

No Visible Results?

[You] shall again take root downward and bear fruit upward. . . .
May you be rooted deep in love.
Isaiah 37:31 amp; Ephesians 3:17 amp

Single parenthood. We single-handedly clean house, cook dinner, do laundry, attend parent-teacher conferences, join PTA groups, and stand in the cold and rain to watch our children play soccer, march in the band, or whatever it is they're doing. Somehow, in the midst of it all, we manage, with God's never-failing support, to cope with whatever arises.

Have we ever stopped to realize that all those challenges are doing something good—priceless, even—inside us? They're developing deep, strong, under-the-surface roots of godly character as we learn to rely on our Lord and Savior through everything we face. When we're forced, by sheer circumstance, to trust God for strength and wisdom, we grow—whether we realize that or not.

The hard work of single parenting is no illusion. It's tough. Really tough. Yet those very circumstances that challenge us also develop us. Our heavenly Father is causing us to "take root downward" so we may "bear fruit upward."

Father, help me to realize that You're using all the "hard stuff" in my life to build my character—training me to trust You in every way.

Battle of Attu

Her children respect and bless her.
Proverbs 31:28 MSG

During World War II, Japanese forces occupied two little Aleutian Islands. The islands offered very little strategic value to either side. However, a combination of national pride and concern about Japan's possible offensive use of the islands spurred U.S. officials to want to reclaim them.

The Battle of Attu took more than a year to conclude—and it was deadly. Many of the soldiers, who reportedly cried out for their mothers, froze to death.

Many times, we moms feel as if we don't have much impact on our children. The pressures of the world and the desire to conform to it can be as strong as gravity on them. Our kids seem to tune us out. Are we really making a difference?

Yes, we are. We should never doubt the impact we have on our kids. Other influences may triumph for a while, but they never come first or last longest. The old saying is true: A mother is the first book read and the last put aside in every child's library.

Help my children, Father, to cling to You like a baby clings to his mother. I thank You that nothing can rob my children of Your love.

Perfect Attendance

Some people have gotten out of the habit of meeting for worship, but we must not do that. We should keep on encouraging each other, especially since you know that the day of the LORD'S coming is getting closer.
HEBREWS 10:25 CEV

After a full week of activity—mounds of laundry, dinner preparation, parent-teacher conferences, little league games, and everything else that comes with being a single mom—a quiet Sunday morning sounds simply divine. Maybe we can enjoy a leisurely cup of coffee while the kids sleep in. Or maybe a long, hot bath. Oh, how tempting to nourish the flesh rather than the spirit!

Hebrews 10, though, reminds us to stay in the habit of meeting with other believers. We need fellowship to nourish our souls and prepare us for another week of motherly duty. Church is one way that the Holy Spirit helps us to regroup and refresh for a new week.

Church also teaches our children about priorities. They watch everything we do, so if we send a message that it's more important to stay home on Sunday morning than to join with other believers in worship, we can be sure that they'll follow a similar pattern.

As the day of Jesus' return grows closer, let's be sure we're fellowshipping with the rest of His body—the church. It's good for this life and brings eternal rewards.

Jesus, forgive me for the times I want to isolate myself. Thank You for Your reminder that the church—Your body—is one way that You use to meet my needs. Help me to make fellowship a priority.

From Badlands to Glad Lands

I will restore to you the years that the locust hath eaten.
Joel 2:25 KJV

Have you ever tilled a garden in the spring, breathing the earthy fragrance as sharp blades turned the moist, rich dirt? Perhaps you planted seeds and envisioned fresh vegetables: rosy radishes, plump pods of peas, and sweet carrots that taste nothing like their grocery-store counterparts. Or maybe you and your children have patted soil around tomato plants that promise a tasty harvest. Everyone loves flowers; we may get carried away with circus-colored visions of zinnias, marigolds, and petunias.

Then Japanese beetles and green worms discover our gardens and destroy our dreams. Without a twinge of conscience, they bore holes and riddle leaves until our seed-catalog-perfect scene succumbs to their greedy appetites.

When God sent fierce enemies to punish their willful wrongdoing, the Israelites felt as if giant locusts had wiped out years of their lives. His people had invested all their energy in defying God, yet had nothing to show but spiritual, emotional, and physical devastation.

But God still loved them. He even promised to restore the years they lost because of their sin.

When we make bad choices, it's hard to believe anything good can grow in our lives again. But when God plants His seeds and rains His love down on us, we can expect the best!

Lord Jesus, I have not cultivated my life according to Your directions. But You, the Resurrection and the Life, can bring springtime to me today and every day. Thank You, Lord, for raining Your blessings upon me.

The New Me

Therefore, if anyone is in Christ, he is a new creation;
the old has gone, the new has come!
2 Corinthians 5:17 NIV

Are you in Christ? Is He consistently Lord of your life? Then you are a new creation.

Regardless of your past, regardless of the circumstances you may have faced, you're a new creation. All the past guilt is gone—vanished, obliterated—and everything is new.

It's true that some of us live with the consequences of past choices. Maybe our children are the result of premarital sex—but they are nonetheless marvelous miracles of God. Maybe today's health problems result from years of unwise and harmful choices—but God says the guilt is all in the past, gone. Everything is new. What's history is done and over—and Jesus has replaced your old with His new: new peace, new joy, new love, new strength.

Since God Himself sees us as a new creation, how can we do any less? We need to choose to see ourselves as a new creation, too. And we can, through God's grace.

If you are "in Christ," you are a new creation. Be glad. Give thanks. Live each day as the new creation you have become through Jesus.

Father, I'm so thankful that You are a God of grace—and I thank You that I am a new creation. Please give me the spiritual eyes to see myself as a new creation, looking past the guilt of yesterday's choices.

You Are Never Alone

I, the Lord*—the first [existing before history began] and with the last [an ever-present, unchanging God]—I am He.*
Isaiah 41:4 AMP

Alone. In the middle of a crowded room and yet alone. Alone in our parenting, alone in our jobs, alone in our dealings with teachers and doctors, alone for Sunday morning worship. All alone. Or so it seems.

Did you notice what God said of Himself in Isaiah 41? "I, the Lord. . .[an ever-present, unchanging God]." Ever-present. *Always* present. There's nowhere He isn't. That means while you're sitting in the pediatrician's office, waiting for test results, He's right there with you. As you're reviewing spelling lists or helping with science projects, He's there. When your boss cancels your scheduled week of vacation or criticizes your work, God is with you all the way.

Of course, if we choose to, we can focus on our apparent aloneness. But doing so inevitably creates an attitude of "poor ol' me." Why should we fall prey to that thinking when we have a guarantee that the almighty God will be by our side, always present, with us at every turn?

Though at times we'll all feel lonely, we are never truly alone.

Father God, what comfort I take in knowing You are always with me. Because of You, I never have to face life alone.

Like Father, Like Son

He did what the Lord *said was right,*
just as his father Amaziah had done.
2 Kings 15:3 NCV

Whenever we read about kings in the Old Testament, scripture makes a point of telling us what kind of father he was, too. Over and over, we find the words *"just as his father had done."* What point was God trying to make? Maybe that He was just as concerned about what went on in the rest of the palace as in the throne room.

Almost without exception, the sons followed in their father's footsteps as a leader. If the father did evil, the son did, too. Sometimes, even more evil, like Ahab, son of Omri (1 Kings 16:30). If the father pleased the Lord, chances were that the son did, too. Sometimes, even more so, like Jehoshaphat, son of Asa (1 Kings 22:43).

Though there was no guarantee how a son would turn out, there were indicators. It was the cumulative effect of a lifetime as the king-in-training observed his father at work, at worship, at home. Day after day after day. The father's example was profound, and in this case, his influence as a leader rippled through the kingdom. . .and at home.

Every day, we single moms are being watched by our kids. Our influence on them is profound, even eternal. Thus the question we must ask ourselves is, are our lives pleasing in the Lord's sight?

Dear God, there is nothing more important to me than raising my children to love and honor You. May my influence on my children be pleasing in Your sight.

Telling the Truth

"Can any of you prove that I am guilty of sin?
If I am telling the truth, why don't you believe me?"
John 8:46 NCV

Jesus often butted heads with the Pharisees. In John 8, the picky legalists argued with Jesus about His authority to preach and do miracles. Jesus responded by asking, "Why don't you believe me when I tell you the truth?"

Jesus always told the truth—because He *is* the Truth. We can imagine that when the boy Jesus told His parents that He hadn't broken Mary's best dish or lost Joseph's favorite hammer, they believed Him.

We can't always say the same thing about our own children. It's too bad they don't come with a built-in lie detector to sift truth from falsehood: "He started the fight, not me." "I didn't cheat on that test." "They gave me the candy—I didn't steal it."

How can we encourage our kids to tell the truth—always? We can introduce the difference between truth and lies through Bible stories, daily conversation, even impromptu games. Maybe we can find a way to reward truth telling without excusing misbehavior. Most of all, we absolutely must model truth in our own lives. If our children catch us in lies, they'll assume such behavior is acceptable.

The more we tell the truth to our children, the more likely they are to tell us the truth.

Lord, You are the Truth and the Way.
Shape us first to live in truth, that we may show our children the way.

Contentment? Yeah, Right. . .

Be anxious for nothing, but in everything by prayer and supplication, with thanksgiving, let your requests be made known to God
Philippians 4:6 NKJV

The pan flew across the room, hitting the wall and dropping to the floor with a thud. Two squabbling kids at the dinner table stared at their young mother, who stood with tears streaming down her face. "Go to your rooms," she said quietly, as she bent to pick up the pan. They fled.

"Lord," she whispered, "I can't do this anymore."

Most single moms can relate. Sooner or later, almost all of us get pushed to the brink, and scripture lessons on "being content in all things" begin to sound hollow and trite.

Yet we may miss Paul's true message when he writes about contentment. In this verse, Paul encourages the Philippians to pray about their circumstances instead of worrying over them. Believers are not necessarily meant to be content *with* all circumstances, but *in* all circumstances. And being content does not preclude a drive for improvement; rather, it's an understanding that God is always with us, no matter what, and will provide a way for us to work through our problems.

Contentment is not about being weak and accepting; it's about trusting that God delivers and guides us. Commit problems to God in prayer and trust that He will provide deliverance. And thus peace.

Father God, when things are hard, help me remember that peace comes not from accepting where I am but from trusting You will always provide for me.

Time for Kids

*Jesus said, Suffer little children, and forbid them not, to come unto me:
for of such is the kingdom of heaven.*
Matthew 19:14 KJV

Maybe the disciples noticed Jesus' last encounter with the Pharisees drained Him. Or perhaps the noisy, dirty little kids that swarmed around Jesus had runny noses. At any rate, the disciples did not want them annoying the Master. Jesus had been healing crowds of people almost nonstop. He dealt with eternal issues every day. Important people needed answers to their questions. Jesus certainly could not waste His time and energy on children.

Jesus knew every minute counted in His quest to preach God's Word and heal desperate people. Soon He would die on a cross to redeem mankind for eternity. Jesus probably spent extensive time in prayer and preparation for this crucial event.

Yet when His well-meaning disciples shooed mothers and children away like mosquitoes, Jesus reprimanded His followers. He told them the kingdom of heaven was populated with souls like these. Jesus placed His hands on cooing babies and prayed. He hugged chubby and skinny little children close. Maybe Jesus even played a quick game of tag with his junior disciples.

Sometimes we parents, struggling with constant pressures, forget Jesus loves our children and wants to spend time with them. If we invite Him along on a family nature-hike or picnic, He's sure to come.

*Jesus, how glad I am that You are the friend of the children.
Someday we will all sit together on Your lap. For now I am content
that You want to spend time with me and my family, here and now.
Be with my children and me as we go throughout this day.*

OF MOUNTAINS AND MOLEHILLS

For who are you, O great mountain [of human obstacles]? . . .
You shall become a plain [a mere molehill]!
ZECHARIAH 4:7 AMP

Not enough money to last the month. Haven't eaten out in so long you weren't aware your favorite restaurant closed—or that the kids' favorite burger place now offers three flavors of cappuccino. Haven't bought yourself a new outfit since. . .you can't even remember! And the last time you had your car's oil changed was when you got that tax refund check. There's no such thing as extra cash any more. Simple pleasures that once were just everyday expenses are now decidedly luxuries.

It's funny how we get accustomed to certain amenities—and, before we know it, we believe we can't live without them. But it is possible to be content with less. God can teach us to be satisfied with frozen pizza instead of an evening out. . .with thrift-store bargains rather than the latest fashions. . .with the library in place of our mail-order book club. We can be satisfied, grateful, and content—and, even more importantly, we can pass those qualities on to our children.

Sure, at times our financial struggles may seem like mountains. But, in time, we will triumph, and see them as the molehills they really are. And, if we so choose, we can allow our financial challenges to teach us valuable lessons in the process.

Father, please teach me and my children to be grateful and content, viewing our financial struggles as the molehills they really are rather than the mountains they appear to be. Thank You for meeting all our needs.

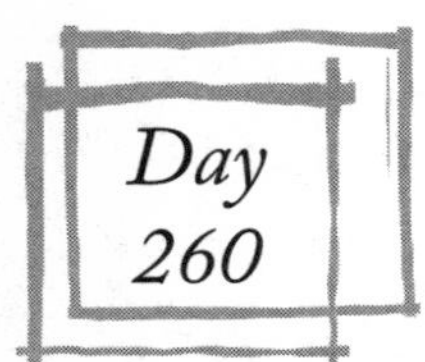

Type-A Prophet

Elijah was afraid and ran for his life. When he came to Beersheba in Judah, he left his servant there, while he himself went a day's journey into the desert. He came to a broom tree, sat down under it and prayed that he might die. "I have had enough, Lord."

1 Kings 19:3–4 NIV

Did Elijah take on too much and suffer for it? He seems a classic Type-A guy. He had a calling. He felt consecrated. He had a plan. He was doing God's work. He had even been part of many miracles!

So how did he end up alone in a remote place, exhausted and depressed, begging God to let him die?

Isn't it comforting to read about a flawed prophet? One with the highest of highs and the lowest of lows. At one point, Elijah led Israel in righteous living! In the next chapter, we read of his bone-deep weariness. James tells us that Elijah was a human, just like us (James 5:17). Elijah was *real.*

God used Elijah, flaws and all. Just like Elijah, we can honor God and be used by Him—flaws and all—if we give Him our whole heart.

Lord God, sometimes I feel so wholly inadequate to do Your work. I don't feel as if I have much to offer, but I give You my heart, knowing that You can do more with my life than I could ever ask or imagine. Use me as You will!

The Least of These

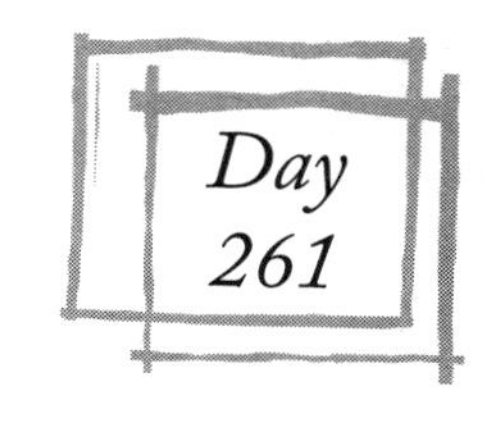

The king will answer, "Whenever you did it for any of my people, no matter how unimportant they seemed, you did it for me."
Matthew 25:40 CEV

Some people act as if children are something to be tolerated, not cultivated. They are signed up for this, dropped off for that, and somehow, in the course of all of the activity, they are supposed to learn and grow into adults with a sense of thoughtful purpose. Do we think they'll teach themselves?

Jesus understood the potential of each child. He knew that their little hearts and minds were hungry for knowledge and truth. He knew that by granting them a play in the game of life, He was investing in the future of the Kingdom of God.

We may never know the full scope of our impact on our own kids, but we are definitely part of God's plan for the development of their young lives. As a mother, you are a teacher, a leader, a confidant, a model, and a source of great love. You have the potential to bless a child's life forever.

And according to the Lord Himself, whatever you do for a child, you do for Him.

Jesus, use me to shape the lives of my children for Your glory. Help me to see these kids as a gift from You—never as a hindrance to my adult pursuits. Please grant me Your wisdom and love.

Voice of the Shepherd

"My sheep listen to my voice;
I know them, and they follow me."
John 10:27 niv

Next time you're around a group of children, watch for this fascinating phenomenon: At Sunday school or the day-care center, even with upwards of thirty kids playing, crying, or quietly looking at books, a child will hear her own mother's voice as soon as she enters the room. As soon as Mom acknowledges the teacher or helper, her child, instantly honing in on her voice, will look up to see her face. None of the other kids stop playing because she's not their mom—her voice doesn't catch their attention. Only a mother's child hears that one special voice above the ruckus.

It should be the same way for us as God's children. We may be engrossed in our day, running after children, throwing supper together, nursing a cold—but when our Lord speaks, we should hear Him because we as His children know His voice.

God's voice is distinct—and when we become part of His family, we learn to recognize it. The more we tune in to that distinct voice, the more we'll hear it.

Let's be like the child, eager to hear a parent's loving voice.

Lord, I know I am Your child—yet often I find it difficult to hear Your voice over the noise of my life. Please give me ears to hear Your still, small voice, and the strength and faith to obey what You say to me.

A New Name

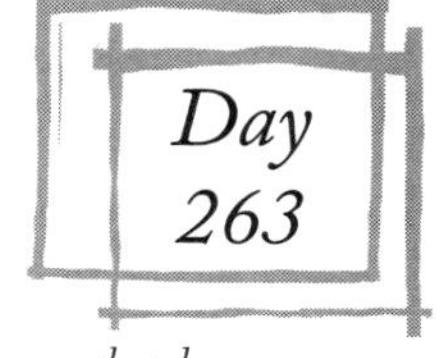

"To everyone who is victorious I will give some of the manna that has been hidden away in heaven. And I will give to each one a white stone, and on the stone will be engraved a new name that no one understands except the one who receives it."
Revelation 2:17 NLT

As a teenager, Darlene didn't like her name. It reminded her of the teenagers portrayed on *The Mickey Mouse Club*. That wasn't her! So she experimented with other names. Around other Darlenes, she used her middle name. She wrote stories under the pen name Heather.

Later, Darlene learned that the sound of her name reflected its meaning: darling or beloved. Not only that, she discovered that her parents had chosen her middle name, Hope, from 1 Corinthians 13:13. Every time they spoke her name, they were saying, "We love you. We have hope for your future." Darlene felt like she had received a brand-new name.

God will give each of His children a new name, reflecting something unique and special in our lives. When Abram, which means "exalted father," was ninety-nine, God changed his name to *Abraham*, meaning "father of many." When Jacob, which means "deceiver," wrestled with God, the Lord changed his name to *Israel*, "he struggles with God." God looks into our inmost being and gives us a name that carries the essence of our new creation in Christ.

What might your new name be?

Dear Lord, I look forward to the day when I will receive my new name, one that reflects the very essence of whom I am in You.

Light in the Darkness

When I fall, I shall arise; when I sit in darkness, the Lord shall be a light unto me.
Micah 7:8 KJV

Being a single parent comes with built-in disadvantages, one of which is not having a ready source for advice.

Often, we just don't know what to do. We need someone to come alongside us and offer a little counsel. But that's a need we seldom advertise. After all, who wants to admit that they don't have it all together?

But we must.

So who do we run to? Who can give us a helpful perspective on our finances or advice on how to handle a school principal? Where do we turn for wisdom on dating issues or learning to live without a mate?

Our first resource should be God Himself. When we present our needs and frustrations to our Father, He'll be a light to us. He doesn't just *provide* light—He *is* our Light. He may use the widowed woman in the back church pew to offer us wise counsel, or perhaps a friend who "just happened" to stop by for coffee. He will always use His perfect Word to be a Light to us.

Though we may sometimes sit in darkness, we always have access to the Light.

Heavenly Father, many times I feel like I can't see where to take my next step. Be my Light, please, and guide my steps.

Hunks of Rust

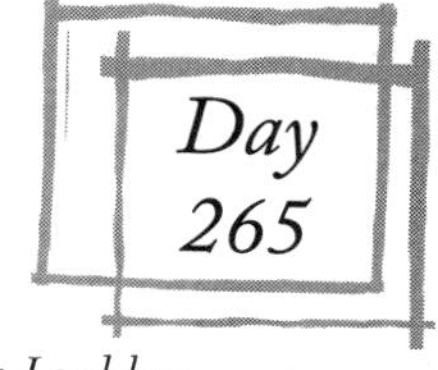

Then Deborah said to Barak, "Go! This is the day the Lord has given Sisera into your hands. Has not the Lord *gone ahead of you?"*
Judges 4:14 NIV

Sisera, a powerful warrior, led a coalition of Canaanite rulers. For twenty years, he had cruelly oppressed the Israelites. He had a fleet of nine hundred iron-plated chariots, chariots that caused dread among the Israelites. What ill-armed, ragged tribe of former slaves could withstand that kind of power? Small wonder no one challenged him.

The Lord told the prophet Deborah it was time for Israel to confront Sisera. General Barak was tapped to lead the charge—but he refused! He insisted that Deborah come with him. So she did—and in a brilliant stroke, God sent rain! Lots and lots of rain. Sisera's greatest strength—iron chariots—became a liability. Oozing mud gripped the chariots like sticky glue.

Barak and the Israelites saw those iron chariots as intimidating, insurmountable obstacles. Deborah saw them as trivial details. She knew that God was sovereign over all things, including the weather! Those iron chariots turned into big hunks of rust.

How do we look at dire circumstances? Do we see only the obstacles? Hopefully, we have the faith to believe that God can turn any situation into a victory. After all, as Deborah reminded Barak, has not the Lord gone ahead of us?

Lord, the very things we fear the most are nothing to You! You are sovereign over everything—material objects, spiritual battles, emotional crises, even the weather. Thank You for going ahead of me and leading me to victory.

TALKING TO GOD

One of his disciples said to him, "LORD, teach us to pray, just as John taught his disciples." He said to them, "When you pray, say: 'Father, hallowed be your name, your kingdom come. Give us each day our daily bread.' "
LUKE 11:1–3 NIV

Ruth was a Christian, but she struggled in her prayer life. How could she be worthy of speaking to the supreme Creator of the universe? He already knew everything in her mind.

Lord, she thought, *I don't know what to say. How can I possibly pray to You? Do You even hear my insignificant requests?*

Yes, God hears—and, although He knows what we need before we even ask Him, He *wants* us to pray. He even gave us instruction on how to pray. Our prayers don't have to be long or eloquent or even particularly organized. When Jesus taught His disciples to pray, the sample wasn't wordy. He simply taught the disciples to give God glory and to come to Him and ask for their daily needs.

But Luke 11 teaches us something beyond just an outline for prayer. The story shows clearly that if we ask God to teach us how to pray, He will. It's all part of the prayer—ask God to lead you, then speak to Him from the heart.

Let's make it a habit to pray every day. Like we tell our kids, practice makes perfect.

Dear God, teach me how to pray. Remind me that my words don't have to be profound. You're just looking for earnest thoughts from the heart.

Starry Skies

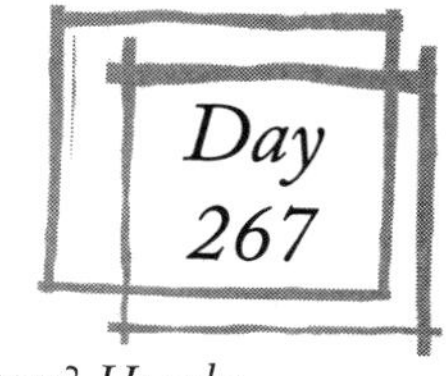

Lift your eyes and look to the heavens: Who created all these? He who brings out the starry host one by one, and calls them each by name. Because of his great power and mighty strength, not one of them is missing.
Isaiah 40:26 niv

The first night of summer vacation found Hanna and Becky enjoying the multitude of stars in the wide sky. The girls giggled while reminiscing over their middle school years, now completed. Thoughts of their upcoming high school years were enhanced by the awesome display above them.

Everyone should spend some time stargazing. When we slow the frantic pace of our minds and look to the heavens, we begin to sense the unmatchable power, the sustaining strength, and the intimate love of God. As we gaze with admiration at the stars, we can drink in the very essence of our heavenly Creator.

It was God who hung every star in place. It's God who knows each star by name. Nothing in the farthest reaches of the universe goes unnoticed by God, because He's a God of order and intimacy.

If God cares that deeply about His starry creation, how much greater is His love for us, His cherished daughters?

Father, You are the Creator of all. I thank You that I can take in the awesome vastness of the universe and rest in peace—knowing that You are not only the master Creator, but that You hold me in the palm of Your hand, caring about every detail of my life.

No Vandalism

You realize, don't you, that you are the temple of God, and God himself is present in you? No one will get by with vandalizing God's temple, you can be sure of that. God's temple is sacred—and you, remember, are the temple.
1 Corinthians 3:16–17 MSG

Church buildings—from giant stone cathedrals to quaint country chapels—pepper the landscape of North America. Wouldn't you be appalled to see any of these beautiful buildings vandalized?

The Bible says we as believers are a type of church building—but even more than that, we're the actual temple of God on this earth. It's amazing when you really think about it: God actually resides in *us*. Our bodies aren't just a temporary dwelling for our spirits—they are the actual home of the God of the universe. So wouldn't "vandalism" of God's temple—our bodies—be even sadder than that done to church buildings?

But how do we "vandalize" God's temple? Maybe by eating that second piece of pie. . .or drinking soda instead of water all day. . . or ignoring physical exercise. (Who really uses a gym membership, anyway?)

Sure, as single moms, it's hard to exercise. Sometimes it's easier to grab fast food than to cook. It's tempting to fill our lonely times with sweets. But our bodies are holy and sacred. Don't vandalize God's temple!

Father, I thank You for dwelling in me, and I commit to take care of my body as Your temple. I will treat it with respect, in honor of You.

Home-Based Business

If any of you lacks wisdom, let him ask of God, who gives to all liberally and without reproach, and it will be given to him.
James 1:5 NKJV

As home-based businesses become increasingly popular, researchers have listed steps necessary to be successful in such endeavors. The top five recommendations: Plan ahead, put money aside, organize your time, organize your space, and stay focused.

We as Christian parents are running our own home-based businesses—the business of Jesus. To be good managers in our homes, we need to plan ahead. Only with careful planning can we set aside time for study, prayer, and teaching. We must be good stewards of our finances so we can serve God with our resources as needs arise.

With proper time management, we will be available to serve our family inside the home and the body of Christ outside. May we always stay focused on our reason (Jesus) and our goal (leading others to Him).

Though serving God is much more than a business, looking at our choices practically can help to bring order to our chaos—and bring success to our spiritual lives.

Father, help me order my priorities and focus my energy with the singular purpose of letting Your light shine through me. Help me to be a good steward of all that You have put in my charge.

Sudden Disasters

We take captive every thought
to make it obedient to Christ.
2 Corinthians 10:5 NIV

Sandra hadn't heard from her son, a freshman in college, for two weeks. Her thoughts raced with worry. *Maybe he's sick, or he's been injured. Maybe he doesn't have his wallet with him and is languishing in a hospital bed, listed as John Doe. What if he's flunking out of college and doesn't want to tell me?*

Moms are very good at worrying. Most of us can go from zero to sixty in under four seconds with catastrophic thinking, especially if we're worried about our kids.

What does scripture tell us about those what-if worries? In his second letter to the Corinthians, Paul reminds us to take every thought captive to make it obedient to Christ. Every thought! We need to hold our thoughts up against the standard of God's Word, just like holding a letter up against a sunny window, to read it clearly. Scripture tells us to "have no fear of sudden disaster or of the ruin that overtakes the wicked, for the Lord will be your confidence and will keep your foot from being snared" (Proverbs 3:25–26 NIV).

What? No fear of sudden disaster? No fear, God says. Even when we wake in the night with a troubling thought? No fear. Even the first time our child drives off with a brand-new driver's license in his wallet? Even then. No fear, for the Lord is our confidence as we capture each thought.

Lord God, take my thoughts—every thought—
and renew them with Your Word.

Restoration

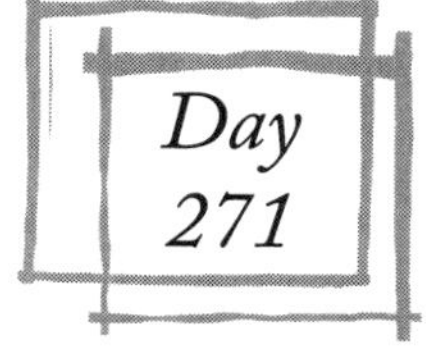

He maketh me to lie down in green pastures:
he leadeth me beside the still waters. He restoreth my soul.
Psalm 23:2–3 KJV

Dumb, helpless, straying sheep. The fluffy creatures don't know any better than to wander away from the herd and get tangled in underbrush. The animals need a shepherd who acts in their best interest and protects them from harm.

That's us—sheep. We wander away from the fold and get caught in the underbrush of the world. We leave the flock and become tired, hungry, and thirsty. Our wandering ways leave us sick in mind, spirit, and body.

We need the Good Shepherd—Jesus. He searches for us when we go astray. He pulls us out of the pits we've fallen into. He removes the thorns from our hides. During the heat of tribulation, He places us in His shadow where we can rest. He slakes our thirst with His living water, the Holy Spirit. He restores our souls. We know His voice and follow Him.

God watches over us day and night, no matter where we are. He tends our wounds, guards us, and builds us back up for the challenges of life. When we are lost, we need only listen for the voice of our Shepherd.

Lord, my Shepherd, I shall not want. Teach me to lie still in Your green pastures and drink of Your quiet waters. Please restore my soul.

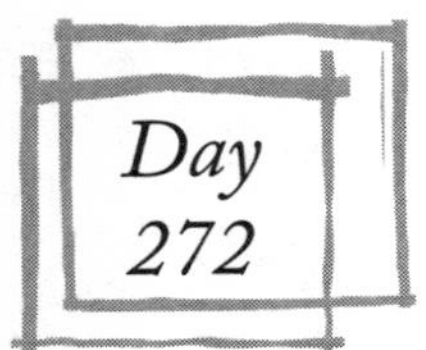

One True Friend

As iron sharpens iron, so one man sharpens another. He who tends a fig tree will eat its fruit, and he who looks after his master will be honored. As water reflects a face, so a man's heart reflects the man.
Proverbs 27:17–19 NIV

Have you found it tough, as a single mom, to have true, genuine friendships?

Many of us lack the time to build such relationships. Sometimes, others shy away from us, perhaps fearing we're "too needy." Maybe we've been hurt so often, we've built walls between ourselves and others.

Whatever the case may be, it's imperative for single moms to form deep, connected friendships. As iron sharpens iron, one steadfast friend sharpens another.

True friends promote the Word of God rather than vengeful thoughts. Honest friends work to remove—not nurture—roots of bitterness. Real friends walk life's path with us, whether that's along a quiet stream of joy and contentment or on a jungle trail full of thorns and thistles.

We all need friends who sharpen us gently so our hearts reflect our Lord rather than our circumstances. Look for that kind of friend. Be that kind of friend.

Lord, You know all things. You're aware that I need friends who are honest and trustworthy. I ask You to supply a wise and honest friend with whom I can share my life, someone who will always point me toward You.

DOING LUNCH WITH JESUS

There is a lad here, which hath five barley loaves,
and two small fishes: but what are they among so many?
JOHN 6:9 KJV

The boy ducked his mother's good-bye kiss, grabbed his lunch, and raced along the Sea of Galilee. He joined the large crowd listening to Jesus. The boy could hardly bear to look at beggars covered with sores, blind people groping their way, and paralytics on pallets.

Jesus will help you feel lots better, he promised them silently.

The boy perched where he could watch Jesus heal people, one after the other. He forgot about lunch as the Teacher told lots of stories. Late in the day, he opened his knapsack. But the Teacher's face stopped him. Jesus looked tired. Probably hungry, too. Though his stomach growled at the fragrance of his mother's bread, the boy took his lunch to Jesus.

"Are you sure you want to give your food?" a disciple named Andrew asked.

He nodded.

The boy never forgot Jesus' smile. For once, he did not care if he ever ate again. He watched Jesus pray, break his bread and fish, and feed thousands. Jesus handed the boy special tidbits. He felt stuffed, as if he'd eaten a holiday feast.

A mother might have prevented her son from rashly giving away his meal. But then, he would not have become part of a miracle!

Lord Jesus, sometimes when my children want to take risks for You,
I try to shield them from sacrifice. Instead, help me encourage them.

This, Too, Shall Pass

Weeping may endure for a night,
but joy comes in the morning.
Psalm 30:5 amp

There may be night feedings that destroy your sleep. Terrible twos that seem never ending. No money for dinner and a movie. Trouble paying the electric bill. Rebellious teens. Disagreements with the other parent. Loneliness, discouragement, physical aches and pains. Being a single mom can be downright tough.

But you know what? Every season has one thing in common—each has a beginning and an end. As with the calendar seasons of spring, summer, autumn, and winter, these "seasons" of your life will pass, too. By God's great design, no season lasts forever. No trial goes on endlessly.

The psalmist eloquently reminds us, "Weeping may endure for a night, but joy comes in the morning." He's not saying that if we can just hang on until sunrise, life will come up roses. The psalm writer is revealing that, though we may go through tear-filled night seasons, we can look forward with joy to the certainty of a new day. A new season of life. This, too, shall pass.

Heavenly Father, I often feel as if my night season will never end.
Thank You for the hope of a new beginning—a new season of life.
I thank You that no trial lasts forever.

A Teary Prophet

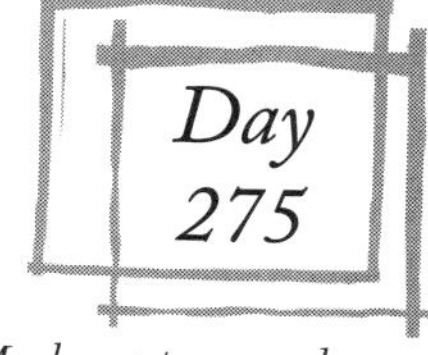

My eyes are worn out from weeping; I am churning within. My heart is poured out in grief because of the destruction of my dear people, because children and infants faint in the streets of the city. They cry out to their mothers: Where is the grain and wine? as they faint like the wounded in the streets of the city, as their lives fade away in the arms of their mothers.

LAMENTATIONS 2:11–12 HSCB

Jeremiah was known as the prophet with the broken heart. He had a mother's heart—tender and compassionate—for Judah. He was a man in tears most of the time. He saw the destruction of Jerusalem and the Babylonian captivity.

When Jeremiah focused on the terrors around him, he felt overwhelmed, even personally assaulted by God: "He pierced my heart with arrows from his quiver" (Lamentations 3:13 NIV). Only when he focused on God's past mercies did he find strength and encouragement: "Yet this I call to mind and therefore I have hope: Because of the Lord's great love we are not consumed, for his compassions never fail" (Lamentations 3:21–22 NIV).

Every day we face crises small and large. Sadly, we often focus on the problem from *our* point of view, which is, of course, rather limited. Incomplete. Earthbound. Missing the big picture.

Jeremiah's perspective changed from despair to hope by remembering God's faithfulness. What a good reminder! We do not face any crisis, big or small, without God's loving presence.

Faithful God, when I feel under siege, turn my eyes toward heaven. Help me remember Your past mercies.

He Already Knows

Let us then approach the throne of grace with confidence, so that we may receive mercy and find grace to help us in our time of need.
Hebrews 4:16 NIV

Isn't it hard to ask for help?

Whether we're in financial trouble, in need a babysitter, or just feeling extra lonely, we don't like to seek help or let others know we have needs. It's not cool to be "needy," you know.

Modern society has created a lens through which the "typical single mom" appears at a disadvantage. So we struggle to try to do it all, be it all, accomplish it all, hiding our weariness behind the pillar of strength we pretend to be.

As Christians, though, we need not appear as anyone besides who we are. God's lens sees through our masks, straight to our hearts. And He's told us we can hold our heads up, approaching His throne of provision and promise with great confidence. We have His assurance that He'll hear us and bathe us in torrents of mercy. He'll give us His grace to get us through our times of need.

God sees us as we are, He knows our needs intimately, and He's well aware of our hopes and fears. Never be afraid to ask Him for help.

Abba Father, I thank You for looking at me through Your lens of love and acceptance, seeing me for who I am and for loving me completely. You know my needs and my heart, my hopes and my fears. Please answer all my pleas as I come to You for help.

A Mother's Voice

My son, keep your father's command, and don't reject your mother's teaching. When you walk here and there, they will guide you; when you lie down, they will watch over you; when you wake up, they will talk to you.
PROVERBS 6:20, 22 HCSB

We carry miniature tape recorders in our brains. At unexpected intervals, they replay bits of instruction we've heard over the years: "Look both ways before you cross the street". . ."Clean your plate". . ."Good girls don't do that." Helpful or harmful, necessary or unimportant, our parents' admonitions stay with us. They are our first and most influential teachers.

Now, we are the teachers—and even our passing comments record messages that will replay in our children's minds throughout their lives. We want our words to guide and nurture our loved ones, not cause them pain. But human nature is such that one negative message can override a dozen positive ones.

We do well to think about what messages we want to pass on to our children. Like it or not, we feed their minds whenever and wherever we're together. How can we lead them on the path they should go? We can tell them, over and over again, "You are wonderfully made. God loves you. Love God with all your heart, soul, mind, and body. And love your neighbor as yourself."

May the words of our mouths always bless our children.

Lord, please put Your words into my mouth.
Let me teach my children with Your gentle, loving discipline.

A Pinch of Salt

Let your speech be always with grace, seasoned with salt, that ye may know how ye ought to answer every man.
Colossians 4:6 KJV

Recipes are detailed and specific, down to the tiniest eighth of a teaspoon. When even that measurement is too large, the recipe might call for a "pinch" or "dash" of a certain seasoning. It hardly seems possible that such a small amount of anything could affect the end result. But it does.

God has given us a recipe for Christian living. We are to be rich in grace, always ready to show love and mercy to others. But we are also to be "seasoned with salt." That's how we effect change in those around us. Without that seasoning, our silence around sin and bad behavior would be a subtle approval of things that grieve the heart of God.

For parents, that means we must sometimes lay aside our desire to be our child's "friend." We'll occasionally need to season our speech with enough salt to convey the truth of God's expectations.

But always remember: Grace is a vital part of making the saltiness palatable. Without God's grace, the salt would be unsavory. Together, grace and salt create a perfect dish that reveals the heart of God.

Lord, please help me to balance my speech with the proper amount of grace and salt. Let my words and my life as a whole be pleasing and effective in the lives of my children and others around me.

Repairing Anthills

Remember my words with your whole being. . . . Teach them well to your children, talking about them when you sit at home and walk along the road, when you lie down and when you get up.
Deuteronomy 11:18–19 NCV

A famous pastor once told the story of a summertime walk he took with his young daughter. The little girl accidentally stepped on an anthill growing up through a crack in the sidewalk. "Oh, Daddy! Look what I've done!" she said sadly. "I destroyed their home."

The father bent down to survey the damage and remarked, "I'm afraid you're right, honey. Their home is ruined."

"If only I could fix it for them—or at least explain it was an accident," she replied.

"The only way to do that," answered her father, "would be to become an ant yourself."

Sensing a spiritual application, the father looked into the girl's eyes and explained, "Honey, people are just like those ants. We have a problem that needs fixed. God knew that only He could fix it. So He became one of us by being born as a Man. His name is Jesus."

The girl smiled as the profound truth dawned on her.

As single mothers, we, too, need to take advantage of such teachable moments.

Father, please let me see the opportunities
You've given me to teach my children Your ways.

Again!

Let the word of Christ dwell in you richly as you teach and admonish one another with all wisdom, and as you sing psalms, hymns and spiritual songs with gratitude in your hearts to God.
Colossians 3:16 NIV

A missionary couple in Africa raised their children with the habit of learning scripture around the breakfast table. The dad would teach the kids a Bible verse, then have them repeat it. "Again!" the dad would shout out, and the children would repeat the verse.

"Now, Tom, you say it!" And then, "Okay, all together now." The dad passed away at an early age, but whenever those kids (now adults) read those verses, they close their eyes and can still hear their father's voice.

That is the very essence of embracing the Word of God deep in our hearts. We learn to recognize and hear our Father's voice.

Loving God's Word—through study, memorization, and reflecting attentively on it as we pray—brings an added layer of depth to our relationship with God. It helps us move closer to the vibrant, effective prayer life of Christ. The prayer life we were always meant to have.

Lord of language, Your Word is a ready-made prayer book. I want to be a better example to my kids of a mom who loves the Bible. Help me make Your Word a sincere expression of my heart.

Million-Dollar Smile

A happy heart makes the face cheerful,
but heartache crushes the spirit.
Proverbs 15:13 NIV

Ever seen a million-dollar smile? You know the one. It shines like the sun—and it's contagious. The million-dollar smile makes everyone else light up, too.

Maybe the face encircling that smile is yours. Or maybe it's not. A million-dollar smile can't spread itself across a face weighed down by a broken heart or a wounded spirit. It can't be faked. You have to have happiness bubbling up from your heart in order to exhibit such a cheerful, honest smile. Where do you find that kind of happiness?

Only God can offer us joy—the true, long-lasting, nobody-can-take-it-away kind of joy that comes from knowing and trusting Him. We may carry a heavy load—but Jesus Christ wants to fill our hearts with joy so our faces shine like the morning sun.

Happy hearts are vital for us as single moms. May our faces reflect the love of Christ in million-dollar smiles that spread like wildfire to the faces of our children.

Jesus, I want my cheerful face to speak of Your goodness. Though I've been hurt and I carry heavy burdens, I ask You to release my heartache. Please cause my face to be an expression of Your joy.

Trust in Him

"The person who trusts me will not only do what I'm doing but even greater things, because I, on my way to the Father, am giving you the same work to do that I've been doing."
John 14:12 MSG

Men had not been good to Jessica. She didn't know her biological father. She had bad luck in dating; then her marriage ended in divorce. Now, she was a single mother with a young daughter to care for. The prospect of trusting anyone was truly daunting.

When Jessica began attending church with a friend, she heard about Jesus—and the importance of trusting in Him. *But how can I trust in God,* she wondered, *if I can't trust anyone else?*

People often fail us. But the good news is that God will never let us down. No matter how many times people disappointment us, God won't. He's always there, always faithful, always looking out for our best interests. He has proven His trustworthiness over and over throughout history. He even gave His only Son so that we could enjoy eternal life.

That Son, Jesus, is our friend and advocate. We can always trust Him—He'll never disappoint us. Give Him a try.

Lord, I have experienced many disappointments in this life. Help me to trust in You and know that You will never let me down.

Christmas List

*Every good gift and every perfect gift is from above,
and comes down from the Father of lights.*
James 1:17 NKJV

Many children eagerly wait for holiday toy catalogs to arrive. They may sit with copies spread across their laps, carefully marking the items they wish to receive for Christmas.

Parents generally take those lists and catalog markings very seriously. They *want* to give their children the things their little hearts most desire, especially at Christmastime, when a little indulgence is welcomed. They don't scowl at their children, telling them to stop being greedy. Instead, they delight in the expectation and joy they see on their children's faces.

When we pray, it's as though *we* are making a Christmas list. But it's not just one time a year that our Father is prepared to fulfill our needs and wants. He enjoys every opportunity to pour out His richest blessings on us, His children.

Our heavenly Father wants us to approach Him with expectation, knowing that every good and perfect gift comes from Him.

*Heavenly Father, I thank You for Your rich blessings and treasured gifts.
Thank You for hearing my prayers and eagerly providing for me.*

Following Rules

"Do not handle! Do not taste! Do not touch!"? These are all destined to perish with use. . . . They lack any value in restraining sensual indulgence.
Colossians 2:21–23 NIV

We all give our children guidelines. Some safeguard them from danger: "Don't play with matches." "Don't eat raw eggs." "Don't drink or do drugs."

Some address responsibility: "Do your homework." "Finish your chores." "Write a thank-you letter."

The problem is that rules alone don't teach our children how to make safe, moral decisions. As Paul comments, "They lack any value in restraining sensual indulgence."

Rules may have "an appearance of wisdom" (Colossians 2:23 NIV), but they don't automatically train our children to make wise choices. We hope our children never commit murder, but they need to understand that even angry feelings can lead to thoughts of revenge and acts of physical harm toward others. We want our kids to avoid illegal drugs, but also to handle household chemicals properly. We want our rules to translate into attitudes.

How can we aid that transformation process? It starts with modeling those attitudes ourselves. We can explain the reasons—biblical, societal, scientific—behind the laws. And, within reason, we can allow our children to experience the consequences of *not* following the rules.

Ultimately, we want to prepare our children to make good choices by having the right attitude.

Lord, You gave us rules to train us in righteousness.
Help us to do the same for our children.

EARNEST ELIJAH

Elijah was a man just like us. He prayed earnestly that it would not rain, and it did not rain on the land for three and a half years. Again he prayed, and the heavens gave rain, and the earth produced its crops.
JAMES 5:17–18 NIV

The prophet Elijah was as human as the next guy, James wrote. The prophet suddenly appeared on the political scene for a showdown with the wicked King Ahab. We don't have much background on Elijah other than that he was a Tishbite from a no-name town. Since he had been given a Hebrew name by his parents, he probably had a godly upbringing. We also know that Elijah was a man of prayer.

James wrote that Elijah prayed earnestly. The dictionary defines *earnest* as intense and serious of mind, not flippant, not trivial. Praying for a drought to ravage the land of Israel was not a casual suggestion Elijah tossed to the heavens now and then. A drought would have serious repercussions, even on him. He took that prayer request seriously. And God took Elijah seriously.

Are we earnest in our prayers for our children? Or do we ramble and whine and sometimes give up altogether? Prayer is the most effective, transforming resource God has given to mothers. It doesn't have to be beautiful or poetic; He'll take our groans! The words don't matter. Our hearts do.

God takes prayer seriously. Earnest prayer is His great delight.

Lord, I want to pray like Elijah, bringing a deeply felt desire to see You act. Lord, You are listening! Hear my prayers.

Almighty Whisper

A hurricane wind ripped through the mountains and shattered the rocks before God, but God wasn't to be found in the wind; after the wind an earthquake, but God wasn't in the earthquake; and after the earthquake fire, but God wasn't in the fire; and after the fire a gentle and quiet whisper.
1 Kings 19:11–12 msg

Have we ever become slaves to inaction because we were waiting for the wrong thing?

As parents, we might want God to force us to move with shouted directions. Wouldn't it be so much easier and clearer if He wrote our next move across the sky, then mightily and unmistakably imposed His will on us?

But God doesn't work that way. He speaks to us gently, through our spirit, while He waits patiently for us to listen and obey His gentle prodding. He never forces us to act because He desires that our actions grow out of our own desire to please Him.

Elijah searched for God in the hurricane winds, the earthquake, and the fire. He expected a mighty God to use all the forces of the universe to announce His presence. In reality though, God was found in none of those things. When the chaos abated, His presence could be realized—and His voice heard as a quiet, gentle whisper.

Almighty Father, help me to hear Your whisper amid the chaos of life. Guide me with Your still, small voice. Thank You for patiently leading me through life.

Powerful One

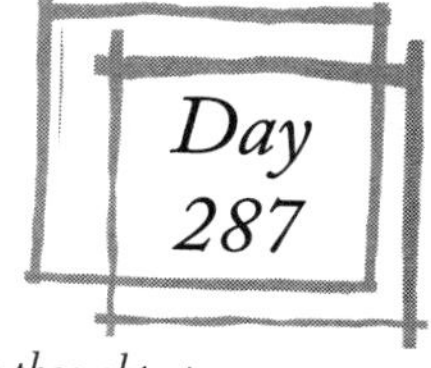

He who forms the mountains, creates the wind, and reveals his thoughts to man, he who turns dawn to darkness, and treads the high places of the earth— the LORD God Almighty is his name.
AMOS 4:13 NIV

Ever pondered the power of our Lord God Almighty? Meditating on God's power can soothe our biggest worries and calm our deepest fears.

The Word of God speaks often of His power—we know He created our universe in less than a week. But if that's too much to comprehend, consider the enormity of a single mountain or ocean. Those vast, mighty things came into being simply by God's voice—and they're only a tiny fraction of everything He made. What power!

The Lord opens the morning curtains to reveal the dawn and pulls the sky shades back at night to bring darkness. He plots the course of the wind, arranges for rainfall, and causes grass, crops, and trees to grow. He feeds the gigantic whales of the ocean, and every tiny little bird. If our Lord has enough knowledge and power to handle these jobs, surely He can (and will!) look after us.

Problems that seem insurmountable to us are simply a breath to Him. Let's not be anxious today—God holds each one of us in the palm of His hand.

Lord God, You are my provider. Thank You for holding such power—and for choosing me to be Your child. Please give me a greater understanding of who You are, helping me to remember that You, the Lord God Almighty, love me.

Unloved

She conceived again, and bare a son: and she said,
Now will I praise the Lord: therefore she called his name Judah.
Genesis 29:35 KJV

Leah, through no fault of her own, found herself in a loveless marriage. Jacob had contracted for her pretty sister, Rachel. But their father, Laban, conned Jacob into marrying Leah as well, plus working seven additional years on his farm. Laban's friends toasted him as a shrewd businessman.

But Leah paid for her father's schemes. Never attentive, Jacob grew more indifferent every year. Still, God blessed Leah with beautiful babies, and she gave them names that reflected her faith in Him despite her pain. She delivered Reuben, which means, "He has seen my misery," and Simeon, which means, "one who hears." Leah named her third son Levi, "attached," hoping for a true bond between her and her husband. But Jacob forever identified Leah with her father's scam. He didn't like losing—and he didn't like Leah. After their fourth son's birth, Leah said, "This time I will praise the Lord," and named him Judah, which means "praise." Although she continued to struggle, Leah did not lose sight of God's love.

She had no idea God planned a special blessing for her: the Messiah, the glorious hope of all mankind, would descend from Leah, the unloved.

Jesus, I want so much to be loved here and now. But until You lead that person to me, help me to cling to You and know Your loving plans are bigger and better than I can ever imagine.

Honorable Heritage

Lord, you are my strength and fortress, my refuge in the day of trouble! Nations from around the world will come to you and say, "Our ancestors left us a foolish heritage, for they worshiped worthless idols."
Jeremiah 16:19 NLT

What Web site was that, Mom? You know, the one where you always used to get Bible verses?"

The teenage girl's mother choked back tears as she watched her daughter type a message of encouragement to a friend. "Does this sound okay?" the girl asked.

"It's great, honey," the mom responded. "I know Erin will appreciate your taking the time to look up verses to share with her."

Seeing her own daughter carry on a legacy of encouraging others through God's Word caused this mother's heart to melt. *What a privilege,* she thought, *to give my child the heritage of serving God in this way. Thank You, Father.*

How often had this daughter seen her mother sharing God's Word to encourage others? Once a week at church? Only when others were watching, or when she could gain some benefit? Of course not. This type of legacy—this honorable heritage—develops by daily displays of parental authenticity.

What a joy it is to pass an honorable heritage on to our children.

Father God, enable me to pass on a lasting and honorable heritage, one that points to You rather than money or fame.

An Eye for a. . . Tooth?

But if there is serious injury, you are to take life for life, eye for eye, tooth for tooth, hand for hand, foot for foot, burn for burn, wound for wound, bruise for bruise.
Exodus 21:23–25 NIV

God gave the law of retaliation to Israel to ensure that punishments fit their crimes. Using clear, spelled-out deterrents, it was intended to preserve the sanctity of human life.

This law was also designed to stop the human tendency to extract revenge. Bitterness has an insatiable appetite—nothing really satisfies it. It's been said that bitterness is a pill we swallow, hoping someone else will die. The truth is, we don't just want someone to pay for his offense to us. We want him to pay and pay and pay. We want an eye for a tooth. We want justice! Not mercy.

Jesus amended the law of retaliation by invoking over it the law of love. "You have heard that it was said, 'Eye for eye, and tooth for tooth.' But I tell you, do not resist an evil person. If someone strikes you on the right cheek, turn to him the other also" (Matthew 5:38–39 NIV).

Forgiveness can be so hard. Only God can give us the desire to forgive. Only God can do the impossible in us.

Father, I need Your ongoing help in this process of forgiveness. Prompt me to pray a blessing on those who've hurt me. Make a miracle out of my heart.

FATHER FIGURES

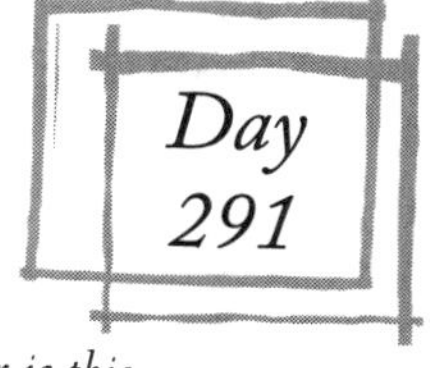

Pure religion and undefiled before God and the Father is this,
To visit the fatherless and widows in their affliction.
JAMES 1:27 KJV

No matter how much we might want to, we as single mothers can't serve as fathers to our children. Some kids are blessed with fathers who remain involved even after a divorce. But many grow up with little or no contact with their physical fathers, due to divorce, death, or other reasons. So we have to look elsewhere for father figures for our children.

Heather had barely thought about the issue when God began to bring father figures into the lives of her children. Men in her divorce recovery group spent time with all the kids during holiday events. Then God brought her adolescent son into contact with an elderly carpenter volunteering for Habitat for Humanity. For her daughter, God provided a pastor who led the girl to the Lord, then discipled her.

As mothers, we should allow such relationships to develop. If it's possible and healthy, we can encourage a continuing relationship with the children's fathers. But if that isn't realistic, we can share our needs with a church family. Let's stop trying to be all things to our families—and free our kids to enjoy the time they spend with godly men.

God commanded His people to visit the fatherless—and He'll bring the right men into our children's lives.

Father, I ask You to bring godly men into the lives of my fatherless children.
I trust Your provision.

He Never Leaves

I will always be with you and help you. . . .
So be strong and brave!
Joshua 1:5–6 CEV

Joshua faced a difficult task. He was to take over for Moses, the man who had led the children of Israel out of their bondage in Egypt.

For years, Moses had been preparing Joshua, teaching him to seek the face of God. Joshua had walked by Moses' side and been through each battle with him. He had been led by the cloud by day and the fire by night. He had walked on dry land through the Red Sea.

Yet with all the training and preparation, God knew Joshua still needed reassurance. So God told him—more than once—"I will be there to help you wherever you go" (Joshua 1:9 CEV).

God tells us the same thing. No matter what we face or where we go, He is with us. He will help us through it all.

Not only has He assured us of His help, He has commanded us to "be strong and brave." So release your fears to Him, and rest in the peace of knowing He is present. There is no need to be afraid or discouraged.

Lord, You are my God and I trust You. Thank You for never leaving me. I draw strength and courage knowing that You are always with me.

Wandering in the Wilderness

Remember every road that God led you on for those forty years in the wilderness, pushing you to your limits, testing you so that he would know what you were made of, whether you would keep his commandments or not.
DEUTERONOMY 8:2 MSG

"I can't *take* any more!" Jamie threw the rancid fried chicken, which cost her last five dollars, as far as she could—then burst into tears. Jamie almost hoped someone would report the crazy lady throwing fast food in the park. Maybe the police would take her away. She'd never have to worry about anyone or anything again.

Like the Israelites in the desert, Jamie seemed to wander aimlessly through a miserable existence. She loved God and tried to put Him first. But she was sick of dealing with her son Will's problems with no help—only interference—from her ex and his cute little girlfriend. Her car invented a new noise daily. Her computer crashed at work. The day before, Jamie had spent hours calling her runaway cat—only to find Yoda purring on Will's lap when she returned.

Now she threw the last greasy french fries, screaming, "Why *me*, Lord?"

Years later, Jamie remembered that miserable day and laughed, giving thanks that God hadn't given her an easier road. The experience she gained helped her manage her new life. Jamie not only survived, but thrived. She even learned to like fried chicken again.

Father, when I feel I am running in a meaningless maze, help me to realize that You guide my steps and make me strong.

FIND JOY IN GOD

Anything I saw and wanted, I got for myself; I did not miss any pleasure I desired. . . . Suddenly I realized it was useless, like chasing the wind. There is nothing to gain from anything we do here on earth.
ECCLESIASTES 2:10–11 NCV

We're all tempted to seek happiness in this world—in materia possessions and worldly pursuits. But those things are all worthles when it comes to true joy.

There's a story in God's Word about a man who experienced al the pleasures of earth, only to realize they weren't worth a thing. Man believe the Book of Ecclesiastes was written by King Solomon, wh tried to grab all of this world's pleasure—but gained nothing. We ca learn from that example.

God has given us many blessings. Our children, for one thing, ar a gift from Him, daily reminders of the miracle of life that He allow us to enjoy. Looking into the eyes of our kids, we can remember jus how much our Father in heaven loves us—and how we can experienc true happiness through Him.

Forget what the world counts as pleasure. True joy is found onl in our relationship with God.

Father, help me to find pleasure and happiness in life through You. Remind me that though the temptations of this world are great, they are ultimately meaningless.

Welcome Back!

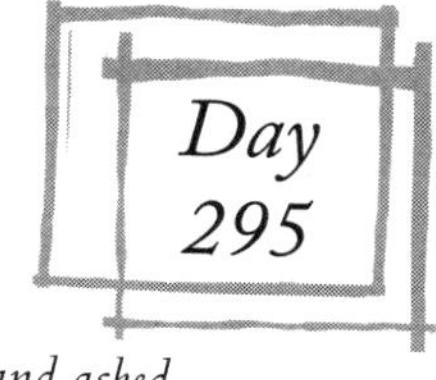

After arriving back home, his disciples cornered Jesus and asked, "Why couldn't we throw the demon out?" He answered, "There is no way to get rid of this kind of demon except by prayer."
Mark 9:28–29 MSG

One afternoon in Galilee, the disciples were arguing with the teachers of the law while a grieving, desperate father listened. When the man saw Jesus approaching, he poured out his problem to the Lord: "Teacher, I brought my mute son, made speechless by a demon, to you. . . . I told your disciples, hoping they could deliver him, but they couldn't" (Mark 9:17–18 MSG).

So Jesus gave the evil spirit its marching orders: "Out of him, and stay out!" (Mark 9:25 MSG). Afterward, He explained to His disciples that prayer was the only way to rebuke that demon.

Was it a particularly difficult demon? The worst of the worst? More likely, the disciples had taken for granted the power given them. Jesus indicated that they had a lack of prayer. His emphasis was *on* prayer.

Somehow, having seen the miracles Jesus performed through prayer, having observed the importance Jesus placed on prayer in His daily life, the disciples still took prayer for granted. If they could do that, the danger exists for us, too.

Lord, strengthen my prayer life! Your Word tells me to pray about everything. I want to pray with a more muscular faith. Forgive me for my silences. Thank You that You still welcome my prayers.

Value of a Child

Jesus called the children to him and said, "Let the little children come to me, and do not hinder them, for the kingdom of heaven belongs to such as these."
Luke 18:16 NIV

Children are an extraordinary and marvelous gift. Nothing else we pursue on this earth can compare to their incalculable value. No amount of money can replace their laughter. No amount of fame can equate to their worth.

Somehow, Jesus' disciples missed that truth. They thought kids were a nuisance and tried to chase them away. Maybe the disciples felt that all the youthful laughter and questioning would interfere with the Master's work. But Jesus rebuked His disciples for such thoughts and spoke the famous words, "Let the little children come to me."

Maybe we need that reminder from time to time ourselves. As single moms, our unrelenting exhaustion can cause us to become impatient and argumentative with our children. We want them to play quietly by themselves, or go to a friend's house—and give us a break. Sometimes we may use day and evening sitters to provide us with our "grown-up time."

While we do need some quiet time, we also need to find the proper balance. Jesus places high value on these little ones. As moms, let's follow His perfect example and place a tremendously high value on our own children.

Abba Father, I thank You for my children. Please forgive me for my impatience with them at times. Help me to be exceptionally loving and gracious toward my children and teach them what is important in the world—a loving relationship with You and each other.

TEACHING OUR CHILDREN

Be an example to the believers with your words, your actions, your love, your faith, and your pure life. Until I come, continue to read the Scriptures to the people, strengthen them, and teach them. Use the gift you have.

1 TIMOTHY 4:12–14 NCV

Everyday life for a single mom is an exercise in scheduling chaos. In the morning, she has hurried breakfasts and the gathering of bits and pieces for school, work, and after-school activities. Through the day, there are meetings, appointments, and practices. At night, she faces homework, baths for the kids, and laundry. A mom barely has time to think.

Where in all this do we find time to teach our children about God? Do we depend only on Sunday school to cover all the bases?

Of course not. Our children *see* our faith—our living faith—at work in us every moment of every day. Children watch adults closely, even when we think they're ignoring us. We send the wrong message if we pray on Sunday, then treat others badly during the week. But our good behavior makes a powerfully positive influence.

In this verse, Paul reminds us that we can *live* faith in five ways: in words, in behavior, in love of God, in reliance on the Holy Spirit, and in the purity of our thoughts and deeds. If we practice these and encourage our children to as well, we'll share our faith and values with them every moment of those frenzied days.

Lord, guide my daily steps in Your ways. Help me show my children my faith and love for You in my actions and words.

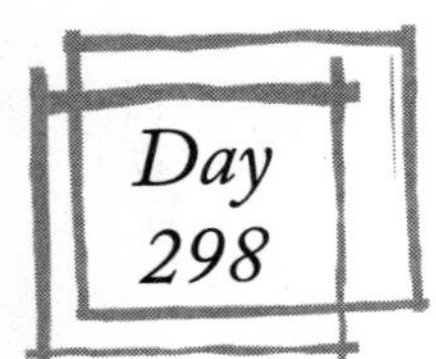

Homely Haven

Let us fall now into the hand of the Lord; for his mercies are great; and let me not fall into the hand of man.
2 Samuel 24:14 KJV

King David made an error in judgment: He commanded his officers to count the number of potential fighting men in Israel, implying that his military success depended on human strength rather than God. But David soon realized his mistake, and he knew just where to turn. The king told the Lord, "I have done very foolishly" (2 Samuel 24:10 KJV).

God let David choose his punishment, from a menu of threes: three years of famine, three months of fleeing his enemies, or three days of plague. David chose the last option, hoping God might be merciful. He would rather fall into God's hands than take his chances anywhere else.

Do our children feel the same way about us? Do they feel secure enough to come to us and say, "I've been really foolish"? Do they prefer any discipline that we mete out over what a school principal or juvenile court might require?

We need to discipline our children—but with mercy. We want to show kindness mixed with justice in our discipline, easing their distress at their wrongdoing.

Ask yourself this: Is my home a haven for my children, a place where they can find forgiveness and be restored to wholeness?

Oh, Lord, show us how to blend mercy with justice to our children.

WARM FUZZIES

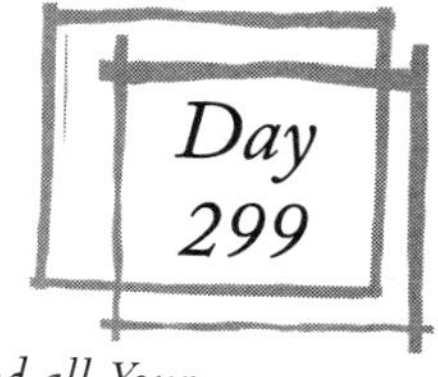

You are near, O LORD [nearer to me than my foes], and all Your commandments are truth. . . . The sum of Your word is truth.
PSALM 119:151, 160 AMP

Have you ever read a scripture and thought, *That's nice. . .but is it real?*

At times, we're all tempted to think God might try to placate His children with tales of comfort or miracles that don't ring true with our day-to-day experience. But that's not the case at all. Whether we need money for groceries or comfort for a broken heart, child care or a car that runs, patience or a paycheck, vindication or a vacation. . .God provides real substance—not just warm fuzzies.

Our God is forever faithful. He'll never tell us, "It'll be okay," when it won't. He is God. Though He may not remove the various difficulties, He has promised to be with us in the midst of them and walk us through to the other side.

As the psalms tell us, God's Word is the sum of Truth. Trusting that Word is much more than a positive thinking exercise. . .it is our faith in action.

Father God, what a comfort it is to know that You aren't simply trying to give me a warm, fuzzy feeling. You care for me and are faithful to walk me through whatever I face.

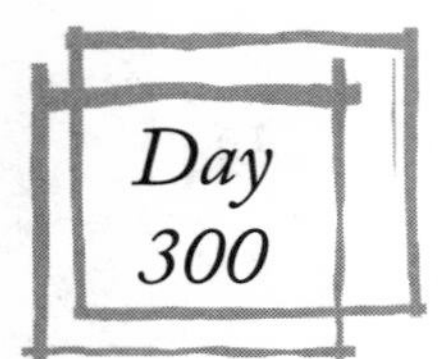

Hagar's Prayer

Then God opened her eyes and [Hagar] saw a well of water.
So she went and filled the skin with water and gave the boy a drink.
God was with [Ishmael] as he grew up.
Genesis 21:19–20 NIV

Hagar must have been one of the loneliest single mothers who ever lived. She was a slave from Egypt, with no rights and less power, forced into a polygamous marriage with Abraham to provide a surrogate child for his barren wife, Sarah.

Some sixteen years later, Hagar was driven into the wilderness with her son, Ishmael. Sarah's plan to "help" God carry out His promise of an heir backfired, badly, as such plans always do. Sarah's bitterness toward Hagar could no longer be contained. So she banished Hagar and Ishmael.

God saw every scene in Hagar's sad life. He heard her cries. In fact, the name Ishmael means, "God hears."

Wandering in the desert, Hagar set her desperately thirsty son under a bush to die. Then she wept. Soon, an angel interrupted her, pointing out a nearby well of water that would save their lives. Hagar named that well the Beer Lahair Roi, or the "well of the Living One who sees me."

Even in the wilderness, God took care of a single woman and her son. He kept His promise to Hagar. He heard her cries and saw her tears. He was with Ishmael as he grew up. God proved Himself faithful.

Lord, open my eyes to how You provide for and protect my family.
I thank You that I am never alone. You see and hear every scene in my life.
You are with me and with my children as they grow up. You are ever faithful!

The Greenhouse Effect

"I am the true vine, and my Father is the gardener. He cuts off every branch in me that bears no fruit, while every branch that does bear fruit he prunes so that it will be even more fruitful."
John 15:1–2 NIV

In a greenhouse, plants grow with a carefully controlled menu of temperature, fertilizer, and pruning. After the plants reach their optimal age and size, most can be transplanted to a more natural environment outside the protective shelter.

A mom is a greenhouse. We protect our kids in our homes, and we provide them with wholesome and nutritious food. We also "prune" them with teaching, guidance, and discipline. Eventually, mom's greenhouse completes its job, and the little sprouts can be released to a new environment.

Jesus is doing the same thing for us. We are constantly nourished and pruned by the Word of God and the guidance of the Holy Spirit. We receive discipline and training as part of the growth process God has designed for us.

God's greenhouse effect is a necessary part of our Christian growth, something He designed as a nurturing pattern for us to follow in our homes.

Jesus, thank You for the greenhouse effect You provide. Thank You for the daily spiritual nourishment and protection You offer. Thank you for Your rich sustenance and even for Your discipline in my life. Help me to advance Your greenhouse effect in my home.

Who's the Boss?

When thou hast eaten and art full, then thou shalt bless the LORD thy God for the good land which he hath given thee. Beware that thou forget not the LORD thy God, in not keeping his commandments, and his judgments, and his statutes, which I command thee this day.
DEUTERONOMY 8:10–11 KJV

Twenty years earlier, Andrea felt like a zero. Her abusive husband left her with a child and no support. She never finished high school, let alone college. But a couple at her church encouraged her to earn her GED and paid for beginning college courses. To her surprise, Andrea found she had a knack for computers. She graduated with honors, and a local business snapped her up. She now owned the business.

Her success kept her traveling and meeting clients on weekends. Because her son was now off to college, Andrea no longer attended church every week. When Christian friends expressed concern, she resented their attitude. Sure, she loved God. But Andrea knew what it took to make it to the top: giving 150 percent to her job.

One day a quiet little voice reminded Andrea that her talents, energy—indeed, her very breath—were all gifts from God. So were the friends who had offered their unconditional love and support.

It was Sunday. Andrea put aside the reports she'd meant to read all morning, jumped into her brand-new car, and headed for church.

Father, You are the author of everything good.
Thank You for not forgetting me when I forget You.

Bugs and Butterflies

"Ah, Sovereign Lord, you have made the heavens and the earth by your great power and outstretched arm. Nothing is too hard for you."
Jeremiah 32:17 NIV

The Lord created the heavens and the earth with glorious beauty, order, and peace. Of course, since sin entered the world, the universe—and often our homes—don't always experience such blessings. But that was God's intent.

We can still find hints of the Lord's perfect creation all around us, though. Take your children to the park in the fall, and see countless ladybugs nesting in the crisp, fallen leaves. Or spend a warm evening on the beach, when most of the world has packed up and gone home, watching the waves roll onto the shore and the birds fly on the horizon. To enjoy such things is to experience the world as the Lord created it: blissfully beautiful, passionately peaceful.

God created this masterpiece of a world for us to enjoy in the depths of our being. Why not take your kids on a "field trip," teaching them of His power and intimate love?

If the Lord could create such a stunning work of art by simply stretching out His hand, certainly nothing is too difficult for Him. Whatever you need today He can accomplish. See His glory in the flowers and the mountains, the rivers and the bugs—and rest in His incomparable grace.

Jesus, I thank You for creating such an amazing masterpiece for my children and me to enjoy. Open my eyes to see the world as You formed it—and help me slow down long enough to enjoy Your astonishing creation.

Strong Enemies Require Stronger Power

He sent from on high, He took me; He drew me out of many waters. He delivered me from my strong enemy, and from those. . .too mighty for me.
Psalm 18:16–17 NASB

The toilet overflows, the car breaks down, work hours get cut, the gas bill is twice what you budgeted for. Taken one at a time, these challenges are minor nuisances. Coming in a bunch, they can send even the strongest among us over the edge.

Though the "strong enemy" in Psalm 18 is a human opponent, our "enemies" as single mothers are just as real. We may face illness in our homes, financial trials, or the strain of raising children on our own. Feeling as if we're drowning in responsibility, these "enemies" can quickly become too mighty for us.

Thankfully, we have an even mightier God! Though the daily issues of life may seem overpowering—even insurmountable—God has promised to deliver us from our "strong enemy," and from those "too mighty" for us. He uses His Word to bring hope to our weary, worn-down souls. He may use a sister or a coworker or a friend from church to send an unexpected check or drop us an encouraging note. Or He may find some other way of helping us, something we never would have guessed.

Of this we can be sure: God is mightier than any foe we face.

Father, sometimes life feels like a raging flood around me. Help me turn to You in my times of trouble, knowing You are able to deliver.

Happy Holidays

What will you do on a festival day,
on the day of the LORD'S *feast?*
HOSEA 9:5 HCSB

Holidays. We expect Christmas and Valentine's Day to resonate with joy. But instead, they often echo with loneliness and pain.

Most single mothers face a time when they spend holidays alone. Our children may spend the day with their other parent, or they may be spreading their wings as teenagers. Even when the kids are with us, the holidays look different than the traditional picture we carry in our hearts.

But single moms can avoid some of the pain by planning ahead. We can use three *S*'s to have a super holiday.

Set aside your expectation to celebrate on the holiday itself. Does it really matter whether you open gifts with the kids on Christmas Eve or Christmas Day? We can make the time with our children special, whenever it occurs.

Simplify. Instead of fixing all our families' favorite dishes for both Thanksgiving and Christmas, divide them between the holidays. Our children can help us choose which traditions mean the most to everyone. We can feel free to let go of others.

Socialize. If our children will be gone for a holiday, we can invite others to join us in their place. Gather with your church family or accept an invitation to dine with someone else.

Our holiday traditions may change. But with a little planning, single moms can enjoy wonderful celebrations anyway.

Dear Lord, as I celebrate holidays, let me not lose sight of You.
May You fill me with joy and peace as I revel in the fact that with You
in my life, I'm never really alone—no matter what the occasion.

Flypaper on the Ceiling

You do not have, because you do not ask God. When you ask,
you do not receive, because you ask with wrong motives,
that you may spend what you get on your pleasures.
James 4:2–3 NIV

Jesus promised that every prayer of a God-seeking person would be answered (Matthew 7:8). Every prayer! So why does it seem as if some of our prayers don't get answered? Why do some prayers seem to get stuck to the ceiling, as if caught on flypaper?

The purpose of prayer is to bring God's revealed will into our lives. When prayers go unanswered, it's wise to examine whether we are just airing our problems or our wishes to God. Without intending to, we may be praying at cross-purposes with what God wants. Or. . .we may not want His answers.

Sometimes our goal in prayer is for change from without: *Lord, please help Ryan make better grades.* God might answer by prodding us to change within: *Lord, help me to accept my son for who he is, not who I want him to be.*

We need to be willing to examine our motives so that we can pray in harmony with the principles of scripture. Are we willing to leave the how and when and why of our prayers to God? Doing so is an indication that we are praying in line with God's will. *That* is the prayer He has promised to answer. "This is the confidence we have in approaching God: that if we ask anything according to his will, he hears us" (1 John 5:14 NIV).

Lord, teach me to pray Your will in my family's life.

Beauty of the Beholder

So God created human beings in his own image. In the image of God he created them; male and female he created them. . . . Then God looked over all he had made, and he saw that it was very good!
Genesis 1:27, 31 NLT

Janet looked in the mirror and winced. *I shouldn't have eaten that extra piece of cake,* she thought as she pinched a bit of fat around her waist.

Janet's not alone. Women tend to find something wrong with themselves, no matter how they actually look. Our noses have bumps. Our hips are too large. Our eyes are too small for our face. We've got wrinkles where smooth skin used to be.

Though there's nothing wrong with presenting ourselves in the best light, we should always remember one important fact: God created us in His image. We don't have to look like the models in a women's magazine to be beautiful. The One who created us loves us exactly as we are!

Those little things we see as imperfections are actually attractive to God. Just as we see our own kids as the most adorable things, God sees us as His lovely children.

When it comes to self-image, let's not view our own perceived flaws as negatives. Let's see ourselves through God's eyes, remembering that His creation is always good.

Dear Lord, when I look in the mirror, remind me that I was created in Your image and that, although I may not always see myself as beautiful, You think I look very good.

Lead Me On

This book of the law shall not depart out of thy mouth; but thou shalt meditate therein day and night, that thou mayest observe to do according to all that is written therein: for then thou shalt make thy way prosperous, and then thou shalt have good success.
Joshua 1:8 KJV

God Himself told Joshua the news of Moses' death. Saddened, Joshua knew he would miss his spiritual mentor. But Joshua also thrilled to the fact that God was talking to him just as He did to Moses!

God had big plans. He told Joshua to guide the Israelites across the Jordan River and conquer a huge area that stretched from the Euphrates River to the Mediterranean Sea. Joshua must have been awestruck, because God lost no time in reassuring him: "As I was with Moses, so I will be with thee" (Joshua 1:5 KJV). But God also commanded Joshua to learn His Law. The Israelites' leader needed to spend substantial time meditating upon God's Word. God promised that if Joshua integrated His commands into his personal lifestyle and leadership methods, he would succeed.

We may find ourselves taking leadership positions in our families or congregations. How will we make it? God gives us the same answer He gave Joshua: Absorb My Word. Let My commands light your paths.

Joshua listened. Many of his people did not.

Will we?

Lord God, help me study the Bible, meditate on Your precepts, and listen for Your guidance each and every day. And as You grant me success, may I give You all the glory!

Spring Cleaning

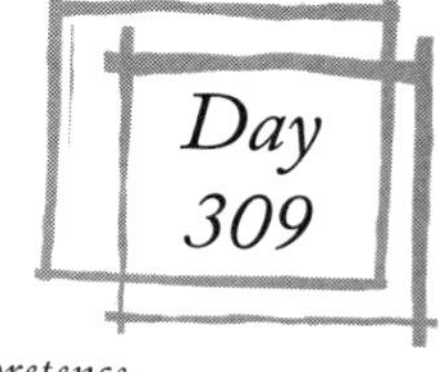

So clean house! Make a clean sweep of malice and pretense, envy and hurtful talk.
1 Peter 2:1 msg

A sparkling clean house may be ideal, but it's not always possible. Whether you have rowdy teenagers or roughhousing little ones, it's hard to keep the house perfectly ordered. With too many hours at work and too few moments of rest, we often just skim the surface in our cleaning—washing the dishes but not cleaning out the frig, throwing the Matchbox cars and Barbie dolls into one big box rather than finding their actual storage places.

Sometimes, we just have to do what we can. And you know what? That's okay. We can occasionally let go of perfection, leaving some dust on the mantel and a stack of laundry in the basket. Single moms have higher priorities than an immaculate house.

In 1 Peter, we're instructed to "make a clean sweep" of malice, pretense, envy, and hurtful talk. The image is of using a broom—but it's not addressing our dirty kitchen floor. God wants us to focus on things that count for eternity.

After all, what do we gain if our kids come home to a gorgeous, flawless, showpiece house filled with anger, bad attitudes, and fighting?

Father, show me where I need to clean house and where I need to let go of perfection. I need Your wisdom to know the difference.

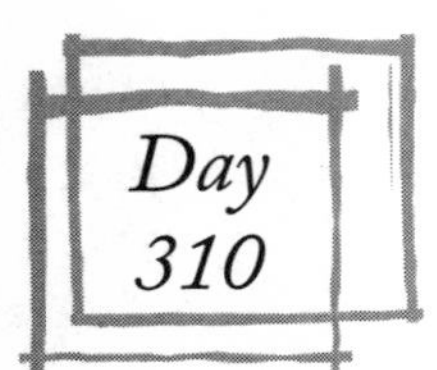

The Last Straw

While Belshazzar was drinking his wine, he gave orders to bring in the gold and silver goblets that Nebuchadnezzar his father had taken from the temple in Jerusalem. . . . They praised the gods of gold and silver, of bronze, iron, wood and stone.
Daniel 5:2, 4 NIV

It was the last straw. Belshazzar, king of Babylon, had taken out the gold and silver vessels that had been looted from Solomon's temple in Jerusalem. He used those sacred vessels for the party of the century. Though *party* might be too kind a word. More like a drunken orgy. Belshazzar partied as his city was under siege.

God was ready to deal with Belshazzar's arrogance. A mysterious hand appeared, writing a message of Belshazzar's fate on the wall. Later that night, he was killed.

Centuries later, our culture is still at odds with what God holds sacred. And it's not just our culture that disregards what God holds dear. Sadly, we can do that, too. Is getting to church, regularly and on time, a firm intention for our family? Do we cut ethical corners at work or on our tax returns? Do we slip up with a careless "Oh my God!" on occasion, or let our kids take the Lord's name in vain?

Let's ask God to reveal any areas of neglect in our lives. Then let's cut out anything—like a cancer—that could lead us to sin.

Lord, I don't want to settle for what the world thinks is right. Search my soul! Show me what needs to change and let me be quick to repent.

Molding His Clay

O Lord, you are our Father. We are the clay, you are the potter; we are all the work of your hand.
Isaiah 64:8 NIV

Many of us have had the chance to make pottery in an art class. Those of us who've tried it know making something nice is much more difficult than it appears. Only a really talented potter can create a work of true beauty.

Clay starts out hard and cold but becomes formable after the potter beats, stretches, and works it over. Eventually, the clay becomes soft and pliable—then it goes on the center of the potter's wheel. The clay is pushed and pulled. Spinning rapidly, it rises up and is shoved back down. Sharp tools make designs and patterns within the developing work of art. Finally, in the right hands, a masterpiece emerges.

We are God's clay. Often, we're beaten down and worked over. But with Him as our potter, in His tender hands, we'll be molded and shaped into something beautiful. Sure, it can be painful and tiring. But we trust that when He is finished, we'll be glorious examples of His workmanship.

Made by tender, loving hands, no two pieces of pottery are exactly alike. And neither are we—as our characters are formed by God's perfect wisdom and knowledge. He always has our very best in mind.

Lord God, You are the potter, I am merely Your clay. Mold and shape me today to become the masterpiece You had in mind when You saw me in my mother's womb. I submit myself to be in Your hands and trust You will keep me there.

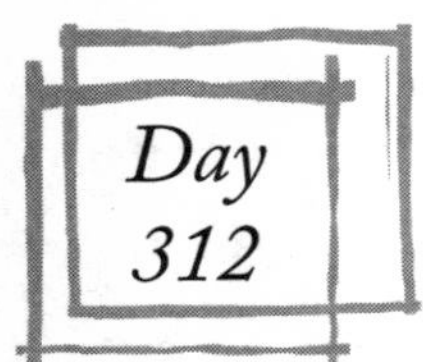

Treading Water

With the crowd dispersed, he climbed the mountain so he could be by himself and pray. He stayed there alone, late into the night.
Matthew 14:23 MSG

Treading water is not a sign of weakness. It's a tactic swimmers employ before their strength begins to fail. When weariness comes on, the swimmer stops pulling herself through the water, instead gently moving her arms and legs ever so slightly to remain above water. No progress is made while treading water, but time is gained for strength to recover. Eventually, the journey will continue.

Single moms often feel like they're drowning—losing strength as the waters overtake them. So "treading water" for a time may be the best choice. We won't make any great advancements during that time—but a conscious decision to take no large steps, address no big issues, and simply rest can be exactly what we need to regroup.

Tread water for a few days, even weeks, if necessary. Reconnect with God through prayer and introspection. Let the Holy Spirit renew your soul and body so you can begin the journey once again with a new vigor.

God will always be faithful to bring you through.

Jesus, please renew and reenergize me as a parent and as a believer. Through rest and prayer, please strengthen me and return me to the vigor I once felt.

Perfect Balance

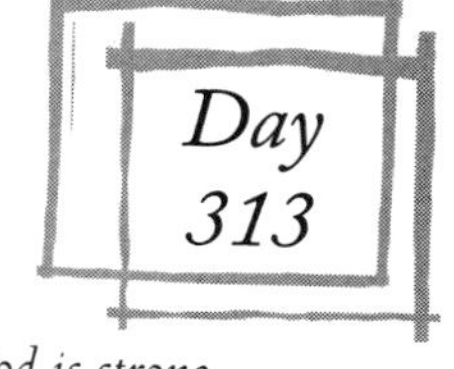

God has said this, and I have heard it over and over: God is strong.
The Lord is loving. You reward people for what they have done.
Psalm 62:11–12 NCV

In two short sentences, the psalmist captured one of the awesome paradoxes of God's nature.

"God is strong." He is powerful enough to accomplish what He requires.

"The Lord is loving." His love directs His strength to work for our good, never against us.

Think how differently we would view God if He lacked one of those two qualities: If He was loving but not strong, we'd love Him like a brother—but not revere Him as the almighty God. If He was strong but not loving, we'd fear Him—but never turn to Him as our Abba ("Daddy") Father.

Because God is both strong and loving, we trust Him with our lives. His reward in our lives grows out of both qualities. He shows us His love by His discipline (Hebrews 12:7–11), but He also remembers our frailty (Psalm 103:13–14).

As parents, we discipline on a continuum between justice and mercy. We might punish heavily for a minor offense or lightly for a serious wrongdoing. Neither extreme benefits the kids.

But God our Father can teach us the perfect balance between strength and love.

Father God, You are strong. You are loving.
Teach us to discipline our children with love and strength.

What Did You Say?

The Lord asked Cain, "Why are you angry? Why do you look so unhappy?"
Genesis 4:6 NCV

This is really an amazing verse. See the example God is setting for us as mothers? He took the time to stop what He was doing and ask Cain, "Why do you look so unhappy?" Wow—it's not as if the Creator of the universe didn't have other things to do. Yet He noticed the sadness of His "child."

Our kids often show anger, unhappiness, or sorrow on their faces. But do we take the time to notice? How often have we yelled across the room, "Not now—I have work to do!" Or maybe we only half listen as our children talk to us. Perhaps the entire day slips away without our really sensing what's bothering our children.

If we're honest, we'd probably say it happens more often than we care to admit. Of course, we aren't being malicious or scheming to make our children feel unimportant. We really do want them to feel cherished—but our careless, hurried attitudes may cause them to think we're just too busy for them and their needs.

Today, let's consider our heavenly Father's example of loving parenting—then take the time to demonstrate how much we care.

Heavenly Father, I thank You for Your example of listening to Your children, of taking the time to notice what's going on in our hearts.

Always?

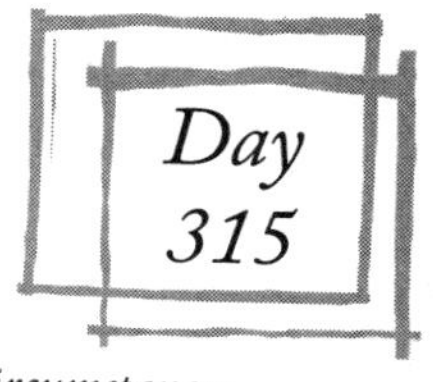

Always be joyful. Never stop praying. Be thankful in all circumstances, for this is God's will for you who belong to Christ Jesus.
1 Thessalonians 5:16–18 NLT

Why is it so hard to pray? Scripture tells us to pray about everything, but it's difficult to believe God wants to hear the humdrum of our everyday life. Why? What stops us from being diligent in prayer?

Maybe our own mediocre experience with prayer hurts us. Sometimes we bore ourselves! We get easily distracted. It can be difficult to even get started. Words fail us.

Keeping a prayer notebook and using it during quiet time—with prayers listed out and dated—is one way of enriching our prayer lives.

What are the advantages of a prayer journal? It can help us realize that God has answered more prayers than we think. It can remind us to lift up people in ongoing circumstances, because we're prone to forget. It can focus our attentiveness. It can expand our faith as we discover God's answers to our prayers may result in an altogether different outcome than we had expected—always better! It can broaden our objectivity, especially important for moms, as we lift up our concerns over our kids and allow His light to shine on our problems. And it can train us in the habit of prayer as a first and immediate response to our family joys and crises alike.

Lord, how good it is to know that when mothers pray, we can be confident our prayers are received and attended to by a loving Father.

Cast It into the Sea

And the apostles said unto the Lord, *Increase our faith. And the* Lord *said, If ye had faith as a grain of mustard seed, ye might say unto this sycamine tree, Be thou plucked up by the root, and be thou planted in the sea; and it should obey you.*
Luke 17:5–6 KJV

The bills that are due total more than the paycheck. The project deadline is approaching—and things look hopeless. The school nurse just called to say Suzie has pinkeye. How can one person take care of it all?

As a single parent, it's easy to feel afraid and alone. It often seems that no one cares or understands what we're going through.

But Jesus said, even in hard times, our faith is enough to get us through. Our trust and confidence in God, even if they're as small as a tiny mustard seed, are enough to change the circumstances of our lives—or our attitude toward them.

When trials present themselves, do as Jesus said: Turn in faith to Him. Then hold on to that faith and believe God for miracles!

Lord, please help me always to keep my faith and confidence in You—regardless of the circumstances. I place my trust in You, knowing that You can accomplish much through my faith.

FORGOTTEN FRAGRANCES

He has made everything beautiful in its time.
ECCLESIASTES 3:11 NIV

Scuffling along a dreary path, Liza and Jane remarked on the cold, dead, sad display of the wintertime forest. The previous summer, the same path was crowded with fragrant, eye-catching flowers. Now, though, the blossoms were long gone, and their gentle fragrance only a distant memory.

But Jane and Liza knew, from years of living through the changing seasons, that the springtime sun would soon warm the air, melt the snow, and cause the flowers and trees to grow once more. The stark, cold quiet of wintertime would give way to new freshness, new beauty, new life.

It's the same for us. God indeed makes everything beautiful in its time—flowers, trees, baby animals, and us. There are seasons in our lives that are dry and cold; we wonder what good will come of our lives. In other seasons, life is radiant and wonderful—and we simply enjoy every minute of it.

If you're in one of those cold, sorrowful seasons of life, don't fear. Soon, God will blow back the gray clouds, revealing the warmth of His Son and making us beautiful once more.

Father, I thank You for the beauty You've given me to enjoy.
You have a time for everything, and will eventually make all things beautiful.
Please keep me faithful, awaiting Your special time for my life.

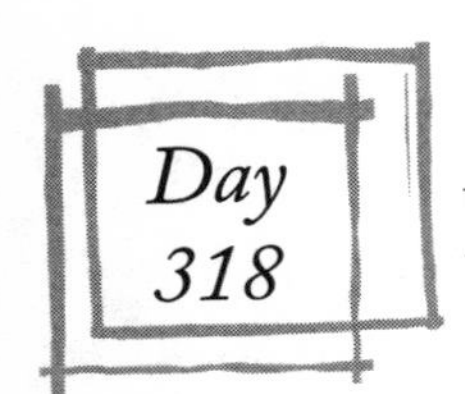

Life's Rollercoaster Ride

"Live in me. Make your home in me just as I do in you. In the same way that a branch can't bear grapes by itself but only by being joined to the vine, you can't bear fruit unless you are joined with me."

John 15:4 MSG

It's exhilarating to ride the first car of a rollercoaster! Anticipation increases as the train slowly climbs to the top of the first hill. Nearing the pinnacle, excitement and even fear grow in the riders. Then, a thrilling descent followed by another uphill climb. People stand in line for the experience.

Parenting is a lot like that rollercoaster ride. Pregnancy is a long, exhilarating uphill climb, with birth and those first days with the new baby the exciting descent. Other uphill climbs toward the milestones of life are sprinkled throughout our journey. We must enjoy the climb, savor the anticipation, and eagerly await the next hill we'll face.

So, who fills that seat beside us? Do we invite Jesus along as we climb the hills and hurtle into the valleys of life? Or is that seat always filled with friends, family members, or coworkers?

Make Jesus your constant companion. The ride will be richer and more memorable.

Jesus, forgive me for those times I leave You behind.
Be my constant companion, and help me to enjoy and savor every moment.

Elbow Grease

It is useless for you to work so hard from early morning until late at night, anxiously working for food to eat; for God gives rest to his loved ones.
Psalm 127:2 NLT

Take it easy! Relax. Don't sweat the small stuff. Life is short. Stop and smell the roses.

Yeah, you've heard it all before. But single moms often think no one else understands. They're not in our shoes. There's just no way to carve out time for some good old rest and relaxation.

Who'll cook dinner if you don't? How will the bills get paid if you don't pursue that promotion? Where will the Christmas presents come from if you don't work overtime? And, yes, midnight is a bit late to be folding laundry—but it has to be done, doesn't it?

Of course those things must be done, and the duties usually do fall to us moms. But would it really be the end of the world if your daughter wore the same pair of jeans twice in a row, or the Christmas tree had fewer gifts underneath?

What *would* be regretful is if you stayed up late every night and continually got up at the crack of dawn, only to find yourself burned-out and angry—even physically sick.

God calls this over-effort "useless." Do what needs to be done and then relax. Take Him up on His offer of rest!

Father God, I am tired of working so hard and feeling so empty. Please enable me simply to relax.

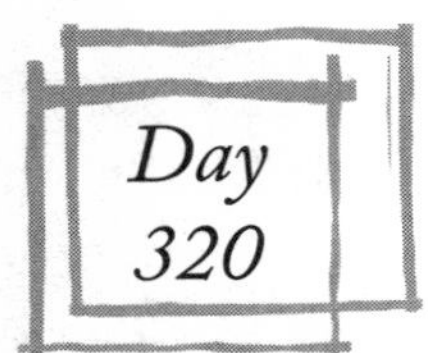

Untidy Prayers

"When you pray, do not say the same thing over and over again making long prayers like the people who do not know God. They think they are heard because their prayers are long. Do not be like them. Your Father knows what you need before you ask Him."
MATTHEW 6:7–8 NLV

When our child falls down, scrapes a knee, and calls out our name, what do we do? We hear that desperate need in his voice. We hear and respond immediately.

When we pray to God in our pain, He hears! He responds!

The Lord loves prayers that burst out of a hurting heart. We are broken, in need of comfort and healing. Our facades are unmasked, our defenses down. Those prayers are authentic, sincere, earnest. Consider how many of David's psalms begin with a cry from the depths of his very human soul.

The Lord listens to those in need (Psalm 69:33). We can pray simple, untidy, not fancy, from-the-gut prayers. We can wail out our most horrible feelings and know God will not be shocked.

God isn't like the grocery store clerk who keeps his eyes lowered and his chin to his chest, tossing out the perfunctory, "How are you today?" God *really* wants to know. How are you doing today? What's on your mind? Tell God! He already knows our real thoughts and feelings, but He still longs to hear from us.

Father in heaven, You gave us ears, both physical and spiritual.
I thank You for the gift of two-way conversation.
I thank You that You both hear and speak to me.

Making Time for Friends

A friend loves you all the time,
and a brother helps in time of trouble.
Proverbs 17:17 NCV

"Feel free to call me any time of the day—even at 2:00 a.m."

That offer gave the new single mom a lifeline. Knowing that someone was willing to stand by her—even through those long lonely watches of the night—made them somehow more bearable.

Single moms need friends, though they can be hard to make and keep. Changes of address or job schedules can alter old friendships. And as for making new friends—well, with running the household by oneself, who has the time?

Make the time! Proverbs gives a basic rule of friendship: "A friend loves you all the time." The flip side is that you need to love your friends all the time, too.

We need to love our friends when they're sick, and pitch in to help them.

We need to love our friends when they're weak, when they cry over the same problem for the tenth time.

We need to love our friends when they're strong, when they get a promotion at work or buy a new car.

We need to love our friends even when it's inconvenient, caring and helping regardless of our own plans and agendas.

Give that kind of friendship, and you're much more likely to get it back.

Our loving Father, I thank You for the friends You have brought into my life, and I ask that You will make me into a friend who loves all the time.

By the River

"Blessed are those who trust in the Lord and have made the Lord their hope and confidence. They are like trees planted along a riverbank, with roots that reach deep into the water."
Jeremiah 17:7–8 NLT

Trees lining a riverbank are often a bit strange. They're twisted and gnarled, growing out of rocks or up through other trees. Rarely standing up straight, they stretch over the river as if to drink or catch a breeze off the water. Though not always beautiful, these trees are strong and well nourished. With water always available, their roots plunge deeper than most other trees—strengthening their firm foundation, making their foliage brighter. Even their smell tends to be more refreshing and sensual than the rest.

God's Word says that if we put our trust and confidence in the Lord, allowing our hope to rest in His hands, we'll be like those strong, healthy trees. True, our circumstances may be gnarled and ugly—but with our roots deep in the Lord, our foundation is firm and unshakeable, our fruit brilliant and refreshing. We'll breathe in the fragrance of our Savior, drink in the river of life, and be strong and confident whatever may come.

Jesus, I thank You for Your faithfulness and ask that You'll help me to increase my trust and hope in You. Like those strong trees by the water's edge, may my roots go deep into Your Word, drinking from the river of life that never runs dry.

Smiles for Everybody

God has blessed me with laughter and all. . .will laugh with me!
Genesis 21:5 msg

Angie grabbed her Bible, then scanned the foyer for her boys. Nowhere to be seen, of course. She returned to the sanctuary, hoping Trent and Thomas hadn't been running down aisles or attempting karaoke with the microphones again. She asked an usher to check the men's bathroom. No sign of her Dynamic Duo. Angie finally tracked her sons to a parking lot football game and herded them into the car, wishing she had a cattle prod. She growled and grouched as they pulled toward the exit. Old Mr. Sanders waved her down. He wanted to tell her his weekly funny story. Angie didn't feel like smiling, but she opened her window and laughed as Mr. Sanders told her his latest fish tale. Angie waved good-bye, then began her usual what-did-you-do-to-your-church-pants interrogation. Trent and Thomas answered in monosyllables. A new wave of suspicion passed through her mind. What were they hiding?

"Mom, why don't you laugh with us like you do with old people?" Trent asked from the backseat.

Thomas's sad, dark eyes melted Angie, the Wicked Witch of the West, down to nothing. She prayed a few seconds, then took a deep breath. "You're right. I'm sorry, guys. Who wants to tell me their favorite knock-knock joke?"

Jesus, I love to make other people smile. And You have blessed me with laughter. Please help me remember my children need to laugh with me, too!

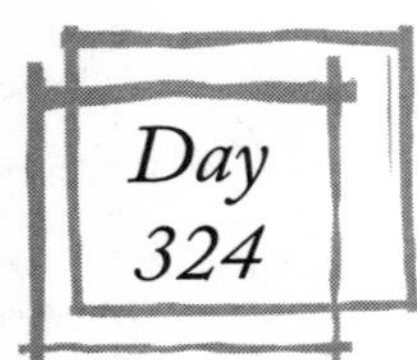

Imparting Gratitude

Let your conduct be without covetousness; be content with such things as you have. For He Himself has said, "I will never leave you nor forsake you.". . . Let us continually offer the sacrifice of praise to God. . .giving thanks to His name.
HEBREWS 13:5, 15 NKJV

Is this all there is? Don't we have any more presents under the tree?"

"All my friends get new clothes when school starts."

"Why don't we eat out more often?"

"Why can't we have a big plasma TV like Jacob's family?"

"But I wanted an iPod, not a CD player."

"Mom, we're out of my favorite cereal."

The rapid-fire requests and complaints pour forth, and we glimpse something troubling in our precious little ones: greed. . .ingratitude. . . a sense of entitlement. We've worked hard to provide for them. We resisted that stylish blouse we saw in the catalog so they could have new school shoes. We volunteered to work overtime so they would have a few extra presents under the tree. What went wrong?

Our hard work may inadvertently spawn such attitudes. When we rush to fulfill every desire our kids have, they begin to expect even more. If, on the other hand, we purposefully allow some perceived need to go unmet, or if we expose them to families who have even less than we have, the kids may learn to be more content and thankful.

Most importantly, we as moms need to model thankfulness in all circumstances—the good, the bad, and the challenging.

Father God, cause us as a family to be thankful no matter what our circumstance. Enable me to model contentment to my children, knowing You are all that we really need.

Basking in God's Presence

By day the LORD went ahead of them in a pillar of cloud to guide them on their way and by night in a pillar of fire to give them light, so that they could travel by day or night. Neither the pillar of cloud by day nor the pillar of fire by night left its place in front of the people.
EXODUS 13:21–22 NIV

How soothing it must have been to those Israelites to feel the warmth of the pillar of fire in the cold desert night. How comforting to be sheltered from the blazing hot sun with a pillar of cloud by day. Imagine how it must have been to have such a visible symbol of God's company among His people. The Lord even spoke to them out of that pillar (Psalm 99:6–7). They were literally able to bask in the presence of God.

Even better than a visible pillar is the gift of the indwelling Holy Spirit—especially for moms! The Spirit gives us a very real advantage over the forces that war against our children each day, but we also benefit personally. The Spirit empowers us to obey God's Word. It helps us to avoid sin. It teaches us to grow in maturity of character. It reveals God's will to us. It comforts and counsels and ministers to us. Christ gave us His Spirit to help us as we pray.

The indwelling of the Holy Spirit is better than any external symbol of God. Unlike the Old Testament holy pillar—remarkable but temporary—the Holy Spirit will never depart from us.

Lord, in all of my family's struggles, may we sense Your nearness. Please show us that You really are closer than our own breath, and that You see and hear everything that happens.

Rely on the God Who Sees

She answered God by name, praying to the God who spoke to her, "You're the God who sees me!"
Genesis 16:13 MSG

The young single mom checked her bank balance one more time, not really believing the total: $1.87. That's it, until the next payday. The bills were paid, and she did have enough food for the week, but the lack of cash made fear grow in her like a choking vine. What if she had a flat? Or what if. . . ?

The temptation to beg God for money rolled over her. She stepped out of her house and onto her patio, which doubled as her prayer closet. She gazed at the bright stars and turned her mind to God, lifting her situation up to Him.

In the midst of her prayer, Hagar came to mind. The young woman smiled. *Of course,* she thought. Her Sunday school class had just talked about Hagar. Terrified and alone, Sarah's servant met God twice in the desert (Genesis 16:7–14; 21:17–19). Scripture never speaks of Hagar marrying after she and Ishmael were evicted from Abraham's household. She remained a single mom, relying instead on her Lord the God who sees.

The young woman sighed as a sense of peace settled over her. God knew her situation. They would make it. "Thank you, Lord," she whispered, "for seeing me."

Father God, thank You for providing for my needs, and help me to remember that You are always with me, seeing and loving me. Amen.

The Blackberry Mom

You know when I leave and when I get back;
I'm never out of your sight.
Psalm 139:3 msg

Just in time, Kristen arrived at her son's soccer game. Her mind, though, was still on an unfinished project at the office. *Fortunately,* she thought, *I can get both things done at once.* Technology provided a remarkable ability to multitask, even while watching a soccer game. When her son, Ryan, sat on the bench, she whipped out her Blackberry and worked.

Unfortunately, each time Ryan looked up to see if his mother was watching him, he saw her head bent over, fingers flying over the type pad.

The car ride home was a silent one. Puzzled by Ryan's bad mood, Kristen asked, "What's wrong?"

Ryan grabbed her Blackberry off the car seat and shouted, "I hate this thing!"

Imagine if God were distracted when we prayed. How would you feel, knowing He was only paying half attention? Feeling as if He had put you on hold for a moment when something more important came up?

Thankfully, scripture tells us that God's attention is fixed on us, available day or night. "I look behind me and you're there, then up ahead and you're there, too—your reassuring presence, coming and going. This is too much, too wonderful—I can't take it all in!" (Psalm 139:5–6 msg).

Lord, may I learn to listen carefully to my children and to give them my full attention when they ask for it or need it. Even when they don't.

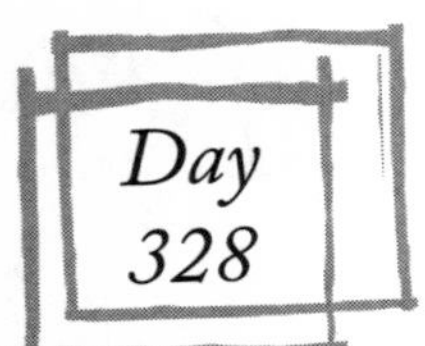

STUFF OF LIFE

When goods increase, they increase who eat them,
and what advantage has their owner but to see them with his eyes?
ECCLESIASTES 5:11 ESV

Stuff—our lives overflow with it. Our desire for stuff goes a long way toward explaining our fascination with garage sales. How often do we buy from our neighbors only later to sell the stuff ourselves?

The writer of Ecclesiastes asked this about stuff: What good does it bring to its owner—except to look at it? Stuff begets stuff. The more we have, the more we think we need.

Single moms know all about stretching their resources. Rising grocery, insurance, and gas costs eat up any increase in salary we're lucky enough to get. But if we're caught up in buying unnecessary stuff—if our "goods increase," to use the Bible's phrase—we'll find the budget getting even tighter. And our stress level will increase accordingly.

How can we value what we already possess—and teach our kids to do the same? Start by thanking God for your basic shelter, food, and clothing—as well as all the extras He's thrown in.

Let's rejoice in God's bounty instead of longing for more stuff. Godliness with contentment is a great gain (1 Timothy 6:6).

Oh Lord our Provider, You shower us with more than we need.
Help us find joy in what we have.

YOUR WORTH

"What is the price of two sparrows—one copper coin? But not a single sparrow can fall to the ground without your Father knowing it. . . . So don't be afraid; you are more valuable to God than a whole flock of sparrows."
MATTHEW 10:29, 31 NLT

But I only had my hamster a week, Mom." The young girl sniffled.

"I know, honey," the mom said, trying to calm her daughter. "We'll get a new one. Hamsters aren't that expensive."

"Why? Why aren't they expensive?" the child asked.

"Because hamsters aren't that valuable. Only things of value cost a lot—you know, like diamonds or a new car."

"Well, my hamster was valuable to *me*!"

Hamsters or sparrows—they all have the attention of Almighty God. A tiny, "worthless" bird can't fall to the ground without Him noticing. But your heavenly Father finds you much more valuable, worth more than a whole flock of sparrows. What kind of attention must He be paying to you?

How valuable are you to God? He willingly gave His only Son's life for the chance to have you as His very own. Will He not now care for you as well?

Father, how precious and constant is Your caring concern toward me. You place value on me. Amazing!

He's Here!

When they came to the other disciples, they saw a large crowd around them and the teachers of the law arguing with them. As soon as all the people saw Jesus, they were overwhelmed with wonder and ran to greet him.

Mark 9:14–15 NIV

Jesus had just come down the mountain after being away with Peter, James, and John for a few days. When He located His disciples, He found them surrounded by a large crowd, locked in a heated argument with teachers of the Law.

And then, scripture explains, everyone saw Jesus. Almost like children running to a parent who's been away, their faces were filled with joy as they surrounded Him.

Tweak this Bible passage a bit, and it plays out like a scene very familiar to moms. We've been away from home for a while and return to the house to hear the kids arguing. But they see us and run to us, relief written on their faces! Happy that we can act as peacemakers for their argument. Happy that dinner will now get underway. Happy, really, just that we're home.

What a beautiful parallel to our relationship to Christ. He's here—even in our homes. He can solve our problems and provide for us. All will be well.

Lord Jesus, thank You for the gift of motherhood.
Your presence in my home is so comforting.

God's Kid

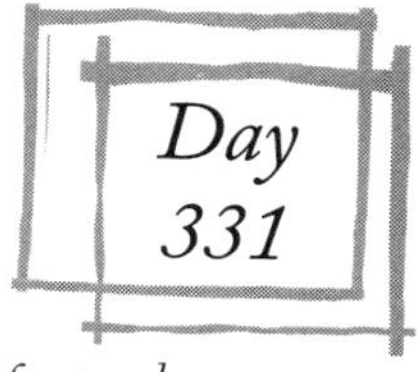

So Daniel said to the steward. . ."Please test your servants for ten days, and let them give us vegetables to eat and water to drink. Then let our appearance be examined before you, and the appearance of the young men who eat the portion of the king's delicacies."
Daniel 1:11–13 NKJV

Mothers worry when new laws, court orders, and other circumstances dictate that their children must spend time in an environment hostile to their values. Many moms deal with ex-spouses who ignore God and live in relationships and lifestyles that defy His Word. How can a child survive with his or her faith intact?

Daniel, an Old Testament teenager who stuck to his standards, gives us hope for the children we love so much but can't always protect. Daniel probably lost his family when the armies of Nebuchadnezzar, a ruthless Babylonian king, raided Judah and took him captive. Instead of executing the young aristocrat, authorities assigned Daniel to a select group who would live in the palace and serve the king. Surrounded by sensual luxury, Daniel experienced new temptations. He even struggled with his diet, knowing Jewish law declared the delicious meats and wine from the king's table unclean. Perhaps other Hebrew captives shrugged off their upbringing and ate. But Daniel, Shadrach, Meshach, and Abednego, the "God Squad" in the Babylonian court, refused to bow to peer pressure. They requested permission to eat vegetables and drink water. God honored their determination to follow Him, and the boys began careers that made an important spiritual impact on their captors.

Father, You know I would shelter my children from evil if I could. But I trust You to walk with them when I cannot.

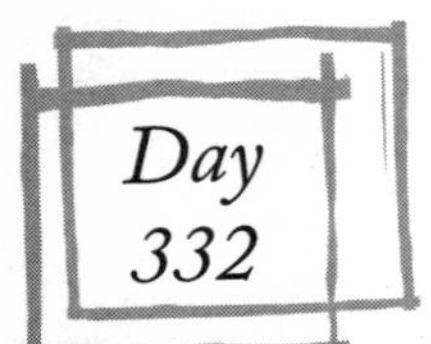

Get Plugged In

For we are God's workmanship, created in Christ Jesus to do good works, which God prepared in advance for us to do.
Ephesians 2:10 NIV

"How can I 'produce fruit' for God, when I'm already so busy?" Ruth wondered aloud as she read an e-mail requesting her help with an upcoming church luncheon. She wanted to contribute but felt overwhelmed with other responsibilities—inside and outside her home.

The Bible often calls us to "bear fruit" by doing good works, showing God's love to others. That's easier said than done when we're trying to squeeze in family, jobs, and other responsibilities. But bearing fruit doesn't necessarily mean we have to volunteer for every church committee. What it does imply is that we should find a way to show God's love every day.

Seek out ways and places to use your talents, as much as you can give now. Take stock of the time you have available to give in a week or month, then set a goal to spend some of that time on church and other activities. Ask where you could be of assistance, and find a place to "plug in."

And if you can't find a plug, make one yourself. Chances are other people might share your interests and want a new place to join in.

Dear Father, help me find a way to be "plugged in" without feeling overwhelmed. Remind me to show Your love every day, and to use my talents for Your good.

Least Likely to Succeed

I will pour out my spirit upon all flesh;
and your sons and your daughters shall prophesy.
Joel 2:28 KJV

Fourteen-year-old Noah poised drumsticks like weapons, ready to inflict noise on the congregation. His mother breathed the prayer that ruled her life: *Please, God, don't let him get carried away.*

Lisa adored her lovable son; yet Noah drove her—and everyone else—crazy. No week passed without a teacher's phone call. At church Noah picked arguments with his peers. The pastor caught Noah leading little boys in a wild wet-paper-towel fight in the men's restroom. Her son also loved to annoy the girls.

Now Lisa wished Noah were beside her, even if he fidgeted as if he were sitting on an anthill. But the youth pastor thought playing drums during the service might focus Noah's energy in a positive direction.

Instead, Noah smacked the drums and smashed the cymbals until Lisa's head throbbed. How could anybody find that much rhythm in "What a Friend We Have in Jesus"? Afterward, Lisa felt a hundred indignant looks prick her as she tried to hurry Noah out the church door.

"I *love* to hear a young man praise God with enthusiasm!" said old Mrs. Richards, blocking their escape. "He's using you, Noah!"

Lisa's son never did learn to sit still in church. But ten years later, as Noah worked in an inner-city center, winning teens to Christ, he didn't have to.

Open my eyes, Lord, and help me see
Jesus working in my children today.

Christmas Comes on Leaden Feet

But you must not forget this one thing, dear friends: A day is like a thousand years to the Lord, and a thousand years is like a day. The Lord isn't really being slow about his promise, as some people think. No, he is being patient for your sake. He does not want anyone to be destroyed, but wants everyone to repent.
2 Peter 3:8–9 NLT

To a child, Christmas comes slowly. Inching along, December 25 takes forever to arrive!

But to a mom, the calendar seems to flip to December every few months. Christmas comes altogether too quickly. It's exactly the same amount of time—but different viewpoints lead to very different perceptions.

In the first-century church, believers were growing impatient. Jesus had promised to return—but where was He? Like children waiting for Christmas, the early believers couldn't experience Jesus' second coming quickly enough.

God, though, sees time differently than we do. In His love and wisdom, He wants no one to perish. He's giving time to everyone to repent from their sins and truly know Him. It's an offer for every single person we love—even those we don't. His agenda, unlike ours, is always perfectly holy.

We have the promise of the Bible that Jesus is coming back. It may seem like a long time to wait—just as our children feel about the arrival of Christmas. But one day, He will return and our long wait will be forgotten.

It's a Christmas morning that lasts forever!

Lord of the universe, You are coming back! May I model patience and expectancy to my family, never wavering in my belief that You will return!

Expert Advice

Don't put your life in the hands of experts who know nothing of life, of salvation life. Mere humans don't have what it takes.
Psalm 146:3 MSG

We read advice columns, peruse parenting magazines, devour the latest books on childrearing, and watch talk shows touting the "experts." How to prevent bed-wetting. . .sex education. . .choosing the right college. . .disciplining with positive reinforcement. . .you name it, somebody's talking about it.

We all want and need help in mothering our children. We may even feel desperate for answers to the tough questions—those that seem completely beyond our ability. But that desperation may work against us, causing us to readily accept *any* advice offered. Let's always ask ourselves, "Whose counsel do I value most? Human 'experts' or God's, from His perfect Word?"

There's nothing wrong with seeking others' opinions on complex parenting issues. But we have to weigh that advice against the unchanging truth of scripture. Mere humans don't have what it takes, according to the psalmist—so let's not put our lives and, by extension, our children's lives, solely at the mercy of human wisdom and reasoning. God has what it takes!

Father, help me to know when I'm listening to the wrong voice. Stop me, and guide me through Your people and Your Word.

The Ant's Lesson

Go to the ant, O sluggard; consider her ways, and be wise. . . .
She prepares her bread in summer and gathers her food in harvest.
Proverbs 6:6, 8 ESV

Working women treasure Saturday mornings. We don't have to rush to work or to church. We can catch a little extra sleep and spend a quiet, contented morning (we hope) at home.

Those times to rest and recharge are necessary. But problems can start when we allow that rest to become our highest priority. We may set our alarm later and later each weekend, then hit our Snooze button once or twice or more. It's easy to act like the man in Proverbs who says, "a little sleep, a little slumber" (Proverbs 6:10 KJV). *No, really—just five minutes more.*

In contrast, Solomon points us to the example of the lowly ant. Think of what that tiny bug accomplishes: She locates food and carries home as much as she can manage. She makes a note of where the rest of the food is located and enlists others to help out. She stays busy and never worries about her next meal. She's already prepared.

What might we accomplish in an extra five, ten, or fifteen minutes a day? Has our quiet time slid by the wayside? Is there a stack of mail needing our attention? Can we play a game with our children or read a book together?

Let's consider the ant's ways, and be wise!

Lord, teach me the balance between necessary rest and laziness.
Teach me to use my time wisely.

At Water's Edge

That which has been is that which will be, and that which has been done is that which will be done. So there is nothing new under the sun.
Ecclesiastes 1:9 NASB

The tide changes, yet its effects remain exactly the same. It waxes and wanes, returning again and again to the shoreline, constantly churning the sand. As the tide returns, it works irreversible changes on the landscape.

So it is with sin. It's the same today as it was when we were young, when our parents were young, and when their parents were young. Sin, like the tide, washes into our lives with temptations and empty promises. It works irreversible changes on our hearts; its effects are equally permanent. There is nothing new under the sun.

Sometimes, our kids want us to believe that times have changed—that tolerance should now determine acceptability. Many parents simply aren't willing to stand and enforce the tried-and-tested guidelines of scripture.

We must help our children become a friend of God and an enemy of this world. We need to stand firm against the eroding powers of sin. May we never allow that unending tide to wash over our families.

Father, please give me strength to battle the tide of sin that will erode my life and my children's lives. Give me wisdom for the battle and strength to withstand the power of the enemy.

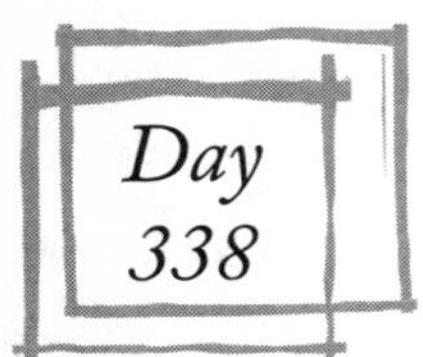

GIRLFRIENDS

Mary arose in those days, and went into the hill country with haste, into a city of Juda; and entered into the house of Zacharias, and saluted Elisabeth.
LUKE 1:39–40 KJV

Mary, betrothed to Joseph, a carpenter, was still trying to grasp the amazing news the angel Gabriel brought her: She would bear a Son named Jesus who would reign over Israel forever!

"I am God's maidservant." Mary gave herself fully to God's incredible plan, yet questions flooded her mind. Her pregnancy left her vulnerable to charges of adultery and the penalty of death by stoning. Would her fiancé believe the truth? What would her parents say? How would her friends react? Mary must have felt very, very alone.

God confirmed His plan with the supernatural sign of her relative Elizabeth's late-life pregnancy. And He gave Mary a friend who not only understood her unique situation, but also celebrated it. The two women could laugh and cry and talk themselves hoarse about their babies. Elizabeth probably prepared her young kinswoman to parent God's Son by sharing the wisdom of her blameless walk with the Lord. Mary, young and strong, helped elderly Elizabeth keep her household together. The months they spent together gave Mary the emotional and spiritual foundation to return to Nazareth and face the wonderful, troubling days ahead.

God blesses women by bringing girlfriends into their lives—to support, love, and cherish each other.

Lord, You never designed us to handle challenges alone.
Please send me a special woman, a friend who will bless me—
whom I can bless.

Timid Timothy

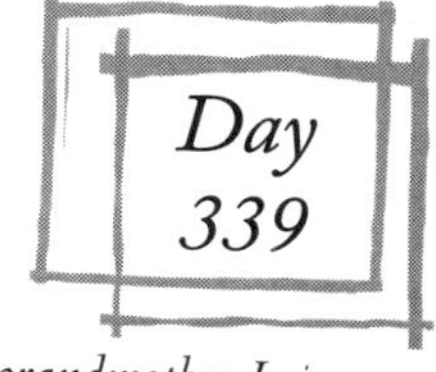

I am reminded of your sincere faith, which first lived in your grandmother Lois and in your mother Eunice and, I am persuaded, now lives in you also.
2 Timothy 1:5 TNIV

Although Paul and Timothy were not related by blood, they were as close as any father and son could be. Converted to Christianity during Paul's first missionary journey, Timothy stood by his mentor faithfully. Interestingly, Timothy struggled with timidity and self-doubt, even stomach troubles, but he earned Paul's high regard. Paul wrote that Timothy was in his prayers day and night.

Timothy's mother and grandmother were Jewish Christians. His Greek father, many scholars assume, was an unbeliever. Still, the faithful prayers of his mother and grandmother changed his life! Timothy provided tremendous support to Paul, became a bishop, and eventually died as a martyr for the sake of Christ.

The Bible offers many examples of parents who believed their prayers could effect great change. Job offered prayers and sacrifices for his seven sons and three daughters, just in case they had sinned! Abraham begged God to bless Ishmael, his outcast son.

The prayers of the righteous are powerful and effective (James 5:16). Prayer changes lives. As parents, we can use that power to claim our children for God. We can pray fervently and with genuine insight. We know them best and care the most.

Lord, Lois and Eunice prayed earnestly for Timothy's future. They trusted You would fulfill Your purpose for him. Help me to envision my children's future, trusting You to fulfill Your purpose for their lives.

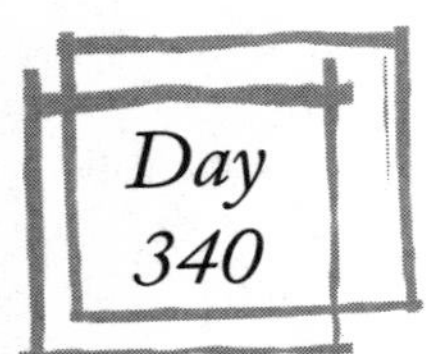

Sit Back and Sing

"The Lord *will conquer your enemies when they attack you. They will attack you from one direction, but they will scatter from you in seven!"*
Deuteronomy 28:7 NLT

Many of us grew up watching Sylvester the cat trying to catch Tweety Bird. It never failed though—Tweety's elderly owner or the big bulldog always intervened, and the cat, usually with his hair standing straight up, would scurry away.

Ever notice that Tweety never seemed worried, even when saying, "I taw I taw a puddy tat"? He just sat on his perch and sang. Apparently, Tweety had confidence that as long as he stayed in his cage, he'd be protected from the "bad ol' puddy tat"—even if his help wasn't immediately apparent.

When our "enemies" advance toward us, we often lose sight of the fact that God is on our side. Taking our eyes off Him, we tend to look at the enemy instead.

Unfortunately, that's totally backwards! We can sit back and sing (praising God), knowing that we're under the protection of His mighty hand. He will conquer and scatter our enemies.

Lord God, I thank You for fighting my enemies for me.
I don't have to fear or worry because I know You are always with me—
and my enemies are helpless against You.

Money, Money, Money

"The servant given one thousand said, 'Master, I know you have high standards and hate careless ways. . . . I was afraid I might disappoint you, so I found a good hiding place and secured your money. Here it is. . .down to the last cent.' "
Matthew 25:24–25 MSG

The Bible is clear: Christians should be good stewards of the resources God gives them. Whether in money or talent, the Lord wants us to use those gifts in a manner that pleases Him.

In the parable of the talents, a wealthy master gave each servant a sum of money. Two of the servants invested what they were given and were rewarded for their efforts. The third squandered the money and gave the master nothing more upon his return.

There's a lesson here for us as Christians. It isn't good enough simply to "hang on" to the things God's given us—after all, everything we have really belongs to Him. We should give back to Him—in money offerings or use of our time—and use what's left wisely.

Hard as it may be for a single mom, the best way to secure our financial future is to plan. Make a list of goals for your family's future: getting out of debt, saving for college, preparing for retirement, and so on. Then make a plan to save a certain amount—even if it's only a few dollars—each month.

Many Christian financial professionals and nonprofit organizations will help you with the planning. No excuses, now—stewardship is calling!

Lord, help me to be a good steward of the monetary gifts You have given me. Help me to plan properly for the future and to give back what is Yours through tithing.

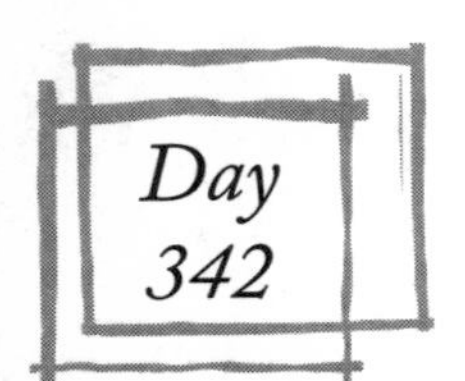

Never Alone

There stood by the cross of Jesus his mother, and his mother's sister, Mary the wife of Cleophas, and Mary Magdalene.
John 19:25 KJV

Mary breathed every agonizing breath with Jesus as soldiers tortured Him on the cross.

He is the King of the Jews! She tried to recall the angel Gabriel's announcement, old Simeon's prophecies, the wise men's worship. . .all affirmations of Jesus' divine nature. But all she saw was her dying Son.

The scriptures do not mention Joseph after Jesus' early life; perhaps he died before His ministry years. Nor did Jesus' half-siblings appear during His crucifixion. But God did not allow Mary to cry alone. Although other disciples hid, John, at Jesus' request, cared for Mary like his own mother. Despite possible danger, Mary's women friends—her unnamed sister; Mary, the wife of Cleophas; and Mary Magdalene—refused to desert her or Jesus. Brave Nicodemus and Joseph of Arimathea asked Pilate for His body. Mary Magdalene, Joanna, and others tried to assist at His burial.

Although Mary could not see beyond those dark days, many of these staunch believers would become her fellow laborers after Jesus' resurrection.

While few mothers share Mary's horrible experience, all of us hurt when our children struggle. Like her, we may not understand their suffering or senseless humiliation, thinking, *Where is God?*

He is there in the tears, hugs, and loving care of friends. And, like Mary, He knows how a Son's pain feels.

Father, when I watch my children grapple with life or death, You never leave me alone. Thank You.

Melting Point

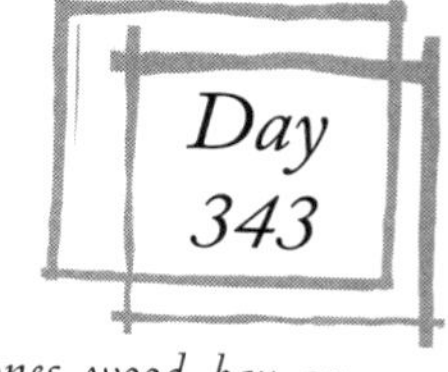

If anyone builds on the foundation with gold, silver, costly stones, wood, hay, or straw, each one's work will become obvious. . .because it will be revealed by fire.
1 Corinthians 3:12–13 HCSB

Wood, hay, and straw—they all burn. We use them as kindling and fuel. Apply a flame to each and they leap to life—providing light and heat until they're totally consumed.

Gold and silver, though, are different. They don't burn; they *melt*. As they turn from solid to liquid, the impurities of their natural state burn away.

In a similar way, tribulation reveals the quality of our inner lives. Trials consume the worthless parts of our character, activities, and spending habits. What isn't consumed melts, turning our stability on its head. Then we're prepared for a reformation of what remains.

When we consider what we say, do, purchase, or pursue, we can use today's verse as our standard. Is our pursuit *ignitable*—temporary and unimportant—or is it *malleable*—something that can be reshaped and used as God directs?

What happens when the fires of tribulation blow through our lives? Do we reach an ignition point or a melting point?

O Lord God, You test me to transform me into the image of Your Son. Teach me to invest in what will last and not that which passes away.

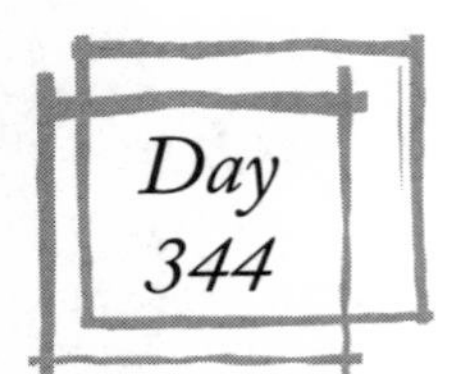

Heart Song

Worthy is the Lamb that was slain to receive power, and riches, and wisdom, and strength, and honour, and glory, and blessing.
Revelation 5:12 KJV

Tiffany's college choir practiced the *Messiah* until she memorized the majestic words, not realizing they came from the Bible. She especially liked the section that began "Worthy is the Lamb that was slain." When she joined the other singers and orchestra under brilliant lights, she wondered if she could ever be the same again. Why did other music pale in comparison?

Years later, Tiffany understood. Her cousin shared her faith in Christ with Tiffany, and the *Messiah* came alive afresh. But then her husband, Manuel, pulled out in front of a semitruck and died a month afterwards, leaving her with little Jake. Tiffany lost her full-time job; her company didn't tolerate her absences. Working two part-time jobs to put food on the table, Tiffany didn't have time to think about grand oratorios. Grief and loneliness tightened her throat to a whisper. She didn't try to sing when she heard the "Hallelujah Chorus" on the radio. But Tiffany pulled a *Messiah* CD from a Christmas grab bag at church. Her eyes filled with tears at the opening notes.

I can't sing it, Lord.

But the words of praise slipped from her mouth almost before she knew it: " 'Worthy is the Lamb that was slain to receive power, and riches, and wisdom, and strength, and honour, and glory, and blessing'!"

Lord, even when my world falls apart, You are God. Help me to praise You, trusting in Your love for me.

Levite Mom

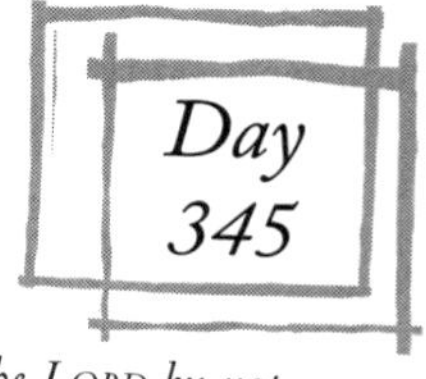

"And as for me, far be it from me that I should sin against the LORD by not praying for you. But I will teach you the good and the right way. Only fear the LORD and be faithful to worship Him with all your heart."
1 SAMUEL 12:23–24 NLV

The Levites of old were set apart, a chosen tribe of Israel. In their priestly role, they helped bridge the gap between a holy God and a sinful people. While serving in the temple courts, they taught the Word of God, pronounced blessings, led worship, received confession, presented offerings and sacrifices on behalf of the faithful, and ensured that the lamps that symbolized God's presence were always lit. Morning and night, day after day.

Like the priests of Old Testament times, parents are invited to fulfill a priestly role to our children. We moms know our kids so well and love them so fiercely that we can plead on their behalf to God in a very meaningful way. We're on the front lines—their first line of defense.

Our homes are where we serve the Lord. In our kitchens, we teach our children great truths of scripture. At the dinner table, we set good examples of confession and worship. In the carpool, we remind them of God's love and faithfulness. Tucking them into bed, we ask for God's blessings. Morning and night, day after day.

Lord God, Samuel felt it was a sin not to pray for Israel. Father, help me become like Samuel. Make me a spiritual leader to my household.

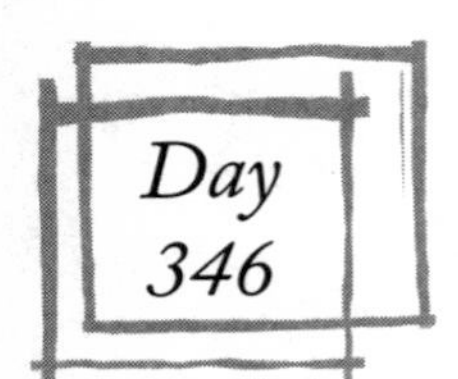

Ups and Downs

Anxiety in the heart of man causes depression,
but a good word makes it glad.
PROVERBS 12:25 NKJV

It was Wednesday, and Marcie wondered how she would get through the end of the week. Her long list of what needed to be done wasn't getting any shorter—and she was beginning to feel anxious. Marcie really needed some help just to get through the day.

"Life is just a bowl of cherries," an old saying goes. But not every day is happy and beautiful. We have bills to pay, jobs to attend to, kids to run around, and life to live. And being a Christian doesn't make every day easy and carefree.

The good news is that we don't have to be anxious. When life becomes too much, we have a God who listens to our worries and speaks words of encouragement back to us—through His Spirit and through His Holy Bible.

The next time anxiety creeps up on you, go to the one true source of joy and peace—our God. Take a minute and pray for calm. Remember that He loves you and encourages you every day. After all, if He takes care of the birds in the air, how much more will He care for His children?

Father God, I may be anxious about today, but I know that I can rest in You. Help me to find comfort in Your Word and happiness in Your presence.

PAUL'S PARENTAL PRAYERS

Every time I say your name in prayer—
which is practically all the time—
I thank God for you.
2 TIMOTHY 1:3 MSG

Paul wrote this positive line to Timothy, a young pastor of the first-century church in Ephesus. As far as we know, Paul fathered no natural children, but he loved Timothy as if he were his own. In his second letter, Paul describes his prayers for his spiritual son in a ministry model all Christian parents can use—whether they're counting their newborns' toes or cheering their children's twenty-fifth birthday.

First, Paul celebrated Timothy; he did not limit his prayers to times when Timothy was experiencing or causing difficulty. Many times we moms pray for our children only when they are in trouble. How many times do we thank God for our kids and His work in their lives?

Second, Paul did not content himself with an occasional mention of Timothy's name to God. He made prayer for Timothy an essential part of his lifestyle.

Third, although Paul cared about Timothy as an individual and prayed for his well-being, Paul saw Timothy as part of God's overall plan and prayed Timothy would fulfill his spiritual mission.

We as Christian mothers also have access to this wonderful privilege called prayer. "Practically all the time," let's focus our hearts and thoughts on God's will for our kids!

Heavenly Father, night and day may I lift up my children to You, helping them through their life journeys by my prayers.

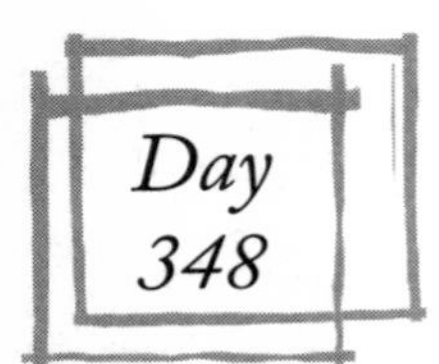

The Gift

For by grace you have been saved through faith, and that not of yourselves; it is the gift of God, not of works, lest anyone should boast.
Ephesians 2:8–9 NKJV

Children receive gifts much better than adults do. When presented with a brightly wrapped package, they spare no emotion and practice no hesitation. Kids tear right into presents, eager to see what's inside. When they find what's inside, they thank the giver (usually with Mom's prodding), and immediately scamper off to enjoy the gift.

Adults seem to think that the longer they wait to open a gift, the more restraint they're showing. Perhaps they feel that tearing into a gift will make them appear greedy—or somehow needy. So they often set gifts aside, even refusing to open them in front of the giver!

Don't do that with the best gift of all. God's grace is freely and completely given to everyone who believes. It should never be set aside or kept in private. Grace is a gift to be opened with childlike abandon, torn into, exposed to the world, and immediately shared with others.

Father, I thank You for the precious gift of Your Son, Jesus, and for the grace You have shown me by forgiving me my sins. Please remind me to share Your gracious presents with others.

"GoogleEarth" Your Life

So be truly glad. There is wonderful joy ahead,
even though you have to endure many trials for a little while.
1 Peter 1:6 NLT

Online computer maps enable us to zoom in to pinpoint specific streets or pull back enough to view entire continents. They're helpful in getting us from one place to another, giving us a better perspective than we have on the ground. They give us "the big picture." What a handy tool that would be if applied to our lives!

You've probably heard the old expression, "Can't see the forest for the trees." Often, we can't see the big picture of our lives beyond our present difficulties. Focused on the obstacles directly in front of us, unaware of the big picture beyond the immediate problem, we can forget the joy that lies ahead.

Is your baby or toddler or teenager causing you stress right now? Consider the big picture: The joy of seeing your baby learn to walk. . . then one day walking down the aisle to the man of her dreams. The joy of beholding that first real smile. . .then seeing his face beam as he reaches for his hard-earned diploma. The joy of observing how each child maneuvers the challenges of college life, marriage, and family—your grandchildren.

What joy awaits us!

Father, Your Word reminds me that there is wonderful joy ahead.
Help me look past the present problems and see the bliss beyond.

Spoiled Rotten

Point your kids in the right direction—
when they're old, they won't be lost.
Proverbs 22:6 msg

Manoah and his wife had never been able to have children. Or day, Manoah's wife received an angelic visitor who delivered the happ message that she would become pregnant. A second visit from the ang confirmed the news to Manoah. The couple asked the angel for guidan in raising their son properly. With such a dramatic start, they kne their little boy had an important future ahead of him. Nine montl later, their little boy was born and named Samson (Judges 13).

Although his parents were a devout couple, Samson suffered a seri of shipwrecks in his life. He cared little for his religion, was consume by lust, and had a violent, vengeful temper. He was easily led into trap by the wily Delilah—and had his eyes gouged out by the enen Philistines.

How did such a strong, gifted man end up with such a wea character? Didn't his parents ever discipline him as a child, or say no t his many wants? Did Manoah and his wife coddle him with too mar possessions and too few expectations and responsibilities? Was Samsc spoiled rotten?

Amazingly, Samson died well (Hebrews 11:32–39). His fait returned to him in the end. A wasted life, to be sure, but not a waste eternity. Let's aim for both a good life and death for our kids!

Lord, hold tight to my children all through their life.
Don't let them go!

Bodybuilding

Now to each one the manifestation of
the Spirit is given for the common good.
1 Corinthians 12:7 niv

Single moms have a lot in common. But each of us is also a one-of-a-kind, original design of the Creator God. No one else can contribute to life quite the way you do.

In his letter to the church at Corinth, the apostle Paul said that each Christian is a part of the overall body of Christ. Each member performs a unique function within that body—and to assume that we should all think and act alike would be disastrous. "If the whole body were an eye, where would the sense of hearing be?" Paul asked (1 Corinthians 12:17 niv).

Each member of the body of Christ represents a different muscle, limb, organ, sense, you name it—and the body can't afford to lose a single one. For optimal function, every piece must work in unity with the others.

Though single mothers face many demands on their time, we should still fulfill our part in the body of Christ. The church ministers to us in many ways—from financial and emotional support to Bible teaching and discipleship—and we, in turn, are to contribute our part for the "common good."

Ready for some bodybuilding?

Creator God, teach me to know myself
and my role in the body of Christ.

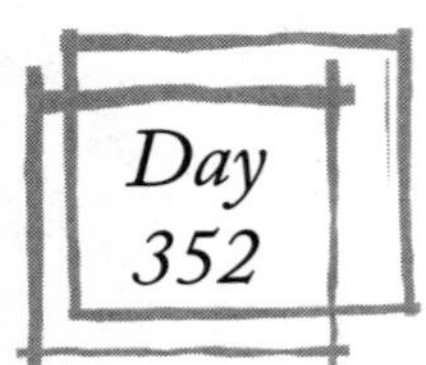

Share the News

I pray that you may be active in sharing your faith, so that you will have a full understanding of every good thing we have in Christ.
Philemon 1:6 niv

Joy was seated on a plane, awaiting takeoff. She was headed toward home—and her children—after a weeklong business trip. This was a chance for a little shut-eye before seeing her family once again.

Joy was about to doze off when a talkative older woman sat down in the next seat. It didn't take long for Joy to realize her traveling partner needed to hear the good news about Jesus Christ. *Not today, God,* Joy thought—but she knew this was an opening she had to take.

Sharing our faith with others can be scary. We could be rejected or even laughed at. But we could also help lead someone to Jesus. Either way, we must share the good news.

In his letter to Philemon, the apostle Paul penned a prayer that his reader would be active in sharing his faith so that Philemon would "have a full understanding of every good thing we have in Christ." When we get excited about other important things in our life—our children's accomplishments, a new job—we share them with others. How much more important it is—and how much more joy we'll get—sharing Christ's love with others.

Share that news! The reward is so much greater than the risk.

Father, I pray for courage and boldness in sharing my faith with others. You have given me so many blessings—please help me to share Your love and goodness with others.

All for Him

Whatever you do, work at it with all your heart,
as working for the Lord, not for men.
Colossians 3:23 NIV

We teach our children to do their best. When they're in school, we xpect them to do what their talents allow. It's difficult when children re capable of different levels of achievement—while one may get traight As, another may struggle just to get by. But they're both xcellent if they're working to their full potential.

That's the beauty of Colossians 3:23. We're not all capable of eaching the same bar. Not everyone can preach like Billy Graham or ing in a way that makes the angels dance. We're given particular gifts nd talents, then expected to use them to the best of our ability for od's glory. But the idea goes beyond even talents and abilities.

Whether we're doing laundry or dishes, reading a story to Michael r checking Liza's homework, singing in the choir or teaching Sunday chool to a room full of six-year-olds, we should work with all our eart.

When we determine to work for the Lord rather than the acknowl- dgement of people, our hearts shape up—and any bad attitudes isappear.

Father, I thank You that You called me to work for Your kingdom. When I'm tempted to grumble and complain, I pray that You'll remind me of Colossians 3:23. Help me to align my attitude with Your Word.

The Importance of Authenticity

So when I came to you, I was weak and fearful and trembling.
1 Corinthians 2:3 NCV

Weak, fearful, and trembling. . .what a powerhouse the apostle Paul was!

Couldn't he have hushed up this inner turmoil and told the people of Corinth something less revealing? After all, don't we want people to think we have it all together? To appear always to be "in the zone" of life?

For single moms, it's about hiding just how hard this job really is. When everyone else looks like everything's under control, why should we admit that we cry at night. . .that we could pay only half the gas bill. . . that we yell too much. . .that we long for a hug now and then. . .that we desperately want ten minutes alone. . .that we ask God "why is my life so hard" at least a hundred times a week? Isn't it better to keep the difficulties to ourselves and polish up our outward appearance?

It may seem like the thing to do, but it's definitely not better. Maybe the apostle Paul revealed such authenticity so others would feel safe to do so themselves. When we're all more real, we're better able to love and help each other.

How many single moms are watching us, hoping to find someone to relate to their problems, hoping for a chance to share their own weaknesses? Let's give them—and ourselves—the freedom of authenticity.

Father, whether I'm having a great day or crying through lunch, help me to be real with others.

FAITH FITNESS

Ye, beloved, building up yourselves on your most holy faith, praying in the Holy Ghost, keep yourselves in the love of God, looking for the mercy of our LORD Jesus Christ unto eternal life.
JUDE 20–21 KJV

Physical fitness takes center stage in our country. Stores teem with books full of advice to help us look better, feel stronger, and live longer. Everyone wears workout suits and jogging shoes. People spend thousands of dollars on exercise equipment. Not content with a basement full of fitness gear, we pay out thousands more for gym memberships.

So we can conclude all Americans are physically fit, right?

Unfortunately, our interest does not necessarily transfer to our actions. Judging from the number of sports channels, we love to watch other people exercise, but sweating it out ourselves? That's a whole 'nother ball game.

In the same way, we Christians often fall short in building ourselves up spiritually. We buy millions of Bibles and tons of literature, attend conferences and seminars, even purchase sweatshirts with scriptures on them—but we don't practice daily spiritual disciplines that make us strong. Jude, the half-brother of Jesus, urges us to devote time and energy to fervent prayer in the Spirit. He tells us to maintain intimacy with Jesus, which the Lord Himself defined as keeping His commands (John 15:10). If we also exercise our faith daily by focusing on His mercy and grace, this regimen will keep us fit for God's heavenly purpose.

Lord, help me stay on top of my spiritual, as well as physical, conditioning. Thanks for Your concern for me.

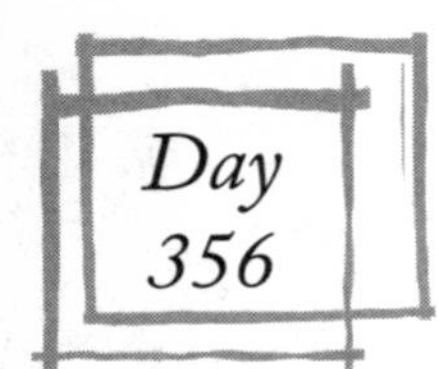

Day 356

The Lord's Prayer

*"Pray like this: Our Father in heaven, help us to honor your name.
Come and set up your kingdom. . . . Give us our food for today.
Forgive us for doing wrong, as we forgive others.
Keep us from being tempted and protect us from evil."*
MATTHEW 6: 9–13 CEV

Jesus provided a perfect, logical structure to help us pray. He wasn't telling us to recite a prewritten prayer. He was simply explaining the components that comprise an elegant and appropriate prayer. Jesus' words are a guide for us to use as we develop our own prayer habits.

First, He gave glory to God by identifying and praising Him. Jesus then recognized that everything the Father does is focused on working His will in our lives. Desiring the kingdom of God and surrendering to His will is a necessary part of our prayers, as Jesus showed. He also prayed for sustenance and daily needs—our health, employment, and relationships would all fit in this category. Clearly, God cares about everything we care about!

Finally, Jesus prayed for forgiveness and the grace to forgive others, as well as freedom from sin.

Our Lord taught us to pray, so that we could confidently approach the Father with our needs. Let's teach our own children to pray by living out an example for them to follow.

*Heavenly Father, thank You for Your powerful lesson in prayer.
Please help me to make the time to pray, and help me to be an
example as I teach my children how to pray.*

God's Armor

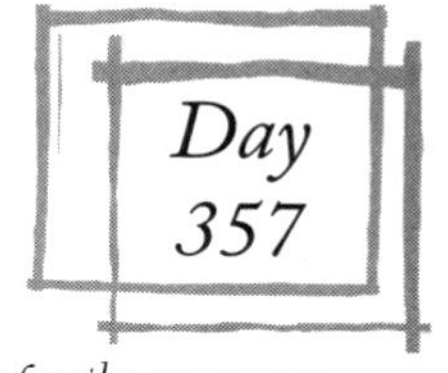

Therefore put on the full armor of God, so that when the day of evil comes, you may be able to stand your ground, and after you have done everything, to stand.
Ephesians 6:13 NIV

Startled by his alarm, the man jumped out of bed. "I'm late!" he said to nobody in particular. Gulping some leftover coffee, he stepped into yesterday's pants and pulled on a sock. Throwing a coat over his shirtless chest, he rushed out the door.

Racing down the snow-covered sidewalk, he thought, *I may be only half-dressed and exposing myself to frostbite and public humiliation—but I won't be late.*

None of us would ever dress so haphazardly. But, sadly, that's often how we put on the armor of God. We rush in, quickly asking God to bless our day and protect our minds, but going no further. As a result, we might end up looking foolish spiritually and exposing ourselves to the lies and attacks of our enemy.

God's Word is clear: We need to put on every piece of armor each day, taking up the shield of faith and the sword of the Spirit. Only then will we be prepared to ward off the enemy's schemes.

Dear Lord, I put on Your armor so that I'm fully protected from schemes of the enemy. From the top of my head to the soles of my feet, I pray Your peace, security, and protection. Keep me in Your presence I pray, Father.

Ever-Present Help

Yet I am always with You; You hold my right hand. . . . My flesh and my heart may fail, but God is the strength of my heart, my portion forever.
Psalm 73:23, 26 HCSB

When God repeats something in His Word, He's emphasizing a point—like when we as moms give our children the same advice or warning over and over again.

One of God's repetitions appears in Psalm 73:23. "I am always with You" rephrases the promise that God gave to Joshua (Joshua 1:9) and Jesus gave His disciples before returning to heaven (Matthew 28:20).

Maybe the apostle Paul had that promise in mind when he commanded us to pray without ceasing (1 Thessalonians 5:17). Since God's always there, why not talk to Him? In the words of Brother Lawrence, a seventeenth-century monk, we learn to "practice the presence of God."

Holly discovered the joy of a constant communion with God through music. In her first months as a single mother, praise songs lifted her spirit when everything else failed. She would hum the tune that accompanied words like, "You are the strength of my heart." Later, she would sing, "Let the weak say 'I am strong.' " Whenever she felt the need, she turned to God through music—and He always met her there.

Whether we seek God in song, scripture reading, or prayer, He'll always meet us there. He will strengthen our hearts whenever we turn to Him.

Almighty God, because I am weak, I depend on You.
But You are strong and always with me. I cannot fail!

Just Trust Me!

Trust in the LORD with all your heart and do not lean on your own understanding.
PROVERBS 3:5 NASB

How often have we told our children, "Don't run in the street"? Or, "Don't touch the stove"? Or, "Do your homework—your education is important"? Or, "Don't fool around with drugs"? Or how about this one: "Just trust me, will you?"

There will be times when we need our children to simply trust us. Times when they need to stop questioning, stop asking why, and simply obey—even when they don't understand the reasons. We tell them to trust that we know best.

In the same way, God wants us to obey Him—even though we may not understand and just can't figure out why. "Simply obey My word," He says. We may not fully "get it," yet He asks us to trust Him in spite of our lack of complete understanding.

We can always trust Him to know what's best. That's what we desire from our own children—and that's what our heavenly Father wants from us.

Father God, if we as sinful human beings show true concern for our children, how could we ever think You would do any less? Forgive me for trusting my own understanding rather than Your wisdom.

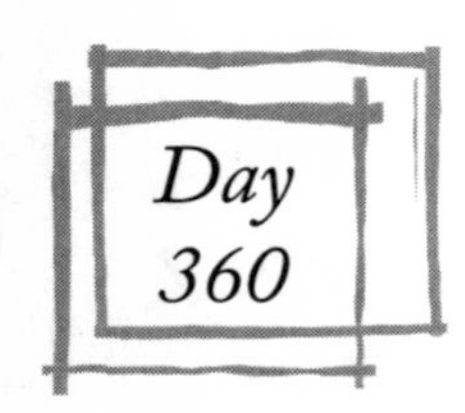

The Right Relationship

But run away from the evil desires of youth. Try hard to live right and to have faith, love, and peace, together with those who trust in the LORD from pure hearts.
2 TIMOTHY 2:22 NCV

The first date is always the hardest, especially for a single mom. Unlike dating in our teens, now we are looking for a relationship that will not only change our own lives but those of our children. It's more than easing our loneliness by sharing happiness and cares. It's more than having someone to trust and rely on.

This time, we're also looking for someone who will love our children.

So the beginning of a relationship is always scary. Will he be a gentleman? Will he be open and friendly? Will he like kids? Most of all, will he love Jesus?

First and Second Timothy are amazing letters that teach young and old alike how to improve their relationships with others as well as with God. Throughout both letters, Paul provides instruction to his young student, Timothy, on how to be a better vessel for God's work. Yet, as in this verse, Paul goes beyond the general to the practical actions that will help.

When we keep in mind what God wants for us in our relationships, the other questions become far less difficult to answer.

Lord, loneliness sometimes overwhelms me. Please guide me as I open myself to new relationships, so that Your desires for me are utmost in my mind.

Beloved Black Sheep

Jacob awaked out of his sleep, and he said,
Surely the Lord is in this place; and I knew it not.
Genesis 28:16 kjv

Many young people leave home to look for a promising future. But Jacob left home because he had bilked Esau, his older brother, out of his inheritance. Jacob also tricked their blind father into giving him a special blessing that symbolized God's favor. Jacob thought he was set for life.

Instead, he became a fugitive. His heart pounded at every rustle behind a rock. Had Esau, the wilderness expert, followed him? The rocks Jacob used as pillows felt less painful than the thought that he never would see his parents again.

During the night Jacob stirred uneasily. *Someone was there.* He felt for his dagger. Instead of Esau, Jacob faced glowing angels on a ladder that stretched to heaven. God Himself stood above it. Instead of judging Jacob as a con man and family disgrace, God promised to give him the land where he stood and bless the world through him. When Jacob awakened from his dream, he called the place Bethel, which means "House of God."

"God was here!" he said in awe. "And I didn't even know it."

Like Jacob, we all have blown it. But God's angels surround us, and His powerful, loving Presence stands ready to bless us far beyond anything we could imagine.

Lord God, how can you offer me, a person who's made so many mistakes,
a glimpse of heaven? Thank You for Your angels surrounding me,
and Your immeasurable mercy.

Refrigerator-Door Treasures

"I promise you that you cannot get into God's kingdom, unless you accept it the way a child does." Then Jesus took the children in his arms and blessed them by placing his hands on them.
Mark 10:15–16 CEV

Little fingers, caked with peanut butter, proudly create a masterpiece with washable crayons and a page hastily torn from a coloring book. Mom declares it to be the greatest work of art she's ever seen. With great care she affixes the paper to the refrigerator door with her very best magnet—the one that says, Mom of the Year.

She could purchase a "real" painting that would get more attention than the childlike effort she attached to the refrigerator. But that's not important to a mom.

Jesus, too, could create better things than the gifts we bring Him. Yet he eagerly awaits our gifts—tokens of our time, talent, and resources—and accepts them as proof that we love Him.

What gifts do we bring to Jesus with the same sense of pride and accomplishment that a child feels when he gives a painting to his mom? Let's go to Jesus like little children, proudly returning to Him some of the gifts He's given us.

Like what? How about the time we spend with our children, and our efforts at sharing His gospel with others?

Jesus, I want to give You the best that I have to offer. Help me to bring You honor and joy. I thank You for graciously receiving my gifts as tokens of my desire to please You.

The Color of Blessing

*"For I will pour water on the thirsty land, and streams on the dry ground;
I will pour out my Spirit on your offspring, and my
blessing on your descendants."*
Isaiah 44:3 niv

Imagine a desert: The ground is dry, showing great cracks and crevices from the lack of moisture. The dirt is rock hard. Plants can't live there—no colorful flowers or beautiful green bushes, just hard, dry dirt as far as the eye can see. It's not a very appealing vision, is it?

Now imagine torrents of rain falling from the sky. The cracks close up and the ground softens. In time, fragrant flowers of every color begin to grow. The barren, dry ground has transformed into a vision of beauty, making our senses dance.

This is a picture of the spiritual blessings God promises to us, to our children, and to our children's children. When the Lord pours His spirit into us, we flourish. The cracks of our souls close up, and we burst forth with the fragrance of joy and peace, blessing and grace. We produce luscious fruit for all to see. We become witnesses to the blessings of Christ.

*Lord, please pour out Your Spirit in my life. There are times when
I am dry and weary, but I know that I can be the mom You desire me to be.
Rain Your blessings on me and my children, Father. Refresh us
and bring a new hope and new peace.*

Radical Hospitality

He is a father to orphans, and he defends the widows.
God gives the lonely a home.
Psalm 68:5–6 NCV

In the western world, most of us expect to live in a single-family dwelling—whether an apartment or a house—rather than sharing living quarters with extended family or even people unrelated to us.

Sometimes, single moms move in with family members until "we get back on our feet." Other times, we share living expenses with a roommate. It might not be our preferred way, but God keeps a roof over our heads. He has promised, as Psalm 68 says, to give the lonely—widows and orphans—a home.

But you know what? God may want to work through *us* to give other lonely people a home. Maybe we start with opening our homes to others who would spend a holiday alone. Then God may push us past our comfort zones into a radical hospitality—perhaps He'll call us to offer guidance and shelter to a troubled teen. Maybe He'll ask us to share a meal, even offer an extra room, to the homeless or victims of abuse.

Whatever the situation, God will give the lonely a home—definitely for us, and possibly through us.

Oh God, our defender, we turn to You when we feel separated and alone.
Guide us to the home You have for us.

Establishing a Vision

Where there is no vision, the people perish.
Proverbs 29:18 KJV

Cookbooks without pictures aren't much fun. Simple words on a page typically don't move us to culinary pursuits. But if that decadent New York–style cheesecake recipe is actually pictured—you know, an image of a succulent dessert, caressed with ribbons of chocolate and loaded with plump red strawberries—we may *run* to the kitchen! Glimpsing a mouthwatering image of what we could create motivates us as the written word could never do.

Single moms, too, need an image of what we're trying to accomplish. What do we see as the end result of all our efforts? What does success in our family, our parenting, our career, our spiritual life look like? We need a vision. Without it, we'll probably walk aimlessly through piles of laundry, stacks of bills, and grocery store aisles.

With a clear mental image of the future, we can visualize where all the hard work of parenthood is taking us—and see, in our mind's eye, the big picture of what God is creating in us and in the lives of our children.

Ask God to give you a vision of your ultimate destination. It'll make worlds of difference in your day-to-day labors.

Father God, allow me to see the vision You have established for my family—embed it into my heart and mind.

Scripture Index

Old Testament

New Testament Scriptures Used

Contributor Bios

Suzanne Woods Fisher's historical novels, *Copper Star* and its sequel, *Copper Fire,* are inspired by true events. Fisher writes for many magazines, is a wife and mother and a puppy raiser for Guide Dogs for the Blind.

Award-winning author and speaker **Darlene Franklin** resides in the Colorado foothills with her mother and her Sia-Ti (Siamese/Tiger) cat Talia. She has two grown children and two grandchildren. She loves music, reading, and writing. She has published novels, magazine articles, and children's curriculum. Visit her blog at www.romancesirens.com/darlene-franklin.

Shelly Kucera Jones is a training specialist with a farm insurance company. Recently married, she lives in Texas.

Rebecca Lusignolo-McGlone is a passionate follower of Christ, wife, home-schooling mother, and freelance author. Her previous work includes the self-published *Devotions for Difficult Days—Thoughts for Those with a Heavy Heart* (available through Lulu.com), as well as writing published in The Billy Graham Evangelistic Association's *Decision* magazine.

Nicole O'Dell is an accomplished writer of books, devotions, and Bible studies. She has been an in-depth studier, Bible-study leader, and teacher for over twelve years. Nicole lives in central Illinois with her husband, Wil, and her small children. She also enjoys Web design and is a member of Mensa.

Rachael Phillips is an award-winning fiction and humor writer who has authored four biographies published by Barbour Publishing. Rachael and her husband live in Indiana. Visit her Web site at www.rachelwrites.com.

A long-time single mom, **Kimm Reid-Matchett** put herself through university while raising three active boys. After receiving her psychology degree, she remarried and now finds her newly combined family of nine to be exhilarating. Kimm continues to work on a plethora of writing projects while volunteering at a women's shelter. She resides in Alberta, Canada.

Ramona Richards is an award-winning author and editor who has worked on more than 350 publications. Ramona's articles have also appeared in *Special Education Today*, *Today's Christian Woman*, and *Chicken Soup for the Caregiver's Soul*. Her devotional books include *Secrets of Confidence* (Barbour) and *A Moment with God for Single Parents* (Abingdon), and her novels include *The Face of Deceit* and *A Muder Among Friends* (Steeple Hill), which received 4½ stars from Romantic Times magazine. She lives in Nashville with her daughter Rachel.

Christan M. Thomas is a writer/editor whose work has appeared in magazines and newspapers across Texas and Tennessee. Originally from the Indianapolis area, Christan now resides in Gray, Tennessee, with her husband Brock and dogs Tucker and Suzy Q. She recently began doctoral studies at East Tennessee State University.

Author Index